# WALKING

### THE

# LINE

# WALKING
## THE
# LINE

### MARIAN BOTSFORD FRASER

Sierra Club Books
San Francisco

Copyright © 1989 by Marian Fraser

Published in Canada by Douglas & McIntyre, Vancouver/Toronto

Library of Congress Cataloging-in-Publication Data

Fraser, Marian Elizabeth, 1947-
    Walking the line : travels along the Canadian/American border /
    Marian Elizabeth Fraser.
        p.      cm.
    Includes bibliographical references.
    ISBN 0-87156-666-4
    1. Northern boundary of the United States—History. 2. Northern
boundary of the United States—Description and travel. 3. Fraser, Marian
Elizabeth, 1947-    —Journeys—Northern boundary of the
United States. 4. Northeast boundary of the United States—History.
5. Northeast boundary of the United States—Description and travel.
6. Fraser, Marian Elizabeth, 1947-    —Journeys—Northeast boundary of the
United States.    I. Title.
F551.F82    1990
917.104'647—dc20                                                    89-37480
                                                                        CIP

The quotation on page 173 is from *Klondike: The Last Great Gold Rush* by Pierre Berton (Toronto: McClelland and Stewart, 1972, p. 142) and is reprinted with the permission of the publisher.
The quotation near the bottom of page 182 is from "The Call of the Yukon" by Robert Service and is reprinted with the permission of William Krasilovsky.

Editor: Nancy Flight
Design by Gabriele Proctor
Maps by Anna Gamble

Printed and bound in Canada
10 9 8 7 6 5 4 3 2 1

*For my parents,*
*Louise and Jack Botsford*

# CONTENTS

# LIST OF MAPS

# ACKNOWLEDGEMENTS

This book began as a series of documentaries for the CBC Radio program "Ideas," a four-hour series in 1986 and a five-hour series in 1987. The opportunity to explore an idea at length and at leisure is a rare privilege, and I am very grateful to Bernie Lucht, Executive Producer of "Ideas," for his support and enthusiasm for this project.

I would also like to thank the International Boundary Commission, particularly the Canadian commissioner, Dr. Alec C. McEwen, and field engineers Dale Dryden and Carl Gustafson and their crews for their interest, information and patience.

I am indebted to the people who live along the international boundary line—librarians and local historians and newspaper editors, and the many, many individuals I spoke to and stayed with across the continent. Thanks also to my agent, Lee Davis Creal, for encouragement and care.

But without the love, loyalty, tolerance (of long absences and an empty refrigerator), good humour (when I was cranky) and support of my family, John and Katherine Fraser, I would not have made it to the end of the line. Thank you.

# WALKING
## THE
# LINE

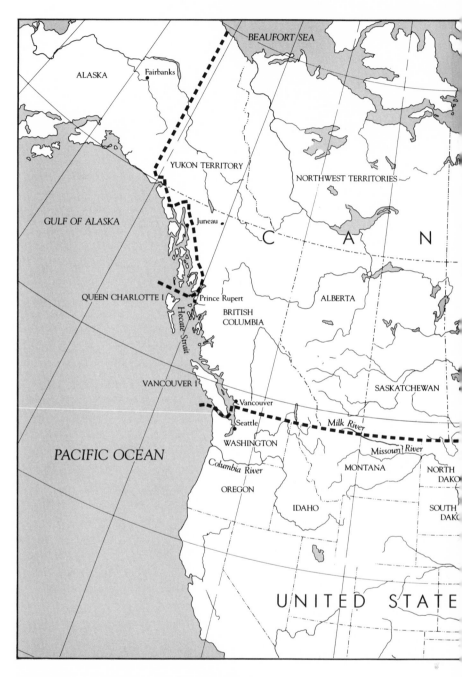

CANADA AND THE UNITED STATES

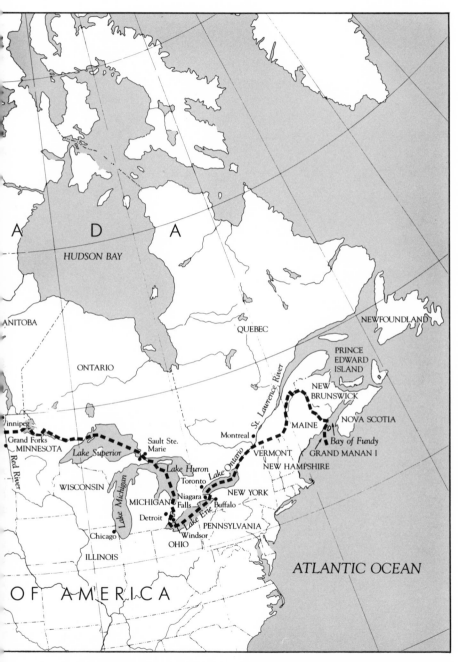

This map is based on information taken from MCR 60 © 1958. Her Majesty the Queen in Right of Canada with permission of Energy, Mines and Resources Canada.

# PREAMBLE

Like many North Americans, I have a family history that moves freely back and forth across the Canada/U.S. border. The Botsford family was originally split by the American War of Independence; some were Loyalists and moved to Nova Scotia or New Brunswick; others remained in New England. My American parents settled in northern Ontario after World War II, but my father had spent large portions of his childhood in Canadian mining communities because his father was an engineer who went where there was work. My cousins are all Americans. As a child, I crossed the border every summer for family reunions in Michigan. I grew up with ideas about funny little differences north and south of the line.

The border is "the line"; it is always called the line by the people who live there and the people who put it there. This book is a journal of my exploration along the line, a grounding of what we refer to as the 49th parallel. I wanted to step outside the official border crossings and discover what the boundary actually is, what it looks like, how it is marked. I wanted to talk to the people who live on the line, to trace the boundary on the ground, to follow it through pastures and line houses, on river banks and over mountain passes, literally to walk the line.

The 49th parallel is a metaphor we use casually in North America, probably more frequently in Canada than in the United States. It signals many things to us, north and south of the 49th—an accent, a cold front, a style in television programming, the look of a face, the cut of a coat. When we talk about the 49th parallel, we visualize a map with a dotted line drawn across the belly of North America. The line, or an approximation of it, is indelibly printed on our imaginations; for me, that means years of looking at maps coloured red on top for the Dominion of Canada and white or with fieldlike pastel rectangles on the bottom for the United States.

In fact, the 49th parallel makes up less than a third of the international boundary. From the Great Lakes east, the border plunges as far south as the 42nd parallel in Lake Erie, then climbs through the lakes to well above the 45th before dropping sharply along the Saint John River valley and out into the Bay of Fundy. In the northwest, in British Columbia and the Yukon and Alaska, the border is a crooked line of monuments perched high on glaciers along the inside edge of the Panhandle and then the fanatical perfection of a 647-mile straight line along the 141st meridian. The total length of the line is more than 5500 miles, or 8891 kilometres.

Almost every foot of the border has been disputed. When you look at a map of North America, it appears that all the little deviations in the border favour the United States, except at the edges of the continent, where Canada held on to Nova Scotia and Vancouver Island. Canada, in fact, did lose most of the boundary disputes; the territorial imperative of the Americans met little resistance from the British diplomats by whose indifferent hands the lines defining Canada were drawn. There are a few long-standing border disputes, and new ones, caused by the extension of the limits of sovereignty in the sea from three miles to twelve miles and now to two hundred miles. For the most part, the boundary is clearly marked and punctiliously regulated.

The border in a sense runs tangentially to two national identities. Historically, it represents many of the flash points in our political histories; diplomacy took place in Washington, London and finally Ottawa, but the War of 1812 and the Fenian raids and the Aroostook War and the invasions of the Hunters' Lodges took place right on the border, in forts and villages and along small rivers. The borderline bears numerous battle scars, signs of urgent settlement and small, forgotten graveyards.

To most North Americans, the border is several things. It is the momentary uneasiness we feel as we approach the Customs and Immigration building at an official border crossing. What will they ask? Will we be searched? What must I declare? When Canadians cross into the United States, they raise their eyes to the gun in the Customs officer's holster and perhaps glimpse the ubiquitous apple-green cars of the U.S.

border patrol, the most powerful police force in the United States. When Americans cross into Canada, they are greeted by blunt signs telling them to leave their guns behind. There is one as you drive onto the Detroit/Windsor Ambassador Bridge after paying the toll that seems to imply that you either throw your gun into the Detroit River then and there or face unpleasant consequences at the fast-approaching Canada Customs booth.

The border is also the scene of our smuggling mythology. Everyone has a smuggling story, I learned as I travelled across the continent. Everyone has an aunt who lived in Windsor and would come home from Hudson's Department Store in Detroit wearing an extra forty pounds of clothing, or a grandfather who tried to smuggle margarine across at the Sault in the fifties. Everyone knows about the fast cars of Prohibition days and bottles of rum stitched into leather upholstery and the funnel beneath the Detroit River and the corrupted Customs officials just about everywhere, it seems.

But the Canada/U.S border is also a series of local cultures that in some places embrace the line and in others are isolated by it. In the east, communities have grown up around the border, and bits of mythology stick to it like burrs to a hedge. The farther west you go, the less relevant the border becomes; it loses its dynamism and becomes little more than an isolated gate bringing focus to an empty landscape. To the native and Metis people, more than for any of the European immigrants, the border is a symbol of disruption and destruction.

Visually, it is a long, long line of numbered monuments. Marking the line began in 1798, with a hoop of iron around a yellow birch tree, indicating the source of the St. Croix River in Maine/New Brunswick. It ended in 1912, when the final bronze monument was placed beside the Beaufort Sea on the 141st meridian between Alaska and Yukon Territory. The boundary is a series of joined straight-line segments called courses, which vary in length from 23¼ inches, on the Maine/Quebec border, to the 647-mile straight line of the 141st meridian.

The surveyors of the International Boundary Commission visualize and define the boundary by monument number. Every summer, they walk the line, clearing the vista, repairing cracked monuments and installing new ones, ordering the destruction of impinging lilac bushes and hedges, patiently resurveying every point. The story of laying down the line is a record of endurance, precision and co-operation; for surveyors, the mathematical precision of the line and its physical realization as a chain of perfectly surveyed monuments are passions uniting men (and a small handful of women) over two centuries.

This book is a record of my travels over eighteen months along selected segments of the border, not every inch of it. The book is organized from east to west, but I did not make an unbroken journey from one coast to the other; my travel took place at different times, in different seasons. I went to places that I thought might have special significance and then for the most part allowed myself to be guided by the interests and preoccupations of the people who live on the border. So the stories are their stories. I did not stray very far from the actual boundary line, except in the Northwest. I did not allow myself to be distracted by places and events if they were not relevant to the border.

The Canada/U.S. border is a peculiarly vital strip of shared mythology and landscape, stretching right across North America. If there is a conclusion, I will come to it when I arrive at the end of the line.

# A YELLOW BIRCH TREE HOOPED WITH IRON: MAINE / NEW BRUNSWICK

Dawn on Grand Manan Island in the Bay of Fundy: one by one, the fat-bellied dories come on home. High in the bow, low in the stern, they cut mirrored waters, purling fine white streamers of foam behind them.

I sit on the damp, oiled wharf at Seal Cove, waiting for Preston Wilcox.

The previous day I had taken the ferry to Grand Manan from Blacks Harbour, New Brunswick, south and west across the deep, dark chop of the Bay of Fundy. The ferry barely glanced in the direction of Passamaquoddy Bay, where Samuel de Champlain sought refuge for an entire winter in 1604, on Dochet Island, and where in 1817 the first joint international survey of the borderline islands was carried out. The island survey was never completed; there is a local story that rum and rough weather prevailed. As a result, there is almost forty-five miles of open water in the Bay of Fundy where the boundary between Canada and the United States has never been precisely delineated. And it was here, on the farthest reaches of the Grand Manan archipelago, on Machias Seal Island, that border trouble blew up like a sudden squall in the summer of 1986.

On a map of the international boundary, Grand Manan Island is an inkspot at the end of the flourish of the St. Croix River, between Maine and New Brunswick. (Machias Seal Island is invisible.) In 1783, a search for the source of the St. Croix River marked the beginning of the establishment of the Canada/U.S. border. Two hundred years later,

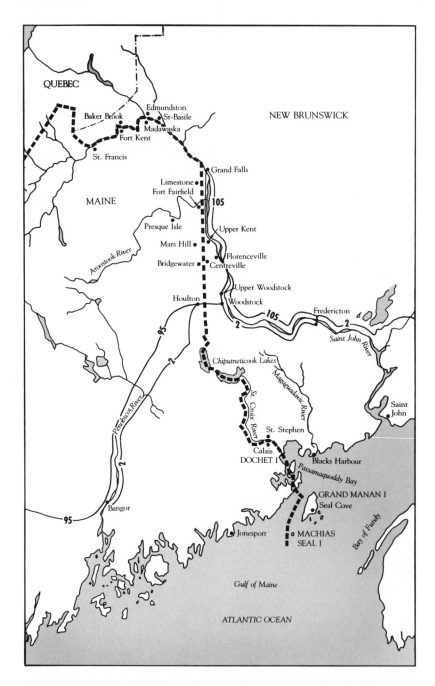

# MAINE/NEW BRUNSWICK

here in the Bay of Fundy, little more than one hundred miles from the source of the St. Croix, the boundary line is still undefined and problematic.

It is a one-and-a-half-hour journey on the ferry to Grand Manan; people who knew each other well chatted and ate chili and drank coffee, and I was like a stranger in a small neighbourhood café. The subjects were herring, the weather, free trade and the ferry schedule; I was the only one who even glanced at the notices about church services and AA meetings. In a book about Grand Manan, I read about Loyalist settlement on the island from the 1780s, about how to bait a lobster trap, about making lip gloss out of iridescent herring scales. I studied tide charts and maps of the Bay of Fundy.

The tides here are so powerful that there is always talk of harnessing them to make electricity; the difference between high and low tidemarks on the shoreline is sometimes thirty feet. You can stand on a beach and watch the tide push the waves up the shore, just as if a tap had been turned on to fill up a basin. Life is measured by the tides; time on the coastline of Maine and New Brunswick is an overlapping calendar of fishing seasons, nesting seasons, breeding periods, set on the monthly grid of spring tides and neap tides. Life is also taken by the tides; tidal currents, like the Sirens, wrap hapless vessels in their embrace and pull them down onto the hidden shoals and ledges of the archipelago.

As a shipping channel, the Bay of Fundy is split by the Grand Manan archipelago into the North Channel and the South Channel. South and west of the lofty bulk of Grand Manan there is a haphazard chain of low-lying, wind-swept islands—a sailors' graveyard since the early 1800s: the brig *Elizabeth*, 1820; the barque *Wallace*, 1841; the schooner *Gertrude E. Smith*, 1883. Shipwrecks litter the floor of the Bay of Fundy; you imagine them sometimes wrenched by the tide from a rocky outcrop, settling into a cavern of kelp.

Machias Seal Island is the cornerstone of the North Channel. It lies ten miles south by southwest from Grand Manan Island, closer to the coast of Maine than to the coast of New Brunswick. It takes its name from the Maine river, bay and fishing village, Machias, or "bad little falls." It consists of fifteen acres of rocky grassland, inhabited by puffins, Arctic terns, Leach's storm-petrels, razorbill auks and a few laughing gulls. The island is like a steppingstone in the sea, the waters around it broken only by fishing boats and the gleaming backs of dolphins and baleen whales; almost half of the world's two hundred right whales breed between Machias Seal Island and Grand Manan.

In 1832, following numerous marine disasters, the legislature of the province of New Brunswick established a lighthouse on Machias Seal Island. Since then, the province and subsequently the federal government have maintained a lighthouse there. Generations of Grand Manan families have been lightkeepers for the archipelago. For many years, three lightkeepers and their families lived on Machias Seal Island with a resident schoolmaster. Now there is one lightkeeper on the island, sometimes two.

In nesting season, a Canadian Wildlife Service officer joins the lightkeeper. In 1944, Canada formally declared Machias Seal Island a bird sanctuary. The nesting season has become a tourist attraction, and there are daily excursions to the island from Grand Manan Island and from Maine. For many years, Preston Wilcox of Seal Cove, Grand Manan, and Barna B. Norton of Jonesport, Maine, have taken charge of the regular bird-watching tours. For many years, they have had a gentleman's agreement not to violate the restrictions imposed by the wildlife officer on the number of people who may land on the island during nesting: twenty-five or thirty people each day, half from the hotels of Grand Manan, half from the coastal resorts of Maine.

But in the summer of 1986, this fine, shared sense of guardianship disintegrated into a border dispute.

At Seal Cove, I breathe deeply of the early morning air; it is salty and oily and fishy. The sky is a flushed, young skin with a few dark smudges of cloud. The sun appears, suddenly—a burnished copper dish pulled dripping out of the horizon—and the glassy bay is slowly coloured and warmed. Pale steam rises off the damp tire marks on the wharf, and off the lustrous, raven-coloured coils of fishing nets called seines.

Sounds cluster and settle in bursts of activity. Winches grind, winding twine for the herring weirs ("wares"); the radio on an empty boat spits out a disembodied conversation. Men coming in exchange terse greetings with men going out. Every time a boat slides quietly in beside the pier, a raucous and hysterical crowd of seagulls rushes up and falls upon the boat with bright, harsh cries like audible wing beats.

Preston Wilcox arrives to prepare his boat for the day. He is weathered and sinewy and white haired, and his eyes are watchful under a peaked cap. His voice is a deep baritone, richer than lobster thermidor.

Preston Wilcox and Barna B. Norton have lived all their lives around Machias Seal Island. They have been friendly rivals for years on the fishing grounds of the Bay of Fundy. Fishing shapes life in the Bay of Fundy; for every fish there is a season and a licence, a specialized craft and a perfect pool or shoal or current. There are the big fancy boats for purse seining and scallop dragging and herring pumping. There are simple, cheap techniques for catching groundfish, like drailing, handlining and bugging, all variations on hook, line and sinker—simple in concept, cheap to construct, requiring perfect technique. Close to the edges of Grand Manan, hundreds of weirs stake their claims, spindly frames hung with nets hung with herring and an occasional lumpfish. Between Grand Manan and Machias Seal Island lie rich lobster and scallop grounds. Here Preston Wilcox and Barna B. Norton and their families and neighbours live their lives, as much offshore as on. Preston Wilcox describes himself as a fisherman and naturalist who leads whaling and birding tours to Machias Seal to "take up the slack" in off-seasons, "anything to make an honest buck."

On 16 August 1986, Preston Wilcox watched Barna B. Norton raise the American flag on Machias Seal Island and claim the land for the United States of America. There is a precedent for this seemingly eccentric act; the people of Maine and New Brunswick know full well that an identical event, on the Saint John River in 1827, sparked the border dispute known as the Aroostook War. Preston Wilcox was right there that day on Machias Seal Island; he came ashore from his fishing boat to watch this ceremony, and he didn't like what he saw.

"It was a foggy, blowy day," said Preston Wilcox with deliberation. "It was a whole party of them; they just come ashore and had the American flag flying on the stern of the dory. They went up to the helicopter pad and put the American flag up.

"I wasn't close or anything, but I went up near where they was having their ceremony and listened. They made a lot of formal motions and recommendations; some of them I can't remember." He paused. "But I can remember three of them." He paused again.

"One was to put an American Coast Guard mooring on the northern side of Machias Seal. Another one was a motion to stop the helicopter from landing on the island while it was birding season, and I do agree with that.

"The other one I remember was they were demanding full sovereignty of the island, in the name of the United States."

The gentleman's agreement between Wilcox and Norton had been spoiled by the popularity of Machias Seal Island. Now American yachts anchor offshore overnight, and Barna B. Norton uses his advantages of proximity and a very fast boat. By the time Preston Wilcox arrives from Grand Manan with his cargo of tourists, the daily quota of visitors has already been reached.

"See, the Canadian wildlife officer can ask people not to land, but he has no real authority to prevent them. He has to call Sackville on the mainland and report, see. Now the Americans land, and their government upholds them, saying Canada has no authority. But if I land, my government charges me."

I called Barna B. Norton (B. for Beal) on the telephone. He has in his possession a deed from his great-grandfather Beal, leaving the island to him. He has a letter from the U.S. State Department, dated May 1983, which informs him that Machias Seal Island is and always has been American territory. He says the letter also tells him that he need not abide by the regulations of a Canadian wildlife officer, who has no business being there. He has set up a territorial council for Machias Seal Island. He is unperturbed by my questions about the flag-raising ceremony.

"We did it mainly to protect the birds," said Barna B. Norton, "because Canada doesn't have any authority on Machias Seal. We're very apprehensive about some tour boat from the United States arriving there with eighty or so people and pushing all the birds off the island."

Barna B. Norton does not accept the authority of the Canadian wildlife officer on the island, "because Canada doesn't own it."

"Who do you think does own Machias Seal Island?" I asked him.

"There's no *thinking* about it," he said, as if to a child; "we know who owns it. The United States owns it by treaties, and I own it personally by my deed from my great-grandfather."

Both the Canadian and American protagonists are convinced that their government is behind them. Both cite the authority of treaties; the Canadians point to peaceful Canadian occupation of the island for more than 150 years. The Canadian commissioner on the International Boundary Commission made a special trip that summer to Machias Seal Island and declared unequivocally that this is Canadian land.

It appears to be of small significance, this dispute over the nesting grounds of the razorbill auk.

But look again at the location of Machias Seal Island. It lies in a patch of open sea, between Grand Manan, the Maine and Nova Scotia coastlines and the lip of the Gulf of Maine known as Georges Bank, the site of an earlier fishing boundary dispute. American and Canadian fishermen now share the waters around Machias Seal, tossing bait from boat to boat, helping with broken nets. Beneath the surface, however, there are tides of uncertainty and potential hostility; in the lobster grounds, for example, the Canadians have quotas and regulations, whereas the Americans are unregulated and harvest at will. The Canadians say that the Americans come in, in powerful boats, and clean out the scallop grounds. If Machias Seal Island is declared either American or Canadian, the boundary line will be pulled one way or another, and sovereignty over the fishing grounds set, one way or another. Both lobster and scallops are million-dollar industries for the people of Grand Manan and coastal Maine.

Preston Wilcox was not impressed with Barna Norton's bravura ceremony: "Well, I tell you, I don't think that was any way to settle any border dispute. More trouble will just flare up."

But Barna Norton thinks there is no need for an official resolution to this problem of ownership, because he owns the island.

"It's just time Canada stopped doing the dickering." His short chuckle broke through the crackle on the phone line.

"Canada is great. They're the smartest people I know. They've taken boundaries for two hundred years; they have ignored our treaties. They go in, cause a dispute, and we settle it by capitulating then, or we negotiate and capitulate, or we get the World Court to do it for us.

"My gosh, now they've got Nova Scotia away down past New York City. We've lost our fishing grounds; we've lost our continental shelf. Canada has hers, and she has ours. My gosh, you're smart people."

Barna Norton paused, and I heard another salty laugh. "You know, my uncle was talking to me the other day, and he said, 'Mr. Reynolds has built a house up in Jonesport,' and I said, 'Was he a carpenter?' And he said, 'No, he was a dickerer.' And I said, 'Uncle, what's a dickerer?'

"And he said, 'Well, he's a man that leaves home in the morning with a hen and comes back at night with a yoke of oxen.'

"And I thought to myself, my gosh, that man must be a Canadian."

* * *

In my mind's eye, I see a long stretch of moose swamp. The cool bush of cedar, birch, maple and spruce is an impenetrable screen. The undergrowth is prickly and tangled and springy underfoot. I can almost smell sweet, sharp cedar, and black muck, and the musk of decaying leaves. Shafts of sunlight pierce the gloom; few birds sing.

Through the swamp, a dark old stream trickles capriciously; this is the source of the St. Croix River. Somewhere at the head of this stream, now called Monument Brook, there was once and may still be a yellow birch tree, with a band of iron around its waist, "hooped with Iron," as the old documents say. In 1798, this birch tree marked the end of the first boundary dispute between Canada, or British North America as it was then called, and the United States of America.

Long before the American Revolution, there was a series of territorial face-offs in this part of the continent; the native Algonquian confederation (here, the Micmac, the Abenaki, the Malecite), the English and the French kept circling one another until the music stopped and there was a scramble for possession. Between the early 1600s and late 1700s, the vaguely defined area called Acadia officially changed hands at least five times. The confusion was heightened by the American Revolution, when deeply felt loyalties divided families and sent them to either American or British territories.

In 1783, the treaty at Versailles named the St. Croix River an official boundary between the United States and Canada, that is, between Maine, then still called Massachusetts, and New Brunswick. But locating the St. Croix River on the ground was a more difficult task than merely naming it in a treaty. In 1783, no settlers used the name St. Croix for any river; this was an old name that Samuel de Champlain gave to the river flowing past his winter settlement into Passamaquoddy Bay in 1604. By the 1780s, there were no signs of Champlain's brief and meagre settlement, and the wrangling began. The Americans insisted that the Magaguadavic River must be Champlain's St. Croix; the British said it must be the Schoodic, considerably farther west. Stalemate.

Consequently, in 1794, the first joint boundary commission was set up, by Jay's Treaty; its job was to translate the boundary from treaty language—a litany of landmarks carefully copied from old maps—into real terms, from arbitrary lines scratched on old parchment into real objects like a tree, the foundations for a monument, something that would say to settlers, your country stops here; across the stream is now another country.

The commission ordered excavations on Dochet Island in the Schoodic River and found the brick remains of Champlain's camp. The St. Croix River was traced northwards, through the Chiputneticook Lakes to the end of the old stream, where the yellow birch tree was marked with an iron band. Near here now stands Monument 1 on the North Line of the Canada/U.S. boundary.

In the oldest part of settled North America, this is how the border took its place in history, as a line cut through people's lives, their land, their idea of the landscape around them. It was first decreed and then located, marked, surveyed and named. In Maine and New Brunswick, the border winds through the history of Acadians, Loyalists, Malecite Indians and Yankees and is part of the pattern of the daily lives of loggers, potato farmers and fishermen.

I carried with me the image of the "yellow Birch Tree hooped with Iron" as I travelled in early summer up the North Line and along the Saint John River valley.

The Saint John River is a wide, wide ribbon above Fredericton, and it poured towards me as I drove north and west into the sun. It's a pastoral landscape, coloured in late June by rosy blue lupines and red-winged blackbirds and gleaming satellite dishes, their faces tilted upwards scanning cloud-dappled skies. In the bright summer Saturday twilight, a couple of old men threw a line on the water, not far from the edge of the highway. I passed a tiny Anglican church, white and wooden, and all the gravestones were tall and thin and pointed, like the church itself.

I like this landscape; there's not a mountain in sight. Only to the north, the rounded hump called Mars Hill, a consistent reference point in historical documents and in border negotiations after Jay's Treaty, in which it was named the next important landmark beyond the source of the St. Croix River. It sometimes seems that seventeenth-century cartographers were blessed with aerial vision, that they could imagine then what we can now only see by flying overhead.

The land has recently been radically altered by the Mactaquac hydroelectric power scheme. The dam has swollen long stretches of the Saint John River and almost made a lake out of lower Meduxnekeag Creek, changing its course and dimensions completely. Remnants of early native and French settlement on the river have been drowned. It's as if someone has imposed a new grid on the landscape and shifted the environment slightly around people; from their kitchen window, the view they grew up beside has become an unfamiliar postcard.

At first glance, the countryside is prosperous, the farmhouses big, machinery and vehicles plentiful. But a lot of the old farms are no longer worked; portions of them have been sold off at various times as perches for modest and incongruously urban bungalows. There are empty squares of land sprinkled with random growth, old barns and sheds collapsing inward, their rusting padlocks resisting the flight of silenced machines.

This is potato country, where Maine and New Brunswick farmers bicker over subsidized potato farming. The crumbling, reddish earth of the valleys and gentle hillsides is tilled, planted and consistently pregnant with potatoes. Potato cold storage barns—humps of grassed-over earth covering low cellars that in winter will be chilled by snow—nestle up like offspring to regular barns or other outbuildings. But these days the smart farmers no longer plant potatoes; they invest in potato futures on the stock market.

New roads carve into the shrinking landscape. You can travel up the Saint John River Valley on old 105, on the east side, poking into little forgotten villages like Peel, Bath and Upper Kent. Or you can fly above the landscape on the Highway 2, the Trans-Canada, crossing high over the river on sprung-steel bridges, shuddering in the wake of the long, heavy juggernauts that rule the road. West of Woodstock, the old Houlton Road, winding at its leisure in a bucolic daydream, has become secondary to fast, new, straight 95, a tentacle of Interstate 95, extending over the border from Houlton, Maine, to Woodstock, New Brunswick. I chose the Old Houlton Road.

Woodstock and Houlton are like neighbouring towns, only they happen to be in different countries. They have always attracted each other's young people for pleasure and courtship and, more so in earlier days, marriage. But their connections now are attenuated, their residents isolated from intense local connections by things like satellite dishes and potato wars and the dispersal of families across the continent. Their shared history recedes in the memories of old people and is replaced by strictly mercantile transactions.

On the old Houlton Road near Woodstock, there is a Chinese-

Canadian restaurant on a hill, and at the bottom of the hill I found the Karnes family, who have lived in this valley a few miles from the border since 1900. The valley is known as Karnesville because half a dozen of the original thirteen children live in the houses on either side of the highway. Below the homestead, there is a little building beside the road, once a teahouse, now a bed and breakfast cottage. Because it was early in the season and I was alone, I was invited to sleep in the house.

Narrow stairways, small neat rooms; the farmhouse has changed very little since it was transported to this spot by the grandparents of Vivian, Alice, Gertrude and Don Karnes. A screenporch has been added, various floorings have covered one another and there is still a wood stove. The wallpaper in my bedroom, stately mansions and courtly mauve figures in powdered wigs, is one I remember from the house where I grew up in the 1950s in northern Ontario.

One of the sisters, Gertrude, started a bakery in the thirties; the old patchwork tin building is still standing, but behind the house there is a modern concrete bakery, to which a spur line runs bearing carloads of flour. A couple of Canadian National cars sit on the tracks that stitch a curved line across the back yard. I imagine the dizzy bliss of a childhood with real trains coming right into your own back yard.

In front of the modern bakery there is a small neat pond, where geese float, bloated with bread crumbs.

Gertrude's bakery was taken over by her brothers after the war; the sisters then opened a teahouse for which they did all the baking. Every Sunday, large parties would drive over from Houlton for Gertrude's Nesselrode and lemon meringue pies. The bakery became famous as far south as New Jersey for its brown bread, but it is now owned by Eastern Bakery in Saint John, and the family imagines that little bread is sold in the States anymore.

Members of the Karnes family, like many others in this area, have moved back and forth across the border as it suits them. Alice, now ninety, is an American citizen and worked for thirty years as a housekeeper in New York. Vivian was a secretary; Don worked on the railway. They are a quiet, serious family. We all sat in the living room for a small glass of wine before lunch.

Vivian kept an eye on the pots from the kitchen doorway. "Maine people have a very strong accent, you know; the minute you enter, you know you're talking to someone from Maine. And it's different from Massachusetts. Is it Yankee? I just don't know." She disappeared to stir something.

"Well," offered Alice, "it used to be that Houlton was lighted up more than Woodstock, and the houses were bigger." She rocked gently, steadily, in her corner.

"Oh, yes," said Don, "at one time Houlton had a couple millionaires. But these border towns are hurt on account of the exchange, even down as far as Bangor. And their potatoes aren't so good right now."

"The potatoes are a sore spot," said Vivian, "And you can't blame them for that." There was a long pause; we watched cars pass.

"But it's friendly, very friendly," murmured Alice, who seemed anxious about any idea of hostility.

"Canadians are more conservative," said Don. "The Americans get a dollar and they spend it." Don gets a small pension from the American government, which he spends, carefully, in the United States.

"I can't say why, but I'm a Canadian," said Vivian. "We shoot over, once a week, and we can bring back up to eight dollars' worth of groceries. It's all very friendly, a friendly attitude."

"Yes," said Alice. "It's very friendly." In the silence, the clock chimed. Vivian went to cook the fiddleheads.

Alice rocked. I saw in her fragile-boned, serene demeanour the not quite tragic flaw of English-Canadian society. Niceness. A fine word for our compulsively tidy state of mind, all the dreams and dust and unpleasant bits thrown away or swept under. Something Canadians share with New Zealanders, an inheritance from a certain class of British forebears: forbearance. History forgotten, pangs of longing for a brighter horizon ignored. Not even here, so close to the Americans, was this niceness tainted with exuberance or vulgarity or imagination, the things that I think of as American. Another country, another culture, just a breath away, but the lace curtain was neatly drawn.

Early Sunday morning, I drove up to the old Customs point, which overlooks the new one on the new highway, where there is a shiny modern duty-free shop full of perfume and bone china in the middle of open farmland. I walked up to the end of the old road, climbed across a log barrier and up onto a rock pile, where there were butterflies, buttercups and dandelions. This was the first of many times I would want to cross the border illegally, just to see if anything would happen.

The sporadic Sunday traffic below suggested the casual intercourse between the two countries, here where the border is merely a turnstile on an open road and a time change; Maine is on eastern time, and New Brunswick is on Atlantic time. The suspense I felt watching traffic approach the Customs booths melted in the morning sun; I saw a monotonous pattern of bugs crawling to a stop, blinking briefly, then crawling on towards the Howard Johnson's in Houlton or the tourist information booth ("interpretive centre") on the road to Woodstock. The duty-free shop drew cars like a pile of sugar draws ants.

My own surreptitious route towards the border, which I pictured as a line drawn through the wild hedge of poplars just ahead, was blocked by boulders. I stopped, suddenly uncertain of my rights. I felt that I was being watched from below.

I returned to Woodstock, where I had an appointment at the old courthouse with Ken Homer of the Carleton County Historical Society. Woodstock is an old Loyalist town; on the outskirts, you can see farmhouses dating from the 1820s, with an assortment of outbuildings in various states of disrepair, sometimes a brand new barn. To my eye, Woodstock and towns in Maine are very similar; their signatures are churches, the high-humped bridges that allow for flooding, ice-filled rivers in the spring, and red brick main streets with elaborate and unnecessary one-way systems. In Woodstock, there are rambling Victorian mansions on the hill, their view of the river now obscured by gas stations and an industrialized river front—Woodstock has burned to the ground at least once. The original grandeur of the town has diminished, but it is still a busy, pleasant service centre.

White clapboard houses with shrubs, a brick Catholic church with double spires, a Wesleyan church and a county courthouse; to my westernized eyes, this is all very eastern. The original courthouse was being meticulously restored to its 1860 state by the Carleton County Historical Society; it is in Upper Woodstock, just off the main street, not far from Hardscrabble Store.

The floors of the courthouse had just been varnished, in honour of the imminent visit of Princess Anne. So Ken Homer and I met in a small cottage across the road; it was also being slowly restored. Much attention is given to authentic detail by the Carleton County Historical Society. Paints are mixed according to nineteenth-century recipes. A chimney cap will be rebuilt (after the royal visit) because it is a little small. The fence has been built to the original specifications. The cottage rooms cry out for a warming hearth, a fireplace. But there will be no fireplace; at the time that the cottage was constructed, in 1820, wood stoves were in vogue.

Ken Homer was formal, thoughtful and reserved. His resonant, measured speech was that of an old-time broadcaster, and I have since heard his voice on archival CBC material. He has lived in Woodstock for about forty years, and in local eyes, he is still a newcomer.

We sat on small antique wooden chairs that creaked. The room was unlit, but not gloomy; we bent over the faded text of an old leather-bound history of Carleton County.

"Woodstock was settled first in 1783, after the American Revolutionary War," said Ken Homer. "Members of the provincial regiments were granted this land northwest of Fredericton, and the population was later increased by immigration from Britain. When Houlton, on the American side, was settled a few years later, most people came through Woodstock and got help in settling from the people here.

"During the War of 1812, there was an agreement between the towns of Woodstock and Houlton that there would be no local hostilities as long as folks behaved themselves.

"As a matter of fact, there never was any problem about the border from its beginnings here up as far as Mars Hill. It was up there that the first major border conflict arose—the Aroostook War, in the late 1830s."

The Aroostook War (so named after the Aroostook River, a tributary of the Saint John north of Fort Fairfield) grew out of disputes about logging rights and settlement around the Saint John River. It was a strange combination of tough-young-state muscle flexing and international diplomacy, finally resolved by the Webster-Ashburton Treaty in 1842. Ken Homer, as a newcomer, was cautious and noncommittal.

"According to documents of the time, the citizens of Woodstock had real fears about the war; it would really have been almost a civil war.

"But Sir John Harvey, the lieutenant governor of New Brunswick, and the American General Winfield Scott were old enemies from the War of 1812, and they came to a gentleman's agreement before any shooting took place."

He paused, and the glimmer of a grin flitted briefly on his face.

"Local folklore has it that the only casualty of the so-called bloodless

Aroostook War was an American soldier, who shot himself in the leg in a Houlton tavern during the celebrations following the calling off of hostilities."

I headed north, up the river on the Canadian side as far as Florence-ville, then over the border to Fort Fairfield, to find evidence of the Aroostook War.

Sometimes, on the winding road beside the river, climbing ridges, catching a glimpse of gabled farmhouses set in groves of poplar, I was reminded of the valley of the Dordogne, in southwestern France. The white clapboard farmhouses in mid-distance in a hazy siesta light look like turreted medieval castles and monasteries. The heated fragrance of a midsummer day is laced with romance and tradition. But then sud-denly there is Florenceville, set in concrete, low to the ground. And the appalling smell of potatoes eternally frying at the McKean's plant. Be-side the highway, men with big, square faces under peaked nylon caps eat thick slabs of homemade meat loaf in truckers' cafés. On the radio, the plaintive whine of country music from CJCJ Woodstock and heavy metal from Maine is cut with commercials for "As the World Turns" and treatments for athlete's foot.

The dream landscape of the Dordogne faded.

Fort Fairfield lies in a wide, beautiful valley, the Aroostook valley, just above Mars Hill. Here the Aroostook River flows into the Saint John, and right in the middle of the town, across from the elegant Carnegie Library, there is a reconstructed blockhouse commemorating the Aroostook War. Stuart Duncan lives close to the blockhouse; he's brown and thin, in his seventies, a member of the Fort Fairfield Heritage Society, and he has the key to the blockhouse. He took me inside.

It's a small, cool building with thick pine log walls; sunlight streams through the dust in the late afternoon. The society has rebuilt the blockhouse with some attention to detail. The hewing is "a bit of a fib"—the wood was sawn before it was planed by hand—but the build-ing is mortised together. The upstairs overhangs the ground floor by about three feet; the long, narrow openings for muskets are now glassed over.

The museum houses a motley collection of pioneer artifacts—a yarn-rolling machine, a broken bedstead, photographs and the rusting tools of lumbermen and blacksmiths. Yellowed, handwritten signs are dis-integrating into dust.

"Do people around here still know about the Aroostook War?" I asked.

Stuart Duncan paused beside a row of thick pottery bowls. "The older folk do, but not the younger generation. It was a very meaningful thing for the folk of my kid days. Everyone knew about the Aroostook War. Common thing, everyone talked about it."

He moved on, caressing the dimpled wooden surface of an ax handle. "This was not a little thing, by the way, to many of them that were military men of those days. See, the folk in Maine considered the king of England was stealing their lumber. That was the whole deal. There was a lot of scrapping in these woods." Stuart Duncan stepped abruptly to one side, to stand beside a musket.

"But it was a bloodless war, the Aroostook War," he said firmly.

"No shooting, no casualties?" I asked.

"Oh, a gun did go off as the story goes, and a man who was sowing oats across the river was killed."

We climbed the vertical stairway into the upper storey, our footsteps reverberating in the silence. We walked around, peering into unlit corners at curling maps and fading photographs of forgotten people. Stuart Duncan confided in me the relationships he imagines between this man's top hat and the lady's bonnet hanging downstairs. The intimate domestic objects sat in visual dissonance in the crude military structure. A large linen flag was tacked to a wall.

"And this flag? It's an Acadian flag, isn't it?"

"I'd better not talk about that."

There was a hush. Motes of dusts rose slowly, spinning in shafts of sunlight. Curious teenagers, laughing and whispering, piled through the open door below, and the spell was broken. I headed out into the flagrant June sunshine, across the Aroostook River and north again.

On Highway 1 on the American side, from Fort Fairfield north to Fort Kent (where there is a blockhouse identical to the one in Fort Fairfield), the countryside is not at all prosperous. The border states are perhaps largely the runt end of the American economy, politically and geographically isolated from the power centres. The road is rutted, the farmhouses unpainted, and there is little traffic.

At the town of Grand Falls, the Saint John River becomes the boundary as the river bends off to the west and north. Here it is distinctly French on both sides of the river, and an intensely local culture flourishes around the border. As the Loyalists moved into the lower Saint John valley in the late 1700s, they pushed the French—the Acadians—farther north to settle finally on both sides of the Saint John River in what is known as the Madawaska territory. Madawaska (the land of the porcupine) was inhabited for several centuries by the nomadic Malecite tribe before being claimed by the displaced Acadians. The Acadians of Madawaska are distinctive, linguistically and culturally different from the Acadians to the north and east; they are known as *les brayons*, "the flax beaters."

On the radio, French talkback jostled with the American Top Twenty. In sudden rain, I passed a household shrine, the Holy Mother in a circle of rocks, with a satellite dish right beside her. The house was painted bright blue and white, the firewood tumbled outside the front of the house, and an assortment of vehicles—three cars, an RV and a truck—sat like a gang of bikers in the back yard. I saw bungalows with garages made to look like miniature barns.

The billboards are unexpected in the United States: Nadeau for sheriff, a Cyr *épicerie*. The Daigles seem to be doing everything on both sides of river; on the American side they are carving gravestones, and on the Canadian side they are producing milk. There are buildings with bright-coloured stone and wild tarpaper patterns, a large church that appeared to be papered in stone and houses papered in brick. Then a modern, square, truly brick state building, under an enormous American flag, and in front, an alarming, larger-than-life crucifix.

At Fort Kent, I crossed back into Canada as the rain stopped. I drove down beside the river to an old homestead that had been moved here and transformed into a community museum. FERMÉ.

I wandered beside the river in the afternoon sun, water glittering, the river so shallow in places it looked as if you could just walk across and scramble up the bank on the opposite side and no one would notice. There was no traffic on the river, only the sound of freight trains rattling across the scrubland with loads of scrap metal. I was just a few miles upriver from Baker Brook, where an American named John Baker settled in the 1820s in the midst of the French community. For the people of Maine, John Baker was the hero of the Aroostook War.

Sitting on the edge of the homestead porch, I imagined a conversation with John Baker as he might have sat on his porch in the 1850s, looking at the river, which has changed very little since then . . .

"Yes, I'm John Baker; I'm a lumberman, an American patriot and an entrepreneur." I pictured a square-jawed, stocky man sitting in a hand-hewn wooden rocker, the kind my grandfather Botsford used to make.

"When I first came up this way from downstate, my brother Nathan was already here, on the Méruimticook Brook, what they now call Baker Brook. Liked the country around here; it's a peaceful bit of river, you know, and back then, in the early 1820s, this upper part of the valley was a real lumberman's paradise. Thick with big timber, pines so straight and fine you could just picture them rigged with a full load of sail. Seemed to me this part of the country should be part of Maine, so as I could hold proper title to it. And it wasn't just my own thought; there were quite a few of us then, kinda got to thinking of ourselves as the Republic of Madawaska." He laughed. "Well, I recall for a while there they were calling me the George Washington of Madawaska.

"So I wrote to the Maine legislature to get them to grant me the land, round about what you now call Baker Brook, and they did. Got a letter, granting me ownership, in spite of any protests I might hear from New Brunswick authorities.

"This got them kind of riled down in Fredericton, and darned if they didn't slap a tax on us, what they called foreigners. And they seized our lumber.

"Well, that called for retaliation. Sophie, my wife Sophie, stitched up a real flag. Not the stars and stripes as you now know it. This one had a white background, big American eagle and a semicircle of stars, red stars."

John Baker's square face softened, and he chuckled again. "It was the fourth of July, 1827; we always had a bit of a party for the Independence. This day, though, we got ourselves a real celebration. Americans came from all around the valley, and a few others, too. 'Course we invited the French, the Acadians, you know, but they weren't too keen on joining in. Well, they took in the dancing and a little rum later on, but just in fun, I guess.

"Anyway, we raised that brand new flag on a nice straight spar; chose it myself. Bunting snapping in the sunshine—hot day but kinda breezy, like today. Right in front of the house, by the river. I made a speech, too, and invited all attending to sign our declaration of fidelity to our own little American republic. And 'to resist by force the execution of the laws of Great Britain.' "

John Baker's face lit up with the memory of his personal triumph over the tyranny of British rule in the backwoods of North America.

"Well, sir," he said, "they must have heard the cheering and shouting and clapping clear down the Saint John valley in Fredericton. Because a few weeks later, there was a justice of the peace knocking at my door, and I don't know as to who did it, but someone had hoisted up that flag again. Well, that Fredericton justice of the peace took one look and said, 'What's that?'

" 'That's the American flag,' I said. 'Did you never see it before? If not, you can see it now.'

" 'Pull it down in His Majesty's name,' said he.

" 'No, I will not,' I said. 'We are on American territory and Great Britain has no authority here.'

"Well, he tore the flag right off the pole and took it off to Fredericton. Sophie got straight down to St-Basile and bought more linen and had a new flag up again quicker than you'd credit.

" 'Course the next I knew there was a big posse coming up the river from Fredericton on barges and men lying out in the woods around the house overnight. Grabbed me at dawn, they did, and took me down to some damp hellhole in Fredericton debtors' prison. Lay there seven months before they got around to a trial, despite the fuss raised back in Maine."

John Baker reached behind him to a nail on the porch wall, from which hung a shiny, battered leather pouch. He took out a soft, yellowed letter and carefully unfolded it.

"And it wasn't just the folks in Maine who were behind me. You'll know about Henry Clay, secretary of state of the American government. He wrote to our Governor Enoch Lincoln of Maine; kept me a copy of the letter. Look, right here it says, 'John Baker's arrest . . . on the disputed ground, and his transportation to Fredericton at considerable distance from his family, and his confinement in a loathsome jail, cannot be justified. I am charged therefore by the President [President John Quincy Adams] to demand the immediate liberation of Baker, and a full indemnity for the injuries he has suffered in the arrest and detention of his person.' That's when Maine first started mobilizing the troops down Houlton way."

At this point John Baker shifted a little in his rocking chair, knocked his pipe on his oiled boot and looked to the river again.

"So," said I (in my reverie), "you were released some months later, went back up the river to Madawaska, and things were pretty quiet for a few years. Then what happened?"

"Well, they tried to settle up things by asking the king of the Netherlands for his opinion. Well, the king would have given all of Madawaska, both sides of the river, to the British! This was round about 1831, and nobody in Maine was going to accept that. Rumour had it that President Jackson would have accepted it, but then I guess he was looking for some support in Maine, so he was, as they say, dissuaded.

"So we Americans decided to incorporate the Madawaska settlements. But then our own Governor Samuel Smith of Maine would have no part of that—after all that we had done for the state of Maine.

"Anyhow, like you say, things settled down a bit. Oh, there was still a big commotion going on farther west over the boundary around Indian Stream, but we didn't hear too much of that in Madawaska. Then, around 1837, I guess, things heated up again with old Ebenezer Greeley doing census for Maine, all over Madawaska on both sides of the river. Upriver again comes the New Brunswick posse; all told they arrested Greeley three times before things cooled down.

"Then the illegal lumber trade got the attention of the politicians. See, our boys used to get kinda riled at being told this was the king's lumber, or the queen's lumber, as the case might be; you know the king's men used to come all through the Maine woods, marking individual trees for the Crown. I can tell you there was a fair lot of wood floated down the Saint John that no one on either side had legal title to. Well, it was just there, see, and you can be sure there was a market for it both in New Brunswick and in the United States.

"Anyhow, finally it came to a confrontation. There was some tussling between a bunch of New Brunswick lumbermen and one of our Maine land agents and his posse—about two hundred men if I rightly recall—right on the Aroostook River.

"And that was the real beginning of the Aroostook War. Some said they were using a dummy of Queen Victoria for target practice down Houlton way."

He chuckled a bit, stopping to pull a match across the sole of his boot, sucking the flame into the bowl of his pipe. "But," I said to him, over the silence of 150 years, "you Americans got pretty serious about it, too. By early March 1837, Congress had passed a bill authorizing fifty thousand volunteers, steamboats for the northern rivers and so on, and allowing the president to spend up to ten million dollars on the Aroostook War. That seems exorbitant, even in the 1980s."

"Well . . ." John Baker paused to think a little. "Folks then could get charged up pretty quickly about Great Britain; the idea of war was popular then in the Yankee states. And both Maine and New Brunswick were pretty fired up; there were troops all up and down the Saint John River valley on both sides.

"You know those blockhouses still standing in Fort Kent and Fort Fairfield? They had the rivers pretty well covered; wasn't too much lumber going to get past those Maine militia men. Up here at Fort Kent, they even built a little island midstream, and they had tunnels leading under the river. And Lieutenant Governor Harvey of New Brunswick— well, he was sure trying to muster up the troops, too, but he didn't have the Colonial Office taking much of an interest. Guess they just saw it as some kind of backwoods scuffling.

"I tell you, we sure seemed to be heading for a real nasty war. Then along came our General Winfield Scott of the United States Army, and he and Lieutenant Governor Harvey talked things over, and the whole thing just stopped.

"Not a shot was fired," said John Baker.

" 'Course the actual boundary treaty wasn't signed until 1842, after our Daniel Webster and your Lord Ashburton had a look at things and did some fancy negotiating in Washington and a bit of palm greasing around here, so I was told. And we had a few skirmishes back and forth in those years. But Maine did pretty well out of the Webster-Ashburton Treaty. They gave some seven thousand square miles of land to Maine, you know, using the Saint John River as the boundary, which of course split Madawaska in two. And that left, oh, I'd say about two thousand Acadians on the Maine side of the river."

"So," I said, "here, up at the top end of the river, Baker Brook became part of New Brunswick. What did you and your family do then, as somewhat notorious Americans? Cross over and settle in Maine?"

"No," said John Baker. "It's funny, I guess. I'd been in this same spot on the river for almost twenty years. Had my roots here, the mill and all. So I just stayed put. Evenings, I could sit up here on the porch with the sun colouring the clouds and a breeze ruffling up the water a bit, just like it is today. Look across the river to that long bluff on the other side.

Seems a long time ago that we were fighting each other over those trees . . ."

John Baker's spirit may still reside near Baker Brook, but his remains do not. He died in Baker Brook in 1869; in the 1890s, his daughter removed the remains of both John and Sophie Baker down to Fort Fairfield. A large, handsome granite monument marks their place in the Protestant Cemetery, beside the Aroostook River:

JOHN BAKER, JANUARY 17, 1796 TO MARCH
10, 1869. SOPHIE HIS WIFE, MARCH 17, 1785,
DIED FEBRUARY 23, 1883.
THIS STONE IS ERECTED BY AUTHORITY OF A RESOLVE
OF THE LEGISLATURE OF MAINE, A.D. 1895, TO
COMMEMORATE THE PATRIOTISM OF JOHN BAKER, A
LOYAL SON OF MAINE,
IN MAINTAINING THE HONOUR OF HIS FLAG DURING THE
CONTENTIONS ON THE DISPUTED TERRITORY,
1834 TO 1842.

West of Fort Kent, the international boundary leaves the Saint John River and becomes again a surveyed line through the bush. I decided to turn east and go down the Canadian side of the Saint John River, making occasional excursions back again to the American side, if only for gas. I drove in pelting rain on to Baker Brook.

Baker Brook today is surrounded by open scrub and a haphazard spread of stacked lumber, sweet and pungent on this damp day, and crumbling barns. A trailer with slats under it has become a house of sorts. Another has pillars made out of lumps of stone set in concrete; another is made of basically white siding with red bits, to look like brick, but its bottom half disports a wild, multicoloured paper siding. Houses express both poverty and flights of imagination, flouting conventional taste. In the town, there's a solid brick church with a gilded spire facing the river, crying out to be immortalized in oils by a colonial Constable.

Telephone poles march along in the ditches beside the road and railway, swinging at odd angles, some short and stubby. There is an intimacy, an immediacy. Farther south, the Trans-Canada Highway steers you away from the details of hardship exposed here, a haphazard graveyard of lost dreams and opportunities. In Madawaska, there is no scenery, just a long scuffle for survival.

But the actual towns of Edmundston, New Brunswick, and Madawaska, Maine, seem prosperous, cheerful, friendly. The stink of the pulp industry is inescapable; on a still day a haze lies over the land and everyone wheezes. The Immaculate Conception Cathedral in Edmundston has twin spires, and so does the Fraser pulp mill, twin stacks that pour billowing white emissions into the air, like perpetual columns of vertical foam. Community groups try, at intervals, to generate discussion about air pollution; then people say, but this is our life, and there are no other employers. The controversy subsides; the foam does not. Fraser Pulp is owned at a respectable distance by the multinational Noranda.

The towns are really one town cut in two by the river, a rickety bridge and Customs. The pulp is made on the Canadian side, pumped across the river through a pipe that runs along the bridge and made into paper on the American side. There is a constant traffic of logging trucks and people who live on one side and work on the other. "Anything over?" is all the American Customs officer wants to know. You speak French first in Edmundston, English first in the town of Madawaska.

On the outskirts of Madawaska, in a rambling red farmhouse on the river, I met Geraldine Pelletier Chassé. We sat at her dining room table, which was covered with historical papers and Pelletier family pamphlets. At one point, she opened the china cabinet and dug out a bronze disk, once a border monument, that her husband had found in the barn foundations. The disk sat on the table between us.

Geraldine Chassé is a big, warm woman with a round face and clarionlike voice; she slips effortlessly between American English and Canadian French. She's a passionate "local history buff" for whom the Aroostook War and its protagonist, John Baker, are very much alive.

"Oh, yes, the famous John Baker. Now he was the real rabble-rouser. But the French in Madawaska didn't rally behind him. These people, these Acadians that had been shifted from one place to another for quite some time, they'd seen all this before—déjà vu, you know. When John tried to incorporate Madawaska in 1831, he tried to appoint Pierre Lissotte to represent the Acadians at the state legislature in Augusta. But Pierre refused because he was a subject of the British government, and the British had been good to him.

"That's what I think is comical, that the British had really been the problem all along for the Acadians; they kept pushing these so-called squatters out of Nova Scotia and the lower Saint John valley. Then, once they got up here where they thought they were free from being moved again, they were so loyal to the British!

"Just goes to show how contrary these people could be."

For the French settlers in Madawaska, there was not only the political rift created by the establishment of the international boundary but also the ecclesiastical division. St-Basile, on the north side of the river, had been the mother church for the whole Madawaska area from the early days of French immigration, in the 1780s. In 1838 and in 1842, demands were made to the mother church for chapels on the southern, American side of the river, where the population had been growing. But after the Webster-Ashburton Treaty of 1842 determined the boundary, formal connections between St-Basile and the American side were severed.

Geraldine sighed like an opera singer. "See, the tragic part of this is that a people was divided. In our hearts, we're so closely related. Most people here on the American side have relatives from the North Shore, and most of the Pelletier ancestors that settled here are from Kamouraska and St-Roch, St-Jean-Port-Joli. The Pelletiers aren't one of the founding families, of course."

Geraldine caught my puzzled look and grinned. "Oh, I know, it's tragic that we have anglicized the name! And we're always corrected by non-French people. They say, 'Your name is not *Pel-e-teer*; it's *Pel-tee-ay!*' "

Geraldine has the kind of rolling chuckle that Molière might have imagined for one of his characters.

"How easy is it to keep your French, living in the United States?"

"I'll give you an example; I come from a family of seven, and my children are the only young ones who speak French. With a name like Chassé, if they are going to be in business around here, they have to be bilingual.

"I had to leave the valley to realize how fortunate I was. As terrible as my French was (I grew up in St. Francis, Maine, right on the border, and we mostly spoke English), when I went away and travelled, I made friends, mostly European, because I spoke French. I was accused of speaking French like a Russian."

"And your kids?"

"Oh, they mix their genders, you know, they say *elle* when they should say *lui*. We have one son who lives in Arizona, right next to the Mexican border; Jim calls once a week and he always speaks French and he's very proud of his name, Chassé with the *accent aigu*; he has a sanitation service with his name on the side and a big *accent aigu*.

"I'll tell you one thing, though; it wasn't always like that; in order to get state funds for our education system when our schools started in this area, oh yes, some of the teachers would say, 'NO SPEAKIN' FRENCH IN DE 'ALL!' It was so ridiculous, and then the people started realizing— those who were open-minded and not quite as *provincial*, 'cause the Yankee can be as obstinate as your Loyalist in Canada—and so in the seventies they came out with a fourteen-million-dollar bilingual program, the Title Seven program. Many, many bucks poured into French and Portuguese and Hispanic language programs.

"To me, on the bottom line, I think growing up along the border has been a privilege. It's contributed a great deal of pleasure to my life. And when I compare our Mexican boundary, I just can't get over it, the difference, the appearance, the energy on the Canadian side of the river; the people are ambitious and proud.

"Twenty-five years ago it wasn't so, but now there's a strong pride in being a Canadian. The Canadians used to be like the Acadians here; they hid their identity; they were afraid to be looked down on. But not now. There's a good strong spirit there in Canada. I think Lester Pearson did a great deal, you know, with your Canadian flag. And of course Pierre Trudeau did his bit."

The phone rang, and Geraldine hustled out to the kitchen, where she carried on a conversation about the upcoming Acadian festival, slipping back and forth between French and English. She returned beaming with good feeling.

"I feel secure having a neighbour like Canada. From Mexico, we have our wetbacks and our trafficking in drugs. But we don't have to worry about losing our wheels when we cross into Canada."

Good feeling founders on economic issues in Madawaska, even though Geraldine Chassé, like most people I met on both sides, feels sorry about the exchange rate.

"But around here, things are pretty bad now. Just this Saturday, my husband went to another auction, one of these big farmers—everything was sold out from under them because they couldn't meet their debt obligations.

"Of course we've had our blockades at the boundary; our farmers preventing Canadian truckers from coming in with their potatoes, up here at Fort Kent and down Houlton way.

"This happened, oh, in the last five years; they emptied their potatoes right there at the bridge so that people couldn't pass."

Geraldine laughed again, and her round warm face crinkled. "It kind of reminded me of the bloodless Aroostook War there for a while, cousins shaking fists at one another."

The next morning was cold and windy, and there were little whitecaps on the Saint John River as I drove down the Canadian side. Going downriver from Edmundston, you pass the very small Malecite Indian Reserve, and then enter the embrace of St-Basile, a parish with a stout, comfortable convent on the hill overlooking the river. This is the cradle of French settlement for the whole of Madawaska. On the river bank, above the railway line, a small wooden chapel has been built on the spot where the first chapel was built in 1785. The plaque on its wall lists all the pioneer families—the Daigles, the Cyrs, the Thibodeaus. Not far from the chapel, at one end of the old cemetery, there is a row of unmarked white crosses, one for each of these founding families, whose names are still on billboards and signposts on both sides of the river in Madawaska country.

In front of the chapel, there is a slim iron obelisk, about three feet tall; it's one of the original boundary markers. This marker is engraved with the names of the 1842 boundary commissioners, British Lt. Col. James B. Estcourt and the American Albert Smith; they were in charge of the original survey of the boundary after the Webster-Ashburton Treaty. An iron ring is attached to the monument; at some point, it became a place to tie up horses.

Every summer, the International Boundary Commission sends out teams of American and Canadian surveyors to repair old bronze monuments like this one, install new monuments (white squat blocks of speckled granite), clear the vista and resurvey the line. South of Grand Falls (Monument 117), where the boundary leaves the Saint John River and becomes the straight section known as the North Line, I went out on the line with Canadian field engineer Dale Dryden and his crew.

Dale Dryden goes out every summer with a survey crew to a section of the Canada/U.S. boundary like this one. As a surveyor, he takes enormous pride in the accuracy of his measurements of time and distance, in the precision of his instruments and in the efficiency of his teams in clearing a neat, open scar across the landscape. Surveyors are passionate about straight lines. Dale patiently explained to me the virtually incomprehensible intricacies of triangulation and astronomical survey. He glowed with pride as his crews attacked the vista, shearing the outstretched arms of maple trees with the savage blades of a large Rousseau brush cutter, attached to a Bombardier fitted out with a bulldozer blade. It looks like a science fiction machine; the bush demands creative technology.

The vista creates a line of sight between two countries. It is not a no man's land, although that's how people see it; they instinctively stop at the edge of the vista. It is an open swath on both sides of the line of monuments, ten feet on each side. In the words of the 1908 treaty that outlines the responsibilities of the International Boundary Commission, there should be a "twenty-foot sky line" through all the timbered areas.

If you are standing right on the boundary, beside a monument, you should be able to see a monument in either direction; you can't always, but you begin to know what to look for. If a building stands between monuments, the crews place intermediary monuments on either side of the building, so you can always trace an imaginary line, monument to monument. If lilac bushes encroach on the vista, they are cut down.

Along this part of the border, there are still potato fields that straddle the line. Smart farmers with land on both sides keep a barn on either side.

Near Fort Fairfield, the Aroostook Valley Country Club has a golf course that sits across the boundary line. It was built in the 1920s and began as a nine-hole course in Canada, "so close to the border that a hooked ball on Number One or Number Nine went right out of the country!" according to the club's *Official History*. The parking lot and the pro shop are in Maine; the course and the clubhouse are in New Brunswick.

A straight row of conifers fringes the course along the boundary line. Several years ago, when the International Boundary Commission tried to cut down these trees as an obstruction on the vista, a Maine senator intervened. Canadian law empowers the International Boundary Commission to do what is necessary to keep the vista clear; there is no equivalent American law. The trees remain.

When Dale Dryden looks at this landscape, he sees the mathematically determined line of sight set in the vista, picked out on the ground just as it is drawn on a map. From beneath old monuments, he clears away the rubble of history, the foundations of an old line house or hotel, bits of barbed and woven wire fences, the rock piles formed during the clearing of fields, a cache of rusted horseshoes.

In the late afternoon sun, south of Fort Fairfield, Dale Dryden and I cut through a field in the four-wheel drive and pulled up close to the vista. He can always find his way to the border; we were south of Monument 79 on the North Line. We stopped the jeep and walked through the long, sweet-smelling yellowing grass. The power lines sang. Grasshoppers rushed up and flicked past our knees. The blackflies made volatile little clouds.

Right on the line were the remains of a small house, just foundations and pieces of tin and tarpaper and crumbling concrete. Broken beer bottles and a rusting Coke billboard and an old stove, its door hanging off. Around the house, there was a garden once; its seeds have billowed out over the empty, fertile fields and settled in a rash of indiscriminately lovely blooms. Bachelor's-buttons and yellow lilies, poppies and lupines, the scented memorial of families long forgotten, spilling across from Maine into New Brunswick and back again. Only the nettles prevented us from walking into another country.

We walked down the hill. There, bent over double in the grass, a tiny, bony woman in a cotton print dress scrabbled for wild strawberries. A cigarette perched on a dry lip, a small plastic bowl in which a few perfect, pale orange strawberries rolled.

This field used to be planted with potatoes, she said, but it's been like this for years. The house was pulled down forty-five years ago, when she was in grade school. Once when she was up here, picking strawberries just like today, the U.S. border patrol came up. Really quietly; she turned around and there they were.

Near Limestone, Maine, just up the line, an abandoned missile silo lies about one hundred yards from Monument 97 on the North Line. The survey crew just stumbled across it one day when they were blasting out the foundations of old monuments.

At the Bridgewater/Centreville border crossing (Monuments 48 and 49), there is a plaque installed in waist-deep wild roses:

THIS INTERNATIONAL MONUMENT SYMBOLIZES THE
BEGINNING OF THE CITIZENS WAR ON POLLUTION
IN WESTERN NEW BRUNSWICK AND EASTERN MAINE,
AND MARKS THE SITE WHERE AROUSED CITIZENS
BUILT AN EARTHEN DAM TO STEM THE FLOW OF
POLLUTION FROM THE VALSING INC. COMPLEX
IN EASTON, MAINE.
9TH JULY, 1968.
THIS DATE MARKS THE BEGINNING OF OUR WAR ON
POLLUTION.
THE WAR CONTINUES . . .

The last line is scratched out.

The following day, Dale Dryden took me to see Gerald Trafford, a protagonist in the border pollution war.

We arrived just before noon at the farmhouse. The property runs right to the border; there are potato fields, woods, open pasture. The land has been in the family for three generations. It is not, to the unschooled eye, a prosperous-looking property. Remnants of past ventures are strewn everywhere—a pile of scrap metal, forms for making barrels, the outline of an old mill still clinging to the banks of a little stream. And a modest hill family members call Trafford's Mountain; they make jokes about putting the television Walton family out of business.

The farmhouse is old and low ceilinged. Tortoise-shell cats blinked in the sunshine and followed us inside, where Mrs. Trafford—Reva—prepared lunch for Gerald, who would arrive home for his lunch around fifteen minutes past twelve, as he had done every day for more than fifty years.

"He knows every rock and tree on the place, just like his father and his grandfather and his great-grandfather did before him," Reva Trafford said. "It means a lot to him just to go out and wander around out there."

Reva is good-natured, grey haired, a large, comfortable woman. She showed me photos of the most recent wedding and invitations to the upcoming—and, she hoped, final—one. Between them, the Traffords have eleven children, some from previous marriages. The children are scattered across the country. One son, Larry, bought an old property across the road; for less than forty thousand dollars, he acquired one hundred acres of land, an old farmhouse and outbuildings—one of which hides a bomb shelter—a trout pond and a large wood from which he culled enough lumber in one season to pay off his mortgage. Larry comes to his parents' house at least once a day.

"He comes by and gets a coffee," said Reva. "It gives us security to know that he's handy."

Through the kitchen window, I saw concrete and wood and rocks in rubble around a small stream.

"Now that used to be a dam," said Reva, holding a handful of silverware. "About fifteen years ago, Gerald had a mill over there where he used to make barrels. He had about fifteen coopers and ten nailers, but it burnt down. Then he put a shingle mill in and ran it off the water, but then the ice took it out. In fact, the water wheel's laying down there in the river. Our son in Ontario has bought that; someday he'd like to remodel it and put the water back over the dam and get us a mill pond again. But Environment Canada has, well, you know you don't just put a dam wherever you want it; and they'll insist on a fishway, which maybe is good and all. But I don't think we should have to worry about whether in Maine they get fish and all . . ."

Reva set the table, got out the crackers, always moving. By the time the mushroom soup was heated up, Gerald was home and in his rocking chair beside the kitchen table. He is seventy-six and works a full day every day, despite his hearing aid and rocking chair and glinting glasses. When I asked a question about the 1968 pollution war on the Presqu'ile Stream (known locally as the Prestile), the sounds of the dishwasher and transistor radio seemed to fade as we slipped back into a storytelling culture with an accomplished raconteur:

"Well, the first we noticed it, the fish come belly up, belly up, belly up there, right above the dam, and we said, what's the matter with all those fish? So we went down and looked them over and there were a lot of dead ones. A lot of them was suckers, trout, and on the lower side of the dam, all kinds of fish, even eels was trying to get oxygen. So we notified the authorities. Then about the second day it got to be so bad, all these fish were dead, and there was an awful odour to it. You couldn't hardly stand it all along the river.

"So we decided we would put a dam in, right up at the boundary line so as to let the Yankees know we were going to do something about it. We was well aware that they had let a lot of pollution loose up at Valsings Plant—they let these big holding ponds go all at once, and that's what killed the fish. So we decided to get a bunch around and whatever machinery we could; I had an old K-8 bulldozer, and I owned the ground pretty much to the river. We just shoved in wood and brush and all, like a beaver building a dam—it really holds, you know—and by night we had her across and the water was coming up; the dam was eight to ten feet high, so of course the water came up right to the top of it.

"Well, by night there was a stream of cars about a mile long on both sides of the road on both sides of the line. They were coming from everywhere, and no one really tried to stop us; we were right on the line.

"The next day, the wardens were trying to deal with all those dead fish; they sprayed some lime to kill the poison."

"You couldn't even open a window in your house for the smell," Reva added, standing at the sink.

Gerald continued. "In a couple of days, that dam was so loaded with maggots, with dead fish comin' up the front of that dam. Well, then we let the sluiceway out to clean it out. It lasted about a week, I'd say."

"And the water wasn't clear, it was just grey, like a grease film all over it." Reva's face crumpled at the memory, as did mine at the image she painted.

"The plant over there, Valsings, never let out so much again—that was three or four big lagoons of sewage.

"And those fish there going belly up, belly up . . ."

A postman older than time walked into the kitchen.

Gerald barely drew breath as he charged deeper into the pasture of his border memories:

"I was born and brought up on the boundary line. My grandfather also had land on the other side, and my father used to go to school on the other side because it was a mile handier. We would take our butter and eggs over there—to three pretty nice stores. When I was a kid, there was no Customs there. There used to be a Customs at Bridgewater, and you were supposed to report, but nobody did. Along where the Customs is now there were five or six old houses, and I guess they used to sell some booze, rumrunners we used to call them. Gallon cans from the north shore . . ."

"Could you go over there and work?"

"No, but you could get a head tax easily. The wages over there was two dollars a day, where it would be a dollar a day here. When I was ten to twelve years old, I used to skip across and handle potatoes all day and watch for the patrol. I'd cut seed for eight cents a barrel in the spring of the year. Eight barrels was a big day's cut. Now they do forty or fifty and get two dollars a barrel. I'd go over there in the fall of the year, too, and pick potatoes, take a section near the woods so I could dodge in the woods real quick. Eight cents a barrel for picking, too.

"I did used to smuggle a lot. It was a matter of survival; if you made five or ten dollars, that was big money."

"There was a fellow at Bridgewater who said to me one day, 'Gerald, can you smuggle over a bunch of beans?' These were dried beans; they got them in Ontario for a dollar a hundred and had them shipped into Florenceville, about ten tons in all. We turned all the bags wrong side out, see, because they had 'Ontario' stencilled on them.

"I had an old Dodge car with a little trailer, and I made ten trips across the border, a mile on the other side of the line, with those beans. Well, about two days later the border patrol came along. They got wind there was beans being smuggled, so they punched a few holes in some of the bags over there, found out they were from Ontario. Then they built a lean-to, right there on the border, and camped out, to see if they could catch somebody in the act.

"Well, for about a week I never went over, and they got all the beans away out of Bridgewater. But I still had a few hundred pounds left, and I thought I would take them this night.

"I remember I had to go through Vic Ketchum's yard to get across, and he said, 'Gerald, you know there's been a patrol camped over there on the line ever since you brought those beans over last week, until about an hour ago. Well, just about an hour ago, both those officers come up by.'

"Well, I just went on to Bridgewater with the beans."

Gerald shook his head. "I had some close calls."

That evening, once more I found myself on the vista, looking down the cut line through a swamp. I heard the song of a solitary sparrow and tried to ignore the insistent blackflies. Henry David Thoreau walked through this border country in the mid 1840s and recorded what he saw in *The Maine Woods*, published in 1864, after his death. Thoreau sat in swarms of the "perfectly formed" blackfly and contemplated the pure primitivism of the swamp. He followed the trail of the musquash, up to his knees in mud and water, and considered the dilemma of choosing the route for the boundary through these "highlands"—so called in the 1783 Treaty of Paris—"the highlands which divide those rivers that empty themselves into the St. Lawrence from those which fall into the Atlantic Ocean." Thoreau meditated on the folly, to be committed with regularity along the Canadian/American boundary, of choosing land-forms to correspond with treaty language. The "highlands" seemed a considerable fiction to a man standing in a swamp,

> truly an interesting spot to stand on, . . . though you could not sit down there. I thought that if the commissioners themselves, and the king of Holland with them, had spent a few days here, with their packs upon their backs, looking for that "highland," they would have had an interest-ing time, and perhaps it would have modified their view of the question somewhat. The king of Holland would have been in his element.

Not a great deal has changed since Thoreau's journey, here at least; the swamp is a little drier, and the potato fields are tilled by a tractor, which I could hear faintly in the distance. In the softening evening light, the short white boundary monuments came to look like boulders and then disappeared in the dusk that descended from the skyline and filled the vista.

I walked on down the line.

# 2

## THE LIE OF THE LAND—
## THE FALSE 45TH PARALLEL

Big road, this Highway 91 north through Vermont. It looks as if someone got up early and vacuumed it. It is smooth and graded, with
clipped edges, and made of pale, spotless materials, and it takes you in
an orderly fashion across the line, where it merges with Quebec Highway 55, about ninety miles south of Montreal. It has been landscaped;
there are groomed evergreen windbreaks on the median and dramatic
stands of birch on outcroppings of dark grey granite ribbed with broad
white bands of feldspar. The road undulates according to the internal
rhythms of the landform; this is the Vermont Piedmont, east of the
Green Mountains and west of the Northeast Kingdom. Below the road
on the left, there is a cluster of low red farm buildings. On the right, a
sign announces the 45th parallel of latitude, the midpoint between the
equator and the North Pole, about three quarters of a mile south of the
boundary.

If you cross the border on this highway, you are halted by flashing
lights and channels of traffic, imperious signs and a barrage of tightly
belted officials wearing sunglasses and hats, sitting in the narrow boxes
Janette Turner Hospital has described as "upturned coffins." Here you
find order, regulation and clear-cut national jurisdictions.

But if you leave Highway 91 before the border crossing and head instead for Derby Line, Vermont, you drive into a little valley of curving
village roads with sudden dips, past big old houses on well-shaded
streets. Canada is just a breath away in the white houses and white
churches of Rock Island, Quebec. The boundary line disappears into a
cluster of buildings, descends suddenly into the Tomifobia River and

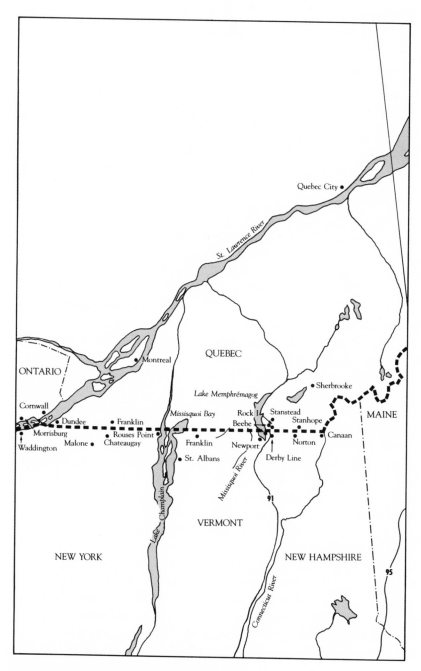

**EASTERN PROVINCES AND STATES**

only becomes recognizable as a border on the outskirts of Rock Island, running over a small ridge. A few miles along, in Beebe Plain, Quebec, and Beebe Line, Vermont, the border runs beside Canusa Road; the houses on the south side of the street are in Vermont; the houses on the north side are in Quebec. Officially, in order to visit your neighbour in what is simply known as Beebe, you are supposed to go to the border crossing at the end of Canusa Road and come back that way, too. (I spent several days in the area, and I only saw one person on Canusa Road.) Up at the end of Canusa Road, the boundary bisects a large granite house before again becoming an occasionally visible line of markers through the bush.

On a map, this is one of three or four straight lines in the entire length of the border. It is an arbitrary 155-mile section, neatly trimming Quebec and touching the states of New Hampshire, Vermont and New York. On the east, the straight line joins the meandering water boundary, Hall's Stream, the northernmost arm of the Connecticut River; on the west, it touches the St. Lawrence River at Cornwall, Ontario. Officially, this is called the 45th parallel section of the line, but the international boundary really never touches the 45th degree of north latitude. Hence, it is known as the false 45th; its tidiness is a triumph of cartographical precision, but not, as I discovered, a model of surveying accuracy.

This is one of the oldest official borders in North America; it was noted as a boundary line as early as 1606, in the Plymouth Company Charter, and even briefly proposed at one point as the entire boundary from coast to coast. In the 1760s, the 45th parallel was named part of the border between Lower Canada and New York, both British colonies at that time. It was surveyed in the 1770s by John Collins of Lower Canada and Thomas Valentine of New York. It took shape as a long row of blazed trees, with a large pile of stones every three miles.

In the decade following the survey, there were murmurings on the American side that the boundary was south of the 45th. An American clergyman claimed that the boundary line was so far south that the state of Vermont was deprived of more than seventeen townships.

In the Treaty of Paris of 1783, after the American War of Independence, the 45th parallel was declared to be part of the international boundary. But in the usual style of treaty-defined boundaries, it was only named, not located on the ground. After the War of 1812, the Treaty of

Ghent stipulated that the 45th be resurveyed. It was then discovered that the surveyed line was from a quarter mile to one and a quarter miles north of the true 45th parallel. Near Rouses Point, on Lake Champlain, the Americans were building a fort just below the surveyed line to defend themselves from Canadians in what was in fact British territory.

Various reasons are given to explain how an official survey, carried out over several years by two skilled and conscientious men, could have been so completely, consistently wrong. Certainly by modern standards, the instruments were primitive, and much of the survey was carried out in harsh winter conditions. The dutifully kept records reveal that the sundries required for one portion of the survey included plenty of rum, wine and six gallons of French brandy. There were confrontations with the Abenaki Indians, who were displeased about the encroachment upon their hunting grounds around the Connecticut River.

In 1831, the king of the Netherlands proposed a compromise whereby the boundary would revert to the true 45th parallel, with a bubblelike arc made around the American fort, later named Montgomery. The Americans would not accept this proposal. In 1842, Daniel Webster and Lord Ashburton settled for the old surveyed line, known as the Valentine-Collins Line, as the permanent boundary.

What on maps looks like a neat, straight line is in fact a crooked row of stitches across a patchwork quilt of farmland, woods and small towns. The false 45th parallel intersects cemeteries, houses, beds, even bodies as it stitches itself across the land. Simply walking the line is not possible here. This is a border that belongs in fiction, not Kafka, but perhaps D. M. Thomas, or John Irving. It is the kind of border you would find in a dream and, upon awakening, be unable to describe. It has its own set of conventions, acknowledged unconsciously in the daily life of villages intertwined like the fingers in a handclasp.

The north/south alignment of the land is powerfully felt even on this gently rolling landscape—the two long lakes, Memphrémagog and Champlain, and the Richelieu, Connecticut and Hudson river valleys still defining the movement and settlement of people. On the Quebec side, the area east of the Richelieu valley is known as the Eastern Townships. In Vermont, the upper right-hand corner of the state is referred to as the Northeast Kingdom.

I made a loop around the Northeast Kingdom on a frosty Sunday morning in late October, listening to Handel and Corelli on Vermont

Public Radio, where the Eye in the Sky weatherman talks about Sher-BROOKE in his picture-story weather forecasts, and where Quebec is just another state in the fundraising drive. CBC Stereo, I thought, rarely imagines any audience outside Canada. As I made my way east, crisscrossing the border on quixotic minor roads, I contemplated the idea of a single, undifferentiated culture, all historical distinctions blurred or simplified.

In Stanhope/Norton, I inadvertently slipped into the United States; without warning, it is Vermont. There is no marker; I drove anxiously down a hill and around the back yard of the U.S. Customs building. Next to the car window, the gun hit me at eye level; then the body bent and acquired a face. All American Customs officers must wear guns; for American Immigration officers, a gun is strongly recommended, but not mandatory. It will probably become mandatory because "of all the things that have been going on around here recently."

Several years ago, there was a manhunt in the Northeast Kingdom; a man described as a veteran of the Vietnam War, armed with four or five machine guns, was camping along the border, zigzagging along from side to side, eluding capture by moving between countries. This now almost mythical deranged figure suits the Northeast Kingdom, a shabby, run-down corner of poor farms on indifferent land, where hunting shacks and temporary houses with no foundations sit like birds poised for flight on the edges of swamps. In Canaan, where Vermont, New Hampshire and Quebec collide, there is a French church and a large plaque to commemorate those who died in the Korean, Vietnam and Second World wars. Canaan, "the birthplace of Ethan Allan Furniture," had a population of less than eleven hundred in 1965; from here one hundred men went to die in Vietnam.

From Canaan going towards Maine and New Brunswick, the boundary was assigned to Hall's Stream, truly a stream, narrow and flat, rippling across snow-dusted fields. Here again, definition and location of the boundary are out of synch; Hall's Stream has wandered from its course as much as 750 feet since 1845, when the stream was surveyed as the boundary. In 1783, the Treaty of Paris declared that the "northwesternmost head of the Connecticut River" was to join the 45th as part of the border. Several streams laid claim to that distinction through their settlers, and disputes led to the brief, proud tenure of the Republic of Indian Stream, between 1832 and 1836. The republic was subsequently absorbed by New Hampshire, and Hall's Stream became the boundary. It was surveyed in 1845, again in 1914–15 and in 1979, by which time more than half of the 467 turning points in the original boundary line were now on land, the stream itself having moved on. But in the boundary game, as in all sophisticated board games, there are rules of hierarchy; precedent supersedes accuracy, and mathematically defined points outrank mere place names and physical description. Regardless of changes in the physical landscape, "the international boundary remains mathematically fixed."

The once hotly disputed land between Hall's Stream and Indian Stream looks to be a wooded ridge of absolutely no significance whatsoever. The front yards in the little settlements along the stream display a demoralized jumble of poverty. Young girls, their features blotted out with make-up, walk along the highway on a Sunday morning glaring at strange cars and smoking.

I turned west and drove back towards Lake Memphrémagog.

This section of the border expands to embrace in its daily compass the entire length of Lake Memphrémagog, a long, narrow lake, about twenty-seven miles from stem to stern, in both Vermont and Quebec. People in Georgeville, Quebec, on the northeastern shore of the lake, drive some thirty miles to buy groceries in the mammoth shopping centre at Newport, at the southern end of the lake, and they have an identity as part of the Stanstead/Rock Island border community. To a certain extent, everyone makes use of the proximity to another country. The Americans come over to the doctor and the dentist; the Canadians regularly cross over for gas and to go to the supermarket. Some keep a post office box on each side of the line.

Valerie Cerini and Howard Smith were for several years the editor and the publisher, respectively, of the Stanstead *Journal*, "Quebec's Oldest Weekly." They had an apartment above the *Journal* office in Rock Island and still have an old family cottage at Georgeville. I sat with them one evening at dusk; across Lake Memphrémagog, we could see the lights of the red brick stagecoach inn at Knowlton's Landing; it is now called L'Aubergine. Persian cats prowled around us. Howard is mild mannered, soft-spoken and given to gentle pedantry; Valerie is uncompromising, blunt of manner, warm of heart. They love this area, know its history well and are delighted to talk about it.

"The Anglophones all insist on telling us we're all Loyalists," said

Valerie. "Well, we're not, because this part of the border was shut. The Loyalists came into Missisquoi County, and they were in the Maritimes and Ontario, but this section of the border was completely shut."

Howard jumped in. "The whole area that is now the Eastern Townships between 1784 and 1790 was a forest buffer zone, declared by Governor Haldimand to be an Indian neutral state closed to all settlement. And in fact, when a group of Loyalists did come up the Champlain valley and settled in Missisquoi Bay on the northern end of Lake Champlain, the British government in Montreal tried to burn down their farms and force them out. They fought back. So Missisquoi County is the only Loyalist county; the rest of the townships may have Loyalist families, but they are people who came here *after* the Loyalist migrations."

Valerie seized the initiative. "The only Americans around here are Yankee land grabbers; 1815 is the oldest dated building in Georgeville, and that's the barn up behind the Murray Memorial Centre. The people who came here were opportunists, and they did a little bit of everything. Georgeville was important at least until 1871, big enough to get Lord Dufferin here. And Sir Hugh Allen and the Molsons; they all had cottages."

"They ran a stagecoach from Boston to Montreal, up until the 1860s anyway," said Howard. Valerie took over. "It came through Rock Island, Stanstead, down through Fitch Bay, hopped on a ferry here at Georgeville and went over to . . ."

"Knowlton's Landing," they said in unison, "which is right over there—see, where the light is shining?" Howard pointed across the darkened lake.

The lake is half in, half out of Canada, and loosely patrolled compared with the roads. "Well, now the Customs officers are unionized, see, so they no longer do so many lake patrols," said Valerie. "Now it's the obligation of the person to report. If you have a boat, you take your boat registration and get a boat pass, and then you can flash up and down the lake as much as you want, and they don't care now."

"Which is a far cry for the old days," she added, "when they had the *Anthemis*, the big steamer on the lake. The Customs officers would always come on board and wonder why the ladies had gained forty pounds on their way home, because they'd been shopping for dresses in Newport!"

To officially enter Canada by road at Rock Island/Derby Line, you cross the small bridge over the Tomifobia River. The border is just beside the thirty-mile-per-hour speed limit sign before the bridge; it runs across the brick corner of a dilapidated apartment building and then along the river. I walked down a steep, narrow track just inside Canada, through garbage, debris and brush, to the old Lay Whip Factory on a grassy river bank. It is a four-storey, pale grey frame building, a wooden shell holding windows as fragile as cobwebs. Dark, stilled machinery is barely visible inside. A pale tan and white cat guards the property. The river rushes past, sliding down a staircase of black stone plates; the water curls yellow at the edges of the curves. At one time, a canal steered some of this water through a short detour, into a mill on the opposite bank, but the mill, too, is now an empty, dangerous place.

These factories and the abandoned Butterfield Tap and Die Factory down the road, which is half in Canada, half in the United States, were the small industries around which these border towns flourished in the latter half of the nineteenth century. Historically, Derby Line, Vermont, Rock Island and its neighbouring village on the hill, Stanstead, Quebec, were key villages in a transportation system and the textile industry. The current Canadian Customs and Immigration office in Rock Island, a dull brick and concrete building, was constructed on the site of one of the old textile factories; there was at one time a pulley system overhead to bring bales of cotton directly and illegally into Canada from a twin factory on the American side.

The Customs officials in Rock Island have plenty of time to talk between cars. "In the 1920s, there were as many as twenty textile factories right here; they were smuggling in custom-made shirts, cloth, shoes, you name it. Then there was a big scandal, and some pretty important people in Ottawa were implicated, and the whole industry shut down overnight."

The attrition visible here is common on both sides of the border; small businesses began as natural extensions of local agricultural activity, expanded as a result of brisk local trading and in response to major events such as the American Civil War, and then were left by the wayside in the subsequent rush to mass production to the north and south.

Now, this bend in the Tomifobia River is neither productive nor lovely. It is forgotten. Its history is obscured, built over and built over.

The old river buildings, the mill and the factories are frail sentinels; their guts have been worked over by vandals and time. The IGA supermarket and its parking lot sit over the river above the ruins of the mill; under the sidewalks it is hollow where the canal once ran. The centre of Rock Island is rotted at the heart, and the long, straight ridge on the American side, above Derby Line, is a cemetery.

Residents along the 45th parallel have traditionally exploited or at least played with the binational intimacy forced upon them by this line. Buildings, or at least property divisions, usually predated the laying down of the line by surveyors. Nowadays line houses are refused building permits, existing ones are encouraged to fall down and transborder intimacy takes the form of neatly squared-off peace parks with controlled access.

But the Haskell Free Library and Opera House in Derby Line, Vermont, and Rock Island, Quebec, built in 1904, was deliberately placed across the boundary line. It was a gesture of international friendship, a good deal less symbolic than most such gestures. Also, it was conceived by a person, not a bureaucratic group, and is therefore idiosyncratic to a degree unimaginable by a committee. The building was offered to the villages by Martha Haskell and her son, Horace, as a memorial to husband and father Carlos F. Haskell. It was designed by Rock Island architect James Ball; the opera house, which is the upper half of the building, is a scale model of the old Boston opera house. It is a grand building, in the Romanesque revival style, with an eighty-foot hexagonal tower, a glossy slate roof, a lower half built in rough-cut grey granite and an upper half made of a warm, apricot-coloured brick; it is set on a rolling lawn, shaded by copper beech trees.

The library on the ground floor is a series of pleasant rooms finished in shining walnuts and mahogany, marble and granite, lit with chandeliers and natural light coloured by stained-glass windows. The reading room is in the United States; the circulation desk and stacks are in Canada. A thin black line is painted on the floor, not, surprisingly, to satisfy the International Boundary Commission, but rather to comply with the demands made by an insurance company after a fire.

The opera house upstairs is a 450-seat auditorium; about a third of the seats and the stage are in Canada. The black line is carefully marked on the polished wooden floor. The stage is hung with an Italianate pastoral backdrop. In the late 1960s, it was suggested that the Beatles might perform here, at a time when John Lennon was persona non grata in the United States.

If you live in Rock Island, to go to the library you must report to the U.S. Customs, then go to the library, then report to Canadian Customs on your way home. The international boundary line, protected by exclusive access to the library from the United States, cannot be exploited. In most of the remaining line houses, the internal configuration of the buildings is of little concern to border officials. There are no longer the ambiguous commercial establishments like Jimmy Hill's Store up at Morses Line, where during World War II good American housewives would tiptoe across the line on the floor of the store to buy soap and ketchup in Canada; these goods were rationed in the United States.

People walk back and forth across the line here. On either side of the bridge, especially the American side, the Customs and Immigration officials inhabit what look like gas stations. On the American side, too, you are supposed to know that you make a little detour to report to Customs; the station is not stretched across the road, to prevent you from going any farther. This insouciance is counterbalanced by a system of surveillance cameras, sensors and electric eyes, monitoring all the streets in these two little towns where there is not an official crossing. If you were to just walk across the border down there on Sunset Avenue, they say, you'd find the border patrol waiting for you at the bottom of Caswell for sure. For sure.

To the chagrin of local Canadian officials, there is no equivalent Canadian surveillance system; the nearest RCMP constable is posted twenty-five miles from the border, "and what the hell good is that? People know this area; they know how easy it is to cross." Several Customs officials told me that the Canadians were offered the opportunity of sharing the American surveillance system—"it would have cost us no more than twenty-five thousand dollars"—but the Canadian government declined. The Canadian officials are sensitive about their impotence: "If you have to intercept someone on one of those back roads at two in the morning, it would be nice to have a gun. What are you going to do, chase them with a bicycle?"

On the Canadian side ("just went to the library"), I got out of my car and went inside to talk to the officals. The job seems less strenuous here, not like those points where three or four people stand in booths in shifts and face a constant stream of rolled-down windows and uncertain, uplifted faces. To do the job here, you come out from behind the counter, go outside, bend down to the opened window or open the passenger door. It would be pointless to stand outside, waiting for cars. There were some people, though, who were just waved through; no questions, just a glance from the car to the building, a glance returned, an uplifted hand, and the car would drive on. But it is the kind of town in which people, without even trying to, know exactly where other people will be at any time during the day. After declaring a bottle of wine, I absent-mindedly walked away with a pen; later that night, I heard about it over dinner. When I had been in the area for several days, I, too, was waved through sometimes—on both sides of the line.

There used to be two parades, on the first and the fourth of July, with two marching bands and two flags. On the first of July, the parade would start up in Canada, in Stanstead, come down the hill, through Rock Island, and stop at the bridge. Here the Canadian band would change places with the American band, the Canadian flag would go to the back of the parade and the procession would continue up the main street of Derby Line. On the fourth of July, the same parade would take place in reverse.

There are cracks in the sanguine homogeneity. On the Canadian side, there are English-speaking people who barely contain their bitterness and contempt for their French-speaking neighbours. They don't like the few brightly painted houses in Rock Island, which strike an eloquent cultural accent in the predominantly white clapboard picture. The border officials, the small grocery stores, the signs are almost all Francophone. I went to a small shop, where I was the seventh person to be served. Everyone before me spoke and was spoken to in French. Before I said a word, I was spoken to in English.

Yet despite the surface distinctions, courtesies and simmering hostilities, the cross-cultural fertilization is deep; beneath the politics, there is a layer of pragmatic unity, like that in a marriage of many years.

Aurore Mosher owns the line house in Beebe, at the end of Canusa Road. She is a plain, forthright woman in her eighties, with solid brown hair and a strong jaw. Her husband, Leon, is ninety-three, formerly a supervisor at Butterfield's. Aurore has owned this house for fifty-six years. She wanted this particular house very badly; it took her three months to buy it from the Stewart estate, and she had to "use the law a little bit to get it." But "I was entitled," she said enigmatically, without elaborating. The original building once contained both American and Canadian post offices. She showed me an old photo, which depicted a simple, well-proportioned, granite house. It now has a rambling extension on the American side.

"We are five here," she said, five apartments built into the house and over the double garage. The boundary marker is buried in the grass beside the front door. Leon sleeps in the United States, and Aurore sleeps in Canada.

We were sitting in the gathering gloom of an autumnal afternoon twilight. The sky darkened suddenly; Aurore lit the lamps. Her three sisters were visiting, all wrapped up in caps and scarfs and mittens, Albertine and Gloria and the eldest, who dozed inside her warm burgundy wool coat. They all sat with one ankle crossed over the other and hardly spoke a word while I was there, except the eldest, who once said, "We are listening," when Aurore lapsed briefly into French. Her husband speaks not a word of French. He is an American, and she is a Canadian. Sometimes the American Customs or Immigration officer on duty across the street will come and ask her to translate for them, because they, too, speak no French. And she comes and goes daily as she pleases.

"Oh, if I have a big load, I go to the Customs, and of course I don't do any smuggling. Of course if I wanted a fur coat . . ."

Aurore took me outside, walking in her bedroom slippers on the thin layer of snow, to show me the boundary monument planted beside her front steps, part of the garden. She talked about the granite trucks coming all night; all night they come down Canusa Road, she said, with the granite for the Rock of Ages plant up the road. But the house is virtually soundproof, with its walls of thick granite. They never stop, she said, night and day.

In Beebe, granite is used almost casually as a building fabric, not just for churches and big houses. There is a huge granite gateway at the entrance to a small municipal park. Roadside commercial signs look like freestanding gravestones; that of the Emslie Company, for example, is a thick slab of pale grey polished stone with deeply carved letters above the engraving of a truck cab. There are small granite bungalows, and on the outskirts of the village a row of quarrying companies, where the granite is left lying around the yards in loose piles, like lumber. Through one such yard, I saw a small herd of cattle wandering at dusk.

As I drove toward Graniteville, I could smell a tension in the autumnal landscape. Hunters in fluorescent orange vests hung with guns and knives pulled up in gangs beside small cemeteries on the back roads. They wore red and black wool trousers and red caps, and stood motionless behind trees, smoking cigarettes, sudden figures in a landscape. I watched comrades spilling out of pickup trucks to admire the white-bellied carcass of a young female deer, splayed and stiffening beside the road. When I stopped beside the Stanstead Granite Company quarry, I heard several shots, the sound bouncing off a slate-grey sky.

The Stanstead Granite Company quarry looks like a set design for a production of *Das Rheingold*. An enormous rough bowl is being hewn out of the crust. I stood at the edge, beside an aluminum shed that contains the controls for the hydraulic system whereby the rock is cut and moved. In the centre of the bowl stands a very tall metal ridge pole, with wires radiating out and anchored around the edge of the bowl. A long metal arm is attached to the pole, so it resembles an inverted compass. Deep in the curves and ledges and ridges of the faceted rock, there are tiny wooden ladders leaning on the sides of the bowl—I can imagine the Nibelung dwarfs placing their tackle around slabs of cut granite. There are many small dark pools of water laced with ice, and the only sound on a Sunday evening is that of a pump, constantly draining the water out of the bowl.

This is the northern rim of a granite industry that since the early nineteenth century has been carved out of the hills south of here, down the central ridge of Vermont. This was one of the first industries to draw French-Canadian labour south into Vermont. The border counties still have a population that in some areas is 30 per cent French Canadian by birth; this population forms most of the Vermont farming community.

Derby Line, Rock Island, Stanstead and Beebe all get their water from Vermont; there is a watershed about ten miles south of the line, and the rivers flow north. This area drains into the St. Lawrence, through Lake Champlain and Lake Memphrémagog. In 1985, the area was one of a number of sites being considered by the American Department of Energy for a nuclear dump. Twenty-five of the 125 possible sites were within fifty miles of the Canada/U.S. border, five of them in New Hampshire and Vermont, within the watershed.

A group of local residents from both sides of the border formed a vigilante group called Citizens Against Nuclear Dump Usage—CANDU, for short. (The name itself antagonized Canadian politicians because they disliked the intended implication of a connection, in some mocking sense, between this citizens' group and the Canadian nuclear reactor.) The group's sole objective was to prevent the sites within the watershed from making the short list for further and more detailed consideration. Chick Schwartz and Jean Choquette were prime movers in this group, and I spent a morning with them at Chick's farmhouse, between Rock Island and Beebe. Chick is an engineer, originally from Atlanta, Georgia, who has become a ceramics artist and sculptor; he lives here with Marsha, his beautiful, warm wife, who is a potter, and their four big sons. Jean is a Canadian Customs officer, a fiery and outspoken Québécois. It seemed an unusual alliance.

The proposed site that most concerned them was centred about five miles south of the border, in the middle of a lake from which the border communities draw their water. It consisted of a twenty-acre burial site contained within a twenty-thousand-acre no man's land. There was to be a shaft, about a thousand feet deep, leading to four hundred acres of underground chambers—in effect, a mine. Only instead of being used to remove precious metals, it would hold nuclear waste. Twenty trucks (semis) would pass through the area every day, hauling nuclear waste to the dump. At the time of the first phase of the search for a nuclear dump, no geological analysis had been done. But the American Department of Energy imagined a shaft blasted down through granite, an apparently impervious substance within which nuclear waste would be held in containers designed to last for three hundred years.

"Plutonium's half-life is twenty-six thousand years," said Chick. "So in effect they were saying, we'll protect everybody for three hundred years. After that, the river in Montreal will be polluted and Montreal probably will therefore be off the map. Because all the water flowed into the Canadian watershed."

"If they had gone maybe ten miles south," said Jean, "they would have gone into the Connecticut basin, where all the water flows south, into the States."

"The DOE had twenty-some maps, showing population and mines and forests and water. And on every one of them, the land above the Canada/U.S border was white. There was not a river; all the rivers stopped miraculously as soon as they came to the border. You could almost imagine a waterfall there, going over the edge, the border!"

"And Lake Memphrémagog—all you could see was the little back bay of Newport. The map didn't show the twenty-five miles or so of the lake that goes into Canada."

The issue of the nuclear dump site became a transborder concern; in fact, initially the Canadians were not even invited to local hearings, but finally it was they who mobilized the Vermont citizens and apparently informed the Canadian government of the plan. CANDU drew broadly based, nonpartisan public support. And its most powerful arguments came from the people who knew the local geology best.

"A lot of the people who came to the meetings had worked in the granite quarries their whole lives," Chick said. "Men who had retired ten years ago were giving impassioned speeches to these guys from the DOE. About how when you sink a shaft into granite, water comes pouring up like a geyser."

"When you look at a tombstone," said Jean, "okay, it's beautiful. It's been polished. But when you look in a mine or a quarry, everywhere there is water."

"And the DOE map," said Chick, getting heated, "supposedly showing all the lakes on the potential sites, did not even show Island Pond, Vermont, which is not only where Rock Island, Quebec, gets its water, but where Derby Line, Vermont, gets its water. And that wasn't even on their map."

At dawn on the following day, I left Rock Island/Derby Line. To go east towards Lake Champlain along the 45th parallel, you must choose a route around Lake Memphrémagog; I took the Newport route and came back into Canada at North Troy. The old Mansonville crossing is closed; it now sits at the end of a dirt road that runs through rills and gullies and over the bright, cold tributary streams of the Missisquoi River. Just before the old Customs house, which has been converted into a private cottage, the road runs beside an old covered bridge. It is a substantial bridge, painted that familiar soft red iron oxide colour; its interior was warm and dry on a cold, wet November morning. Some of the old bridges bear a sign mounted in 1983, written only in French, which describes the history of these bridges, their construction according to various patent designs, the Town, the Howe, the Kingpost. The signs invoke the mythology of these *ponts baladeurs, ponts hantés,* host to first cigarettes, first kisses and the legends of hidden treasure and phantom cavaliers.

Around the corner from the bridge, on a hill, is a little forgotten cemetery, like hundreds I have seen in this part of Quebec, all the stones facing west in crooked lines. Metcalf, 1864, 1874, many Elkinses, Whitcombs, Henrys, Skinners—old Loyalist families, I imagine. One broken stone, its pieces stacked like broken pottery against a sister stone, is pure white and granular on the inside, like a piece of sugar icing. There are no bouquets, just lovely old stones, in the summer brushed by daisies, red currants, wild phlox and Queen Anne's lace. No church; the cemetery is loosely hemmed in by wire and a wild hedge.

There are numerous small roads here marked "cul-de-sac" that end in a fence and a sign: *Chemin et pont fermé*. People in Quebec and Vermont remember the 1972 Montreal Olympics as the time during which many of these small crossings were eliminated for security reasons.

Near Franklin, Vermont, I found Almon Richard, whose family land sits right on the border. His pale green mobile home, not at all mobile, has settled in a field that in summer is covered with a rash of brillant yellow wild mustard. Today the field is leeched of colour. A red sleigh sits on the roof, perhaps abandoned by Santa Claus. Almon has that tough, drained look of an ex-drinker, slightly shaky hands, a sharp laugh and fingers yellowed from many cigarettes. He is alert, responsive, yet unutilized. His wife has recently died, of cancer; Almon has had at least one stroke and several biopsies. Today his colour is good, his eyes bright. He sits at the kitchen table in the trailer, surrounded by hunting trophies, the tanned skins of otter and racoon, and memorabilia from the Fenian raids. He is the first Democrat in his family, and he is known for his skill in training dogs for hunting, and for his knowledge of local history.

Almon is like an old turtle, with a tough shell, like an armour around a thin bright light. The past, his own and that of his family, are of far greater interest to him than the present, which seems empty, silent, the day inching along with the inexorable slowness of the minute hands on the bronze-faced kitchen clock. His best days were when he and his father were working the farm together; he talks a lot about his father.

"We got into trouble a couple of times, my father and I, through red tape, you might as well say; the Americans are great for red tape. They get hold of a little thing and they won't let go of it, take it to the Supreme Court. Well, we took 'em, my father and I, in the sixties, I think.

"There was an outbreak of hoof and mouth disease in Saskatchewan. 'Course they quarantined the area. That's a very bad disease to get in livestock, nobody wants it. So the United States decided they'd put an embargo on all livestock crossings. They had crews that went all along the border, the Department of Agriculture did. Walked the border to see if there was any cattle going back and forth. You couldn't get any through. So they came here, saw my father and me. I was running the farm at the time.

" 'Have you got any Canadian land?' they said.

" 'Well,' I said, 'I've got some Canadian land I use. I don't own it, but I've got a right of way through there and my cows go through there night and morning.'

" 'Oh,' he said, 'fence that off.'

"I said okay. 'Then there's a little bit of Canadian land, part of that meadow.'

" 'Oh,' he says, 'never mind that little bit.'

"Well, the first time I turned my cows out in that field, the border patrol happened to come through; the cows were just over the border about fifteen feet. On our own land, that little bit they told me not to fence! The border patrol went and got the Department of Agriculture, and they more or less drove some over. They got thirteen cows into that one tenth of an acre, seized them, and they were supposed to be shot right there. But the American officials called the Mounted Police to come and hold them cows because they were on Canadian soil and they hadn't gone through Customs.

"Then they called all the big shots. There were ten, fifteen cars in the yard, officers everywhere, and the Mounties were holding the cows. Then they says to me, 'What are you gonna do? If you leave your cows there, the Mounted Police are going to seize them, and if you bring them across here, we are going to seize them!'

"Well, I said to myself, maybe it would be easier for me if the United States government seized them, not the Canadian government.

"Well, the red tape started there. They tried to shoot them a couple of times, but I'm a little smarter than they, got ourselves a good lawyer and served an injunction against them, so they couldn't shoot them. Went to court, for a year or more, and we were winning! The federal judge in Vermont was for us against the lawyers from Washington. Our governor was for us; our senator was for us. And we had to isolate these thirteen cows, put them in a different barn, because they were the government's cows, for a whole year.

"Finally, I guess they saw they were losing. They approached their lawyer and said that if we would drop all charges against them, they would drop all charges against us.

"My father was in his sixties, and he was sickly. He had served in the legislature over here in Vermont, and he was always a law-abiding citizen and believed in his government. It broke his heart to have his government calling him a liar and this and that, and having to go to court. Finally he said, we quit. So they wouldn't pay us anything; the court cost us thousands. My father said, well, to hell with it.

"I know that's what killed him; he died within a year. And after that when they caught any cows, they didn't shoot any. They didn't dare!"

He laughed, a sharp laugh. "Made history there. There's always something going on!"

In the late 1860s, it was the Fenian raids. The Fenian movement was first formed in Ireland as a rebellion against English rule; after the American Civil War, it became a movement in the United States, its militia members mostly ex-northern soldiers. Because Britain had tacitly and perhaps otherwise supported the South in that war, there was considerable tension between British and American governments, which the Fenians were able to exploit. This was also a particularly volatile period for Canada, poised nervously on the brink of Confederation.

"The U.S. government knew about the Fenian Brotherhood, knew they planned to capture Canada and force England to free Ireland. The U.S. was mad at England, so they just closed their eyes and let it go. The Fenians formed an army and even went to the legislature in Washington, D.C. There were several thousand people involved; they were rumoured to have several million dollars, and they had a formal government set up.

"Everyone that came over here, chore girl or what the hell they were, joined the movement. They took part of their wages, see."

The Fenian raids took place in 1866 and again in 1870, at selected points along the border, into Quebec, at Niagara Falls and up the Red

River valley in the west. The valley east of Lake Champlain was seen as strategic, halfway between St. Alban's, Vermont, a major railway centre, and Montreal, which the Fenians hoped to capture. In 1866, the Fenians met little resistance in Quebec; they camped on the Eccles farm, just across the line from the Richard land, captured four or five towns, burned barns and stole brandy and livestock, until troops were sent down from Montreal.

"General Joseph O'Neill was head of the whole thing. He wasn't here the first time, but the second time, this was the only place they hit. Well, anyone with common sense could see it; hell, it was useless." Almon Richard laughed and drew slowly on his cigarette.

"But O'Neill was going to make one last stab. They had this McLaren, who they thought was a Fenian, but he was really an English spy, keepin' tabs on them. So when the Fenians came the second time, in 1870, the Canadians were waitin' for them. The Fenians walked right into the ambush. They just stepped across the border, and it was over in one day."

"Now, was your family living here at that time?"

Almon savoured his cigarette.

"Oh, yes. You see, it was one of the stories I'd always been told (you know how stories are handed down in a family), and I had always wondered if it was true or just kept being blowed up to make it sound better. My great-grandfather lived in the brick house down here, that's the homestead, built in 1853, about two hundred feet from the border. When the Fenians came through the second time, in 1870, he got the womenfolk and everybody out of the house. His sympathies were with the Canadians, because they were neighbours, his friends. And he did more business over there; he was in the smugglin' business or the trading business, besides the farming.

"The Fenians wanted to come in the house and get up in the attic with the windows facing north. Going to get up there with binoculars and look the area over, but he wouldn't let them in the house. They were here a day or so before the raid. Well, somehow Joe O'Neill himself got in the house and up in the attic. Then the Fenians started firing on the house. Well, something was attracting the fire. So, my great-grandfather, he went up in the attic and there was O'Neill with the glasses. That's what got the attention of the Fenians; they were firing at their own man!

"Well, what I was told was that my great-grandfather threw O'Neill down the stairs and kicked his ass out the door and told him not to come back.

"And later that same day he was standin' out on the porch, my great-grandfather was, when the Fenians shot at him. The bullet went right between his legs and through the front door.

"Well, that was the story that was always handed down to me, and it sounds good. But when we were diggin' in the Montreal library a few years ago, we found this history book and it was right in there, the same story! Verified it. Well, somehow I felt better about it then."

Tagged by a young, barking leopard mountain cur, we drove up to the old house, where Almon's great-grandfather had fended off the Fenians. It is a handsome red brick house with black shutters and a fanlight over the front porch. Almon's ancestors were Dutch Loyalists from the Hudson valley, who headed for Canada after the American Revolution and only got as far as Vermont. The family name was Reikhardt. They would have come straight up the Hudson River into Lake Champlain, then along the Missisquoi River to this land. The family still owns about four hundred acres, in woods and pasture.

I looked briefly into the house: stripped pine floors, stereo and TV, toys, the trappings of a young family—Almon's son and his wife.

I didn't think to ask Almon how much time he has spent away from here. He was born in a wooden house on this property, almost on the border; it has burned down. (The family is like the Traffords of New Brunswick in its tenacity, but the Trafford elders, older, have held onto the reins, for whatever different circumstances and reasons.) Almon's sons no longer farm the four hundred acres; they are contractors. For them, living here, says Almon, is like living on the edge of the world.

We walked up the steps onto the front porch, past the dozing cats, up to the varnished wooden door. "Here's the bullet hole; see, he was standing right there, and the bullet went right through his legs. It's more splintered on the inside, see, where the bullet come out. The Fenians had two cannon; one of them blew up and there was a piece of the barrel right here. I left it on the front porch for a doorstop, but I guess somebody stole it on me."

In the shed beside the house, there is a trap door, hidden under machinery and traps; there is a tunnel to the basement of the house. Almon thinks maybe this was a stop on the underground railway.

Then, with the leopard mountain cur, we walked across the border.

"We can't walk freely like we used to. I still walk across when I feel like it. I don't care; they can take me if they want. My brother-in-law is in the Customs, and he says I could be fined a thousand dollars."

"Do they have a surveillance system along here?"

"They have had; they had a hidden camera or an electric eye, or maybe a camera, too. 'Course kids and people activated it, so they finally took it out. I know my grandson and a Canadian neighbour boy about his age were playing together back and forth. The officer finally caught them one day going through. 'Boys,' he says, 'I know I can't stop you going back and forth,' he says, 'but would you go around in the field, instead of going down the old road? It would be a lot better for us.' "

"What about during Prohibition?" We were standing beside the 1842 boundary marker that stands in waist-deep grass on Almon's land.

"Oh, it was always active here. Let's see, I was born in 1920, and Prohibition ended around 1933. What I remember is these big cars, Cadillacs and Packards, going through, loaded with booze, and the Customs chasing them. We lived in the big brick house then. My father wouldn't co-operate with them. You can't; when you live on the border, you gotta be neutral somewhat. You can't squeal on anybody, either, so you don't say anything half the time. For your own good, or your house will burn or your barn will burn or some damn thing.

"Anyway, one morning we got up, and there was a big roadster sitting back of the house out of sight. Pretty near a new one. All loaded down; you could tell from the springs. We opened up the rumble seat, and it was all full of sandbags. That was the decoy car; they'd send that one through first, and the Customs would go after it, and then a couple more would come through with the real stuff.

"Then, of course . . ." He hesitated briefly. "Well, during the war in the forties, I couldn't get in the service because I was a farmer. There was smuggling going on then, and I helped in that, and I'm not ashamed to say so. I figured I was helping my country. It was meat mostly. You might as well say black market. I helped my country, made a few dollars. I didn't figure that as a crime really, but if you get down to brass tacks, it was really. I wasn't paying any duty. I was just running a cheaper customs house, that's all."

We crossed a slanted wooden bridge over Chickabiddy Creek and into Canada. Through the rusty tangle of what Almon calls wild bamboo, past the final burst of goldenrod stuffing, cloud-white on blackened stems, at rest before flight. There was snow in the air and an icy west wind pouring up the valley. When the west wind was blowing, Almon's father would bring visitors to the break that is the border, and he could say, you see, it really is a lot colder up there in Canada.

We walked past the noisy farm of Hector Messier just beyond the trees; he has a system for sucking the moisture out of corn that is going all the time. "He's a separatist," said Almon, "not like his father." Hector came past the bright turquoise house in a bright turquoise truck and stopped to talk to Almon about the hunting, a two-hundred-pound, ten-point buck shot close to here the other day, and the Lebanese men with the bomb, caught crossing the border from Canada over to Richford.

Here and down at Morses Line there were once tiny villages, rather like Pigeon Hill now, I think, but there are few visible remains. There are five houses now in this valley; Hector Messier is the name on the yellow plastic mailbox in front of the bright blue house. E. Piette and H. Sylvestre are the names on the house beside the bridge with a rack of horns on the door. Beside the garage with the bright blue doors sits an abandoned rail passenger car, red, rusted, with a broken back. Across the road from a barn with snowshoes laced over the door is the Fenian raid monument. Almon opened the gate, and the leopard mountain cur bounded up the small hill.

Contemporary engravings—*Action at Eccles Hill* by John Henry Walker, and *Volunteer Camp at Eccles Hill* by A. Vogt (the latter published in the *Canadian Illustrated News,* 11 June 1870)—show a considerable community in the valley, this little hill covered with small canvas tents, and the tall trees are not there at all.

The monument is massive and simple, in the style of prehistoric megalithic statues. On a base of loosely piled boulders and platters of shale sit two roughly dressed blocks of granite, one on the shoulders of the other. The clean white text cut into the granite reads

THE CANADIAN VOLUNTEERS

AND HOME GUARDS

HERE REPULSED

THE FENIAN INVADERS ON THE

25TH MAY 1870

A miniature cannon is mounted on a block of concrete. The monument was erected in 1902 by the Dominion government, under the supervision of the Missisquoi Historical Society. A nice twist of proprieties. The knoll is grassed, with boulders lying around; Almon sees these as hiding places for the red-sashed Canadians waiting for the Fenians. Except for a jay, a pewter squirrel rippling along the grey maple branches, and the snuffling dog, it was silent. The rocks were furred with moss, the dead leaves ankle thick. A distant shotgun sounded, and leaves fluttered like snowflakes to the ground.

The sky seemed to be moving overhead, thick grey and white backlit clouds billowing rapidly eastward. Patches of sunlight passed quickly across the fields as if caught up by the wind. A stream glittered, a tamarack hummed with sudden golden light. The fields roll into the valley and are folded into the stream, as furled ribs of amber, green and gold. The cedars, invisible for half the year, in autumn give a rich, warm green texture to the far hillside, because the maples are stripped bare. Beyond the grey curtain of branches, I could just see the Richard house and the old wooden silo, built of stacked two-by-fours, stark and open like a medieval tower, and rigid in a mass of crumbled rock and blackened timber, the remains of an old stable.

In 1959, for the 350th anniversary of the discovery of Lake Champlain, there was a pageant on this spot, and the last Fenian raid was re-created. The local Canadian militia and the American National Guard volunteered, about two hundred in all.

"We went for a realistic way of doing it," said Almon. "The funny part was, we were going to use blanks, and a couple days before the pageant the Canadians couldn't get blanks. 'Well, it's going to be some battle,' I said, 'if we are armed and you aren't.' The Canadians had 303s, and we had 306s, so we couldn't just trade ammunition. So we gave the Canadians half of our guns and half our ammunition.

"It went off great. We had about three or four thousand people here, and it was so smooth they couldn't believe it. *I* couldn't believe it myself!"

I drove around the Canadian end of the valley later, having crossed the border formally at Morses Line. There is a tiny crooked sign pointing to Eccles Hill, but the monument itself is unheralded. In a maple woods, thousands of skinny striplings were competing to become big trees, and old sugaring huts were visible through the grey latticework. Again, wind-blown light swept over the ridge and set bright coins rattling on the tips of the poplar trees. The fields glowed briefly, a bright green pile. In an apple orchard of short fat trunks, the thick, braided boughs were pruned into arches that almost touched the ground. The new stems sticking straight up were tender and thin, with no colour at all. The leaves formed a taffeta underskirt of burnt orange against the shuttered maple grove.

This is still a part of the continent that is pleasing to the eye, because there is harmony between the land, its colours and textures, and the human habitation. Many of the houses are made of soft grey wood, unpainted, or are white. There are muted red barns, ingeniously constructed with an upper-storey entrance built over a steep rock hill. There are still fences built from stone, the glacial erratics that littered the land cleared by first settlers. The earth is discreetly tapped for its riches or hosts placid cattle. The roofs here are mostly aluminum, pale grey, gleaming, and the silos are elegant, cool columns, the steeples of this valley, to which the eye is drawn across rolling fields. On the pale grey flat tablets marking one-hundred-year-old graves in the roadside cemeteries, the names are in a flowing script that is slowly being erased by the west wind. There are few dissonant elements written on this landscape, and the heated political and cooling economic climates make their impact almost as gradually as the west wind.

Mrs. Weskit of Stanbridge-East, Quebec, is eighty-five, upright, well groomed, clear thinking and careful in her speech. We drink tea, and she offers me sponge cake and the photos of her children; the house is tiny, piled with the artifacts of a simple life. She was a teacher. Madeleine and Beatrice, the good friends of her daughter (Eleanor, who died of cancer) will take her out on her birthday, and she refers to them several times as examples of how the French and English have gotten along. There was always a French school and an English school with no fence between them; people crossed each other's fields and played together on weekends. Now they still go to the suppers at each other's churches, but out of respect for each other's feelings, they never talk about the difficult politics. There is a degree of dignity in the civil relations between people of two cultures that is not reflected in the struggle over whether or not school signs may be in two languages. But this relationship, too, has been damaged, like an apple that is bruised internally before a blemish appears as a softness under the skin. Spies report small roadside signs in English. Mrs. Weskit regrets the resentment that smolders in this small community, and she does not mourn the passing of René Lévesque.

At four o'clock in Frelighsburg, petite young women come hurrying out of the insurance company on the main street that at one time was a large department store and a destination on an international stagecoach line.

Just as it sets, the sun bends a fury of scarlet colour on the wooden hills, where there is now not a single leaf hanging. But the naked trees blush hot and brilliant in memory of their flagrant display of colour a few weeks ago.

By five o'clock, a full moon the colour of platinum is riding high in an inky sky, trailing clouds like a shredded bridal veil.

I drove through darkness to the farmhouse of Phil and Terry Pierce, between East Franklin, Vermont, and Morses Line. They have invited friends to dinner, Marjorie and Chuck of Franklin; like most of the border county people, they have all grown up here and either stayed or returned. Terry's family came here from Quebec around 1910; her father had worked in the New England shoe factories and moved back and forth across the line before buying a farm down the road from here. This farm has been in Phil's family since 1854 and is now run by his nephew, not his own children.

It's a farm dinner: squash, pork, mashed potatoes, cole slaw, rolls and creamed boiled onions, everything on the table at once in small bowls, and we serve ourselves. Both Terry and Phil are small, neat people. Terry has a Québécois accent; she was sent to a Catholic boarding school in Quebec when her mother died, and she still has family there. Phil is bony and narrow faced and has a strong local accent, says "baseball" with the accent on "ball," talks about jawing; when he travels, he especially notices the different kinds of cattle.

Marjorie is soft and pleasant and garrulous, but not thoughtless. Eventually she expresses her political views; Central America is a bed of communists, she tells me, and it is important that Canada and the United States stick together on these things. I am asked pointblank for my impressions of the current president. Marjorie is not unlike a bourgeois woman of rural France, with firm, narrow, even frightening ideas about the large-scale political scene; yet she is kindly, generous and charitable to a fault in her personal life.

As a teenager, Chuck made sap beer with Almon Richard. Chuck was on the border patrol on the Mexican border and in administration elsewhere, but he is reticent on the subject. Does he want me to probe? I am not successful; he won't describe to me the sensor/electric-eye system.

At the Pierces', there is a sense of security about the border, which cuts through a swamp on the back of their property. People here are accustomed to reading the landscape, and small differences or oddities are as obvious as a new barn roof or a freshly cut field. They simply call the border patrol whenever they see a stranger, and strangers are startling and obvious. When a local boy suddenly came upon a six-foot-tall black man at dawn one winter day, he was so surprised he drove right off the road. When a young couple passed through town smelling of the campfire, unable to speak English, they were picked up at the bus station. When a young German woman was staying at the Pierces', she went for a walk and was stopped for questioning by the cruising border patrol. The three young Lebanese with the homemade bomb over at Richford did not get ten miles from the line.

Here where the landscape is continuous, a tight knit of fields and streams and seamless woods drawn over a north/south grid of mountains and river valleys, two distinctive, deeply felt political histories have evolved. Vermont border people look south for their own politics, but they are knowledgeable about and sensitive to Quebec politics, just as you might know all about a neighbour's family problems but wouldn't interfere. Terry Pierce goes to Quebec for eggs, to pick berries and to go to church dinners with Mrs. Weskit; Phil goes over to the dentist. Vermonters and Québécois, French and English close to the border, are politically active and fundamentally conservative. Phil calls the mayor of Burlington a socialist and proudly describes the Vietnam Memorial in the town of East Franklin, where hostility still simmers towards the hippies who settled here in the sixties.

The next morning, I drove on. Lake Champlain as it narrows and becomes the Richelieu River was known as "the warpath of nations" even before the arrival of Europeans here, almost four hundred years ago. In 1816, on a sandy, shore-bound island on the northwestern shore of the lake, at the narrows known as Rouses Point, the Americans began to build a fort, having successfully repelled a British attack on Plattsburgh, New York, during the War of 1812. Construction on the fort was stopped when it was discovered to be north of the true 45th parallel and

hence on British land, but it was finally completed in the 1840s, after
the boundary decisions of Lord Ashburton and Daniel Webster. Local
people called it Fort Blunder, but it was officially named Fort Montgomery after the American major-general Richard Montgomery, who
occupied Montreal in 1775 and was killed during the subsequent attack
led by Benedict Arnold on Quebec City.

The fort was intended to hold eight hundred men, with five bastions
on an eight-sided structure. But it was only occupied by a small company
throughout the Civil War. Granite from the fort was used to build the
causeway across the lake. The guns were removed in 1910. The fort had
a brief career as an unsuccessful tourist attraction in the 1930s, and it is
now classified as a historic site, but with no restrictions on development. It is owned by a Montreal developer.

The fort is clearly visible as you cross Lake Champlain on the high
steel-span bridge; it looked remote and inaccessible on a cold November
morning. A small yellow boat sat on the grey and wrinkled water just off
the point; overhead, the whirring rise of small flocks of ducks broke the
sheen of a sky like polished steel.

Behind the fort there is a magnificent stand of oak and ash, beech,
some maple, now grey and leathered and bared of foliage. In the distance, the sound of bridge construction, a distant train and passing juggernauts on the perilous high span of the new bridge. The fort is almost
anonymous, an outcrop of rock at the end of an uninviting mud road
marked PRIVATE.

I drove over the rutted, potholed road as far as I dared, parked the car
beside a pond-sized puddle and walked about five minutes farther on the
track, along ruts made by cars, bicycles and motorbikes. Today there
was only the wind and the ducks; I pulled my jacket tightly around me
and thanked my Vermont boots. The track took me across a natural
causeway, past water on both sides, so that the fort could almost have
been on an island. I walked past a series of archways with straight
granite sides, their tops shaped with red brick, some still with wooden
ceilings. At right angles to the row of arches there is the main body of
the fort, a two-storey structure, with galleries and walkways connecting
open rooms, still dry and warm, home to pigeons who flew up startled at
my appearance. Big round portholes open to the south.

The site is a marvellous combination of childhood fantasy fort and
something much grander and more mysterious and more powerful than

the theme-park atmosphere of Upper Canada Village, not far away. There is much graffiti, obscene and childish; there is one room spray-painted green and white, and there are patches of whitewashing. The names of lovers and enemies are writ large: KIETH IS QUEER, SEX IS GREAT, POWERTEX SUCKS, JUDY AND BILL FOREVER. On the open plain in the embrace of the ruin, the grass is flattened, soaked, bright green, littered with fruit-punch bottles and Michelob beer cans and the black cinders of illicit fires. There is extensive defacement and deterioration, and not a single interpretive sign, but the fort retains splendour this autumn morning. I recall a visit to a goblin's castle in the border region of Scotland, a ruin ignored, a monument unsaluted, a place in which imagination can re-create a history.

West of Rouses Point, the vista is a sharply defined hiatus welling with mist between rows of blackened trees. Behind a whitewashed boundary marker, a barn on the line is settling almost visibly into complete disintegration, its shingles like the feathers of an enormous raven, suspended in midflutter.

From Lake Champlain to Cornwall on the St. Lawrence, the border country is tougher and rougher, a prelude to the uncomfortable synthesis of industry and tourism that marks the St. Lawrence Seaway. The Quebec side has become more emphatically French and lacks the genteel gloss with which the Loyalists have coated the Eastern Townships. The Protestant churches are for sale, or have been converted for apple storage. Three miles from the border, in Franklin Centre, there are people who rarely, and with some difficulty, speak English. The Vert Pré restaurant is the best place to eat for miles. The young couple, Hélène and André, with pale Québécois faces and black hair, serve carefully arranged platters of simple food and a lunch menu of stuffed croissants. They have returned here from the city; her parents live in the village. At 3:30 in the afternoon, I sat in the window after a late and delicious lunch, watching children get off the school bus at the corner. The native tongue at most of the tables is exuberantly French, except for a table of workmen, whose English sounds incongruous and foreign here.

Yet when I crossed the border, la frontière, into New York two minutes later, I was grilled at length in English by a woman whom I couldn't imagine speaking a word of French. The sense of intimacy, or at least that of neighbourliness, has disappeared; it will rarely resurface between here and Dawson City on the boundary between the Yukon and Alaska. Apart from twinned cities, like Niagara Falls, Detroit/Windsor and the Sault Ste. Maries, the two cultures now run more or less parallel, barely touching, not really connecting.

The colour was seeping out of the landscape; there was a haze of bronze and an occasional bright yellow spill of corn on the road, the clatter of dried corn on pale stalks, the fragrance of manure and decaying leaves. On the Quebec side, you can drive all day on narrow concession roads joining farms at precise right angles. On the front porches sat families of pumpkin people, sometimes just heads, sometimes with bodies like scarecrows, totems derived from ancient, mostly forgotten rituals, suggesting an extended and elaborate harvest festival—All Saints and two Thanksgivings, Hallowe'en and Guy Fawkes, rolled in together and going on for several weeks as the corn is harvested and the last batch of apple cider made.

When I drove south again through one of the few remaining unsupervised crossings, I was harassed by a large barking dog beside a boundary marker defiantly converted into a mailbox. I spent some time looking for a Customs officer to report to.

Near Chateaugay, New York, Dick's Corner Store and Music Oasis advertises

GUNS: HANDGUNS RIFLES SHOTGUNS

AMMO ACCESSORIES

TRADE BUY AND SELL

As you move west, the landscape begins to lack coherence, becomes unkempt. There are a few registered Holstein farms, but there are also swamps and indifferent bungalows. In northwestern New York State, everything lines up with the road, including a long, narrow junkyard of rusting cars not far from Dick's. The solemn baroque music of Vermont Public Radio dissolved into a long afternoon of folk and bluegrass on New York Public Radio.

At Dundee Corner, there are two cemeteries, two Quebecs—one adorned only with a sign stating NO ARTIFICIAL FLOWERS, the other a mile down the road, decorated with numerous formal bouquets of bright pink and red plastic flowers.

Highway 11 takes you east across New York, through small towns, into the Mohawk Reserve area, Akwasasne. Past the Mohawk Bingo Parlour and Video Store. In the small town of Hogansburg, the Lost Dauphin's cottage sits right beside the road and compels me to stop. It is a small A-frame, with remnants of green paint on the window frames and two old cedar trees beside the porch. A birdhouse, a plastic garden chair and a clothesline suggest recent habitation. But it is totally decrepit despite its official, somewhat pathetic sign:

IN THIS DWELLING LIVED ELEAZER WILLIAMS
WHO CLAIMED TO BE THE SON OF LOUIS XVI

On the steps there are bloodstains and a brand new knife sheath, empty. An animal skull swings from a nail on the sagging verandah.

From some distance, you see the pollution pouring out of Cornwall, Ontario, some dozen stacks spewing skyward. Here the 45th parallel section of the boundary ends, and the St. Lawrence River takes over. There is a sharp change in the landscape.

The big, busy international bridge touches down on St. Regis Island, a Mohawk reservation in the middle of the river. For two dollars each, vehicles may quickly pass over the stark symbol of disenfranchisement huddled on this island, the roads of commerce running through but quarantined from contact by high barbed wire fences. I took an unmarked exit and parked on a rutted road overlooking a red farm building with outbuildings, one a bright yellow cabin, surrounded by woods and restless dogs. Mailboxes huddle on corners like village gossips. On the fringes of the island, the stiff river wind has stripped the trees of leaves, and the bones of the landscape are revealed, white and sticklike. In the gullies there is Queen Anne's lace turned black and brown after the first frost, and staghorn sumac with cones of crimson plush left on brittle grey spines. Clumps of white stuffing explode from old cattails whose hearts have burst.

There is something poignant about the reservation, in the middle of the St. Lawrence River, right at the heart of North American civilization. What is geographically and historically a place of some significance has been demoted, passed over. The island looks like a hostel, a motel for the aboriginal people in this heavily industrialized setting, a makeshift accommodation of past and present. Reservations like this are all we have reserved, left over, for what was once a powerful people. We have drawn the circle tight around them.

Beyond Cornwall, the river is no longer a river, but the Seaway, a conduit for goods transported in ships that are worth more than the little towns they slip past. From Cornwall to the Thousand Islands, there are few connectors across the river to disturb the parallel east-west flow of two economies. On both sides of the border, this is land from where attention has shifted. A procession of water towers announces towns in various stages of lingering obsolescence, like Morrisburg, Ontario, and Waddington, New York. On the American side, New York seems an incoherent mishmash of heavy industry, desultory farming, correctional and psychiatric institutions and uncertain tourism. The Canadian side, too, is an odd quilt: lovely old wooden riverside houses and peaceful provincial parklands; horrid little motels and restaurants that seriously offer Jell-O as a dessert. On the car radio, the signal is strong from Montreal; on the motel television, the news comes from Ottawa. The local newspaper moans about neglect, yet again, of eastern Ontario in the most recent throne speech.

Coherence is reasserted briefly through the Thousand Islands, where the stench and clamour of industry is missing and where land forms conspire to bring two cultures close, in the intimacy of small islands. Rich green foliage cloaks chiselled purple cliffs, and the waters are slowed and clear and serene. In the dazzling sunset light, two mythologies compete: that of the native, for whom these islands were the garden place of the great spirit; that of the conquerors, for whom these islands are the playground of the rich.

History has passed through many of these border communities; it will not be back this way again.

# 3

## A BRIGHT LINE OF SILVER:
## THE GREAT LAKES

The *douces mers;* the "sweet seas"; the Great Lakes. Other sections of the Canada/U.S. border can be held in a mindspan like strips of measuring tape. Elsewhere, the limits of each country butt up against one another; you can straddle the line, walk across a bridge, put a light in the window for a foreign neighbour. But on the Great Lakes, almost a third of the entire length of the border, the neatly trimmed symmetry breaks up; there can be no cut line on water.

The border holds tight at the pressure points—Niagara Falls, Detroit/Windsor, Sault Ste. Marie—and then opens around the perimeters of the lakes, stretching as wide as 150 miles around Lake Superior. If you stand on the Michigan shore of Lake Huron, you see a bright line of silver between water and sky; if you stand on the shore of Lake Ontario at Toronto, you see a faint illumination to the southeast that must be Rochester.

Horizons instead of borders.

Tracing the line with a pencil on a modern map of the Great Lakes is child's work. Beginning, as the first surveyors did, at St. Regis, where the 45th parallel hits water, the Long Sault Islands go to the United States. Then, up the middle of the St. Lawrence River into the magical pre-Cambrian clutter of the Thousand Islands, where small pieces of broken rock crust nudge the line gently one way or another. At the mouth of Lake Ontario, Wolfe Island goes to Canada. A neat succession of dots across the bellied waves of Lake Ontario, then a sharp-angled turn southward into the sheltered mouth of the Niagara River. Like a spawning fish, the border travels up the Niagara River, through gorges, skirting whirlpools, along the spine of a rainbow to Goat Island between two waterfalls, the one on the left a graceful ragged curtain, the other a massive curved wall. The Niagara River hinges on the Falls and swings open around Grand Island, the border taking the western channel. Then it is spun like nylon thread across the shallow saucer of Lake Erie, looping around the tip of Pelee Island and up into the Detroit River. More diplomatic dodging of islands—Bois Blanc and Fighting Island hoarded by Canada, Belle Isle held close to the chest of Detroit. Across Lake St. Clair like a zipper; bisecting the lazy curves of the St. Clair River. Arching in a long, strung-out parabola through Lake Huron, running parallel to Manitoulin Island, bending backwards around Drummond Island and slipping between St. Joseph and Sugar islands, which wallow like twin brothers in St. Marys River. Like a flat skipping stone across the depleted Sault rapids and then like a bird, a bullet? a laser beam, soaring over the vacant, profound depths of Lake Superior for 350 miles, tacking up around the eye of the wolf (Isle Royale, to the United States) and down into the tumultuous mouth of the Pigeon River.

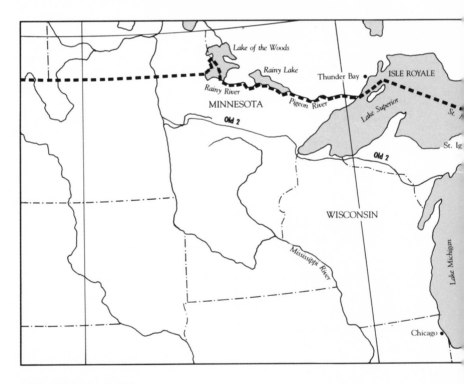

## THE GREAT LAKES

Like the encroachment of white settlement, the delineation of the boundary moved from east to west, backwards against the flow of water. The Great Lakes make a mockery of the notion of a mathematically precise boundary, but they were surveyed as conscientiously as the rest of the border—landmarks noted, monuments built, islands designated with a rough justice, the dotted line drawn on charts and maps. Much of this survey was carried out by an explorer and sometime employee of both the North West and Hudson's Bay trading companies, David Thompson, who realized that the treaty language in this case favoured the British. Simply choosing the deep channel would have meant that most of the islands would have gone to the United States because in Europe and in North America, "the deep channel for 5 miles out of 6 miles will be found on the north side of the river." When the Americans became aware of this, they attempted to enforce the physical law instead of the treaty language, but they were not successful.

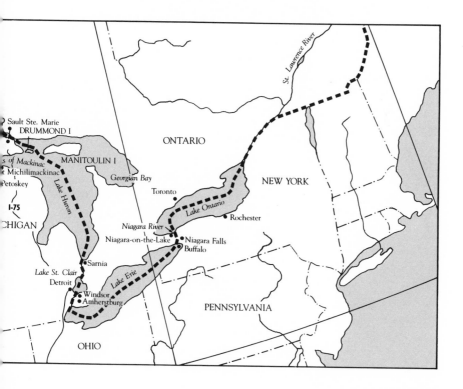

The careful assignment of islands gave both countries toeholds in the fast-flowing Great Lakes rivers, but the extension of territory is illusory; all river channels and the lakes themselves were designated international waters in 1842. In any case, control of the border beyond the pressure points is the loose patrol of moving objects on a fluid surface as tangible as air. It's almost anarchy out there on the water; only landing counts.

It took ninety years, from the Treaty of Paris in 1783 to the final survey in the 1870s, to tie together the threads of the boundary around the Great Lakes. In this period, large and indeterminate portions of North America were flipped like poker chips—from France to Spain to France and finally to the United States in the 1803 Louisiana Purchase. The northern boundaries of this land had never been clear; the position of one French diplomat was that they were "lost in the vast wildernesses in which there is no European settlement and in which it seems that even the necessity for boundaries is unknown."

The War of 1812 tossed the balance of power skywards. Borderline forts changed hands like Monopoly properties: Michilimackinac and Detroit to Britain; Fort George and Fort Erie to the United States; York (Toronto) burned; Buffalo destroyed. But the Treaty of Ghent, which ended the War of 1812, declared that the holdings of the United States and Britain were to revert to prewar positions, and that the boundary as determined in the 1783 Treaty of Paris was to be formally surveyed, end to end.

Between 1817 and 1827, American and British survey parties diligently worked the line from St. Regis on the St. Lawrence to Lake of the Woods, a linear distance of fourteen hundred miles. At times, the joint survey foundered on inhospitable terrain or intractable politics. The memory of the recent war infected decisions about strategically important islands. Marshy, undrained shores and scanty supplies bred illness; in 1819, a British boundary commissioner died of fever at Amherstburg, during the survey of the Detroit River. In the course of this initial survey, only two monuments were erected, one at St. Regis and one on the Northwest Angle, a tiny peninsula in Lake of the Woods. And once again, the imaginative but inaccurate maps that had informed the imperious definition of the boundary in the 1783 Treaty of Paris proved useless and debatable, especially in the swampy acres of bush between Lake Superior and Lake of the Woods and beyond.

The 1783 Treaty of Paris had blindly imagined that a line from Lake of the Woods would intersect with the Mississippi River due west of the Northwest Angle. The Mississippi was strategically important; Britain had been granted access for navigation and therefore demanded a boundary on the river. However, in 1798, David Thompson discovered the source waters of the Mississippi at 47°39' north latitude, one hundred miles south of the Northwest Angle of Lake of the Woods. In 1803, the Hawkesbury-King convention was drawn up between Britain and the United States; this treaty would have taken the boundary line south from the Northwest Angle to the "nearest source of the River Mississippi," or the 47th parallel.

But in 1804, President Jefferson persuaded the U.S. Senate to delete the article of this treaty referring to the international boundary. Instead, Jefferson insisted that in 1713, the Treaty of Utrecht had named the 49th parallel the line of demarcation between what were then French and British territories. Jefferson's claim was a careful blend of rhetoric and hearsay; the 1713 Treaty of Utrecht named no parallel as a boundary line, referring only to the more general concept of drainage basins. But in 1818, Jefferson's notion remained undisputed and was never questioned; it became the foundation for settlement of the western boundary along the 49th parallel.

It should have been relatively easy to unravel a line from Lake Superior, through stiff swamps and tiny dark lakes, briefly across land and over a watershed, then down the Rainy River as far as Lake of the Woods. It wasn't relatively easy; it was very difficult. According to George Classen, in his book about the history of the boundary, *Thrust and Counterthrust*, the negotiations on this little corner of the border were as vexatious as any. (Most of the border disputes were over funny little corners of land that ultimately seem almost useless, like real estate deals that fall through because of a squabble over a chandelier.) Both Britain and the United States made elaborate arguments for outlandish claims in order to gain control of the fur trade. In 1842 Daniel Webster and Lord Ashburton chose the Pigeon River as the exit route from Lake Superior, with a toll-free portage for both nations.

It was not until 1872 that the line was pushed by surveyors up across Lake of the Woods, forming the Minnesota Bulge to accommodate the Northwest Angle, and then dropping straight south to intersect with the 49th parallel, agreed upon back in 1818 as the western portion of the boundary as far as the Rocky Mountains.

The Great Lakes would seem to be the most natural section of the international boundary, a division along geographical features instead of an arbitrated drawing of lines along theoretical lines of latitude. But borders are seldom about geography; they are about cultural sovereignty. It can be argued that a border parting the waters of the Great Lakes is a patently artificial division of a geologically coherent region, the identity of which is further dissipated by the internal divisions into provinces and states. Certainly the acceptance of this continental split in the 1814 Treaty of Ghent cut against the grain of history, settlement and trading patterns, and alliances with the Indians; in many senses, it was as arbitrary a choice as the 49th parallel.

The argument for continentalism arose in the United States in the 1840s, when Manifest Destiny was seeding and sprouting in the American imagination in a variety of forms. Different Americans meant different things at different times when they talked about Manifest Destiny—new states, a loose association of independent republics and everything from gradual settlement to conquest and occupation. Specifically, Manifest Destiny meant annexation—of Texas, the Oregon Territory, sometimes all of Mexico and greater or lesser portions of Upper and Lower Canada. The dream was complicated by the spectre of slavery, bellicose anti-British sentiment, political opportunism and an incipient sense of moral superiority in America, the "asylum of the oppressed." Also, simple hunger for virgin land.

In politicians and journalists, the concept of Manifest Destiny excited metaphors Biblical and poetic, images of soaring eagles, striding giants running rampant midst the treasures of the Halls of Montezuma, and the Stars and Stripes impaled in polar ice. An Indiana congressman imagined the British lion running "his nose in the talons of the American eagle, and his blood [spouting] as from a harpooned whale." John L. O'Sullivan, the flamboyant politician and writer to whom the phrase "Manifest Destiny" is attributed, wrote in 1845: "Texas, we repeat, is secure; and so now, as the Razor Strop Man says, 'Who's the next customer?' Shall it be California or Canada?"

The American idea of Canada at this time encompassed principally those British provinces east of the Great Lakes; the Oregon Territory was still jointly occupied, and Rupert's Land was still in the hands of the Hudson's Bay Company and did not become part of Canada until 1870. Upper and Lower Canada were considered by some to be ripe fruit. In the *National Intelligencer* of 1845, a navy lieutenant writing as "Harry Bluff, U.S. Navy," declared:

> Look at the map: the eastern waters of Lake Huron reach within twenty or thirty miles of Lake Ontario; a straight line . . . from one lake to the other is the natural boundary of the United States. It was never intended that a great country like this should have its parts separated, as they are here, by the most military and grasping nation in the world. . . .
>
> Should ever war again rise between the two countries, no exertions on our part should be spared for the conquest of this part of Upper Canada. . . .
>
> In a military point of view, and simply as it regards national defense, the importance of Texas sinks into utter insignificance in comparison with this tongue of a British province. [With a canal from the Mississippi to Lake Michigan] there is nothing to prevent us from conquering and annexing "the State of Toronto." The people in it would be glad to join the Union.

The focus of Manifest Destiny was erratic and its proponents not organized. Attention soon shifted from the shores of the Great Lakes to the more open frontiers of the Oregon Territory and California. Both nations immersed themselves in what might be seen as adolescence, a period of industrial growth, population expansion and uneasy politics. The provinces of Canada began their torturous progress toward nationhood, and Americans entered the long, deep vortex of uncertainty and conflicting ideologies that would culminate in the Civil War.

Around the Great Lakes, two nations settled, built cities, roads and railways, dug sewers, mines and canals, burned coal, smelted iron ore and poured their waste products into the water.

The size of the Great Lakes is both their triumph and tragedy, the source of their power and the cause of their destruction. The International Joint Commission, the body set up in 1909 by the Boundary Waters Treaty to monitor international waters, has identified at least three hundred chemical compounds contaminating the Great Lakes. But regulation of pollution is made almost impossible by the profusion of official bodies involved, the complexity of the pollution agents and the difficulty in administering penalties and laws. The marking of the border could be seen as one of the many steps in the exploitation of the lakes, and the division of responsibility between two nations a factor in the continuing and appalling indifference to the lakes' destruction. The apparently static nature of the lakes creates a false sense of security, and the stigmata of industry and settlement belong to the other country's shores. The effluent and debris of the two nations make their impact insidiously, separately, over time.

The Great Lakes are no longer the sweet inland seas; they are burdened with the sludge and sediment of settlement and industrialization, in most places covert and invisible, in other places (the Niagara Love Canal, the Cuyahoga River near Cleveland) like running open sores. Toxic rains blow in from the south and the north and penetrate even the waters of tiny lakes on isolated islands like Isle Royale in Lake Superior. The coastline is weighed down with dense settlement; the original forests have been razed and replaced with farms and fast-growing timber that never has the chance to mature into a forest. The waterways themselves are incessantly manipulated, the flow of rivers reversed, the levels of water constantly controlled by switches flipped in deference to the requirements of enormous ships. The gods are hydroelectricity, heavy industry and superfreighter shipping.

Responsibility dissipates, dissolves. Only the silent, slow-moving waters carry horrible secrets from the bays lined with taconite slag in western Lake Superior to the cancer-riddled brown bullheads in Lake Erie and to the feet of a child on a closed Toronto beach, chasing seagulls under a summer night sky stained yellow.

But consider the impact on this region of an even more homogeneous economy.

The two nations front up to each other in three places: Niagara Falls, Detroit/Windsor and Sault Ste. Marie.

## NIAGARA FALLS

Niagara Falls, from *Onguiaahra*, meaning "throatway." The Indian word yawns and yowls like the waters rolling over the edge of the gorge. Even in their modern depleted condition, whereby more water is diverted around the Falls than is permitted to flow over, the Niagara Falls pull us to the edge of the abyss and give us pause.

Louis Hennepin, in 1678: "I could not conceive how it came to pass, that four Great Lakes, the least of which is 400 Leagues in compass, should empty themselves one into another, and then all centre and discharge themselves at this Great Fall, and yet not drown a good part of America."

The wonder is not simply in the volume of water but in the collusion of elements. Water boiling cold, then rolling into a thick, green, glassy curve over glittering hard rock. Wind, and white spume thick as snow, and tinted spray dancing a high tango. A perpetual sound and fury machine, residual testimony to the casual violence done to the landscape by glaciers twelve thousand years ago.

Rupert Brooke, in 1906: "Niagara means nothing. It is not leading anywhere. It does not result from anything. It throws no light on the effects of Protection, nor on the Facility for Divorce in America, nor on Corruption in Public Life, nor on Canadian character, nor even on the Navy Bill. It is merely a great deal of water falling over some cliffs."

The Falls are at the centre of a thirty-mile-long seam between two lakes, and the international boundary runs up the centre of the Niagara River. It is an odd, discrete section of the border, part fertile plain, part lofty escarpment. Once geologically dynamic, and historically of enormous strategic importance, the region is marked with scar tissue, historical and geological. But now the area is most notably a side trip for tourists. It suffers from prolonged bouts of industrial depression, and most of its important functions have gone underground, or elsewhere.

Only half of the water that enters the upper Niagara River reaches the lip of the gorge. The modern guardians of the Niagara Falls are two tall concrete monoliths above the falls on the Canadian side; imposing as medieval drawbridges, they are the emergency head gates poised above the cavernous intake channels for the power stations seven miles downstream. (There are similar, more modest gates on the American side.) The two functions (power and beauty) of Niagara Falls are manipulated by the same switches in the International Power Authority control tower, also above the falls on the Canadian side. Here the precise quantities of water in each of eighteen sluice gates in the cascades is monitored, and adjusted if necessary, in fifteen-minute intervals. The Falls have a day shift (100,000 cubic feet per second from eight in the morning until ten at night in the summer), and a night shift (half that every night and all through the winter). The modern Falls are merely a sideshow, a surface diversion, while the bulk of the water is channelled around them.

And elsewhere; since the early 1800s, the Erie and Welland canals have by-passed the Niagara River, the border and the Falls—new waterways reorganizing geological history around the economies of two nations. What took nature thousands of years through the excruciating ebb and flow of glaciers took teams of engineers just a few years to imitate and make efficient. There is a difference of 327 feet between Lake Erie and Lake Ontario; eight massive locks on the Welland Canal make the transition of freighters possible. The Erie Canal by-passes the St. Lawrence system altogether, heading due east, straight for New York. These shifts away from the Falls and the river explain in part the anachronistic feel about the Niagara Peninsula on both sides of the border.

Beyond the gaudy precincts of the two towns called Niagara Falls and their carnivals of commerce and artifice, this section of the border bears a considerable burden of shared history. The Niagara Peninsula, more than any other section of the border, stands for the War of 1812. Battles were fought all along the Great Lakes, but the dramatic landscape here makes vivid the events of invasion, occupation, surrender, withdrawal.

There is a frisson of ambivalence about that history, despite a procession of impressive monuments, the politely worded plaques in groomed parks and meticulously restored buildings. We are not quite sure about what was won and what was lost here; Canadian and American history books have not always told the same story. The patriotism typical of historical sites is restrained in Niagara, coloured by proximity to the other side of the story. The great fortresses, Erie, George and old Niagara, are eloquent in their vulnerability, silent witnesses to a dramatic past.

* * *

The Niagara Peninsula on a Wednesday in autumn is spectacular and deserted. Canopies of fallen leaves cover the ground, and shawls of infinite variations on the colour red—cranberry, rust, crimson, scarlet—hang on the shoulders of great trees. A curtain of brilliant amber is softened by silvery green threads of willow, and dark, sober pines. It is a blustery, agitated fall day, and the sweet tang of decaying foliage is an elusive underscent. A cold wind pushes upstream against the water, and a profusion of gulls is buffeted about, swinging on the updrafts, flipping and tumbling into sudden empty pockets of air. They fly in disconcerted crowds, battling the twisted currents of wind and mist, then settle like the contents of a pillow on the water and drift downstream to Lake Ontario.

From Brock Monument on Queenston Heights, the lie of the land is clear. Around low and gravelly beaches at the mouth of the river, yachts make a careless patrol, and the quaint towns of Youngstown, New York, and Niagara-on-the-Lake, Ontario, gracefully hug the shores. History reveals itself with propriety, behind the neat palisades of Fort George, Ontario, in monuments of modest dimensions, in small signs detailing events, mostly deaths. Here is the gully on a Youngstown farm where a French priest was killed by the British in 1759; here is the ravine on the Canadian side where the British launched their attack on Fort Niagara. Here, near Lewiston, is the grassy shore from which five thousand American soldiers set off to scale the opposite cliff. Here, right over the brow of Lake Ontario, is Old Fort Niagara, with its stark, pale chimneys and bolted cannon on a sodden green plain.

Old Fort Niagara began its career in 1679 as the French Fort Conti, facing out over Lake Ontario on the American side of the river mouth. It dominates the shore, especially the building known as the French castle, a splendid piece of fortification added in 1726. In 1759, Britain gained control of the peninsula and possession of Fort Niagara. In 1796, as part of the delayed and fractious resolution of the American War of Independence, the British gave up the fort to the Americans. In 1813, Britain recaptured the fort; in 1815, the Americans were back. No further battles were fought here, but in the 1840s, the riverside of the fort (Fort George is a stone's throw away, on the opposite bank) was provided with a number of heavy cannon directed at Canada; "never fired in anger," says the official Old Fort Niagara pamphlet.

The French castle has walls four feet thick, and on the top floor, a room as big as a ballroom where some twenty cannon are mounted in small overhanging dormers. On the ground floor there is a long dining room, a dark waxed table set between a brace of fireplaces; small paned windows face the water. Here the French surrendered to the British on 25 July 1759. A curious bronze plaque of uncertain syntax composed by a Frank Severance commemorates the surrender:

THE PARADE WAS THRONGED WITH TROOPS, VICTORS AND VANQUISHED.
THE LATTER EYEING UNEASILY THE BOLD AND STEALTHY SAVAGES WHO
STOLE THEIR BELONGINGS AND COVETED THEIR SCALP-LOCKS. . . . THE
OFFICERS GATHERED TO BREAK BREAD TOGETHER AND DRINK A FEW
HEALTHS OF ALL THE SCENES ENACTED IN THIS STRUCTURE DURING THE
THIRD OF A CENTURY THEN PAST. . . . . HERE FRANCE HERSELF QUAFFED
A CUP IN ACKNOWLEDGEMENT OF A CONQUEROR TO WHOM SHE WAS
YIELDING AN EMPIRE VASTER AND MORE POTENTIAL THAN ANY STATES-
MAN OF THAT DAY COULD SEE OR DARE PREDICT.

In the vestibule, there is a deep well, said to be haunted by a headless French officer.

A grand platform above Lake Ontario beside the French castle holds the terms of the 1817 Rush-Bagot Agreement. This treaty is always referred to when there is talk about the "undefended border" as the treaty that completely disarmed the border; it actually guaranteed only the balance of naval power on the lakes. Below the wind-swept platform, there is a visible riff on the water, where the smooth, outflowing river collides with lake waters forcing their way into the shelter of the river mouth. On the far northern side of the lake, across white-crested waves and under a sky of dull pewter, a shining cluster of towers and one fragile spire like a Christmas tree ornament are faintly visible: Xanadu or Toronto?

The wind brought cold gusts of stinging rain, and I drove up the peninsula and crossed over at Lewiston. The terrain rises gradually from Lake Ontario as far as York Road on the Canadian side; this old cross-country route comes to a dead end on a cliff above the river, under the high, overhanging chin of the Niagara Escarpment. Across the river from here the landforms sit exposed like geological diagrams—long, horizontal layers of hard dolostone and limestone, the crumbly Queenston and Rochester shale, the fine-grained Whirlpool sandstone. Parts of this rock face are almost five million years old. Over a twelve-thousand-year period, at the rate of about three feet a year, the Falls receded to their present position more than six miles upstream, in a process of erosion known as sapping.

The power plants, Sir Adam Beck of Canada and Robert Moses of the United States, sit almost face to face across the narrows, giants mirroring each other's sculpted, sweeping concrete façades. Sir Adam Beck is set in the bed of ancient debris or talus known as Niagara Glen. This is as far as boats dare to travel upstream, where the water becomes black and shiny, braiding into itself the bright lather from the whirlpool.

In the early years of this century, there was a scheme to build a bridge across the narrowest part of the Niagara Gorge, above the Niagara Glen. Up until the late 1800s, a resident population of timber rattlesnakes hibernated in the Niagara Glen. The senators of New York State were concerned that once the rattlesnakes discovered the existence of a bridge across the gorge, they would immigrate in large numbers into New York State. So the Bridge Bill was defeated, no bridge was built above the Glen and the Americans were saved from the rattlesnakes. (Although surely a sign would have done the trick, something like HANDGUNS OKAY BUT RATTLES PROHIBITED. As I again clatter across the bridge at Lewiston, I imagine a traffic jam of rattlesnakes patiently waiting to clear Customs, queued up over the Niagara Gorge, their rattles detached and hidden under the dashboard like illegal radar detectors.) A timber rattlesnake has not been seen in Niagara Glen since 1959, about the time that the natural landscape was routed for the road down to Sir Adam Beck. The snake is resident in small numbers in New York State and is legally a protected threatened species.

At the right-angle bend in the river, where the whirlpool sticks out like a thumb, the receding falls have partially excavated a previous geological era, when the waters from the upper lakes took a route known as the St. David Gorge. The rotation of water around the whirlpool is an eternal re-enactment of the change of direction taken by the river during successive ice ages; it's a memory coil, the geological equivalent of a broken synapse.

It is, however, the Brock Monument that commands the river here, especially on the American side, where the Robert Moses Parkway curves right up over the river, right under the pedestal, the tall, tall column, and the farseeing stony gaze and long, outstretched arm of General Sir Isaac Brock. Many Canadians come to Brock Monument expecting the pride of victory; the monument is such a triumph of the imagery of conquest. But this brief and minor skirmish was won by the Americans; General Sir Isaac Brock was killed by a sniper in the woods in the Battle of Queenston Heights. Of far greater significance to the Americans was the capture of their General Winfield Scott; this fact is seldom mentioned in Canadian versions of the war. The real victory achieved by the Canadians was a recognition of the significance of this odd war—a clarification, at least within the area of Upper Canada, of incipient ideas of nationhood.

When Brock was buried, initially at Fort George, Winfield Scott ordered that the guns of Fort Niagara be iired in salute.

According to one American historian, the War of 1812 was "the most unpopular war ever waged by the people of the United States, not excepting the Vietnam War." The long, bloody and inconclusive skirmishes up and down the Niagara River were incidental to the American politicians, who were mostly concerned with suppressing the Indians in the West; it just happened that the game had to be played out where there were players, in the Niagara Peninsula, and on the Great Lakes, where there were battleships.

In the years after the war, the Niagara Peninsula was the scene of unprecedented land speculation, the costly business of laying intricate canals, the exploitation of travellers. The small towns were decimated by cholera in the early 1830s, and in 1837 by bankruptcy and depression and political unrest on both sides of the border.

Niagara Falls, New York, and Niagara Falls, Ontario, sit like aging wrestling opponents on their haunches, with the two sets of falls strung between them. Both cities have constructed elaborate fronts facing the Falls for enticing, capturing and milking the herds of tourists that pass through here, 14 million head a year. The fronts are an amalgam of smoothly clipped, sculpted and flowered parkways and unfettered bad taste. On either side of the river there is a jumble of odd towers and queer devices for getting people under, around and down beside the Falls. Behind the fronts are shabby, run-down cities and a gridlock of motels; around the cities are parks, forests, and pretty, old-fashioned villages and large estates, laced with orchards, vineyards and stone walls.

Above the American Falls, a particularly nasty industrial strip bleeds pollutants by the ton through more than two hundred dump sites into the waters of the Niagara River, a kind of witch's potion.

This is both the most natural and the most unnatural of the border locations, a phenomenon of nature structured entirely into a tourist attraction, contained by gift shops and walkways and fences and observation telescopes and snack bars and viewing stations and parking lots. The water flow is carefully manipulated. The edges of the precipice have been smoothed to ensure an even distribution of water. A submerged weir above Goat Island boosts the water supply to the American Falls. The cracked promontory of Goat Island was blasted away and strengthened with steel rods. The rock bed of the Horseshoe Falls was lowered. The cliff faces have been strengthened to slow the pace of erosion. The temptation to remove the clutter of talus below the American Falls was considered for seven years before it was resisted. (It is now a pile of broken rock two thirds the height of the Falls.)

When people come to Niagara Falls, they stand and stare at the water. The American writer Nathaniel Hawthorne seems to have spent an entire day on Table Rock. Daniel Webster, massive and powerful, came to the water's edge in 1825, and feeling "deep and instant consternation," knelt to wash his hands in the "hurry of the mighty stream." Tourists in national dress swarm around the viewing platforms, taking pictures of one another taking pictures of the Falls. Young couples from Ohio stroll arm in arm, with their Honeymoon Certificates from the City of Niagara Falls crackling in their pockets.

Margaret Fuller, in 1843:

The perpetual trampling of the waters seized my senses. I felt that no other sound, however near, could be heard, and would start and look behind me for a foe. I realized the identity of that mood of nature in which these waters were poured down with such absorbing force, with that in which the Indian was shaped on the same soil. For continually upon my mind came, unsought and unwelcome, images, such as never haunted it before, of naked savages stealing behind me with uplifted tomahawks; again and again this illusion recurred, and even after I had thought it over, and tried to shake it off, I could not help starting and looking behind me.

Clifton Hill is the famous Street of Horror in Niagara Falls, Canada. In one short block: Houdini's Hall of Fame, Reg's Candy Kitchen, the

House of Frankenstein, a Burger King, Ripley's Believe It or Not, Movieland Wax Museum, Castle Dracula, the Louis Tussaud Wax Museum (how many wax museums are there in Niagara Falls?), the Guinness Museum of World Records, Sports Hall of Fame, the tower ride, a miniature golf course and Circus World. On Clifton Hill, you can picture-yourself-going-over-the-falls-in-a-barrel or have-your-name-in-a-Niagara-Falls-newspaper or try something truly alarming like live-you-tightrope-the-big-tent-shot-out-of-a-cannon. They call this the Fun Side of the Falls.

My motel on Clifton Hill is wedged between the Castle of Dracula (SORRY WE'RE CLOSED) and the ferris wheel, silent and immobile. Two tour operators in white jackets shiver in the fall morning air, smile ingratiatingly at me and then return to their conversation: "But it's okay, you know, we're still makin' money." Families wander up one side and down the other, stand irresolutely in front of wax museums, where children beg their parents, "Come on, Mom, please? It's just five dollars!" "It's only four ninety-five, stupid, and that's Canadian!" It's a street of innocent wonders, a carnival of cheap thrills that cost a lot of money to see. Nothing is real or human; even the elaborate Movieland light-studded marquee is a front for a wax museum. Clifton Hill is an orgy of static gimmicks, completely banal and empty of history, satire or even eroticism. It is tacky but not one bit sleazy. At the Falls, considerable effort has gone into balancing the sublime with the ridiculous.

Since 1791, there has been commercial activity at Niagara Falls and international competition for the tourist dollar. The banks on both sides of the river have borne a constant and often ugly trade in spectacle and heavy industrial activity. Distilleries, sawmills, iron foundries and nail factories have tottered on the rapids above the Falls. Entrepreneurs fought over attractions such as Table Rock, Behind the Sheet, even the right to use the term "Cave of the Winds." By the early 1830s there were critics. Two English clergymen, James Matheson and Andrew Reed, wrote:

> On the American side, they have got up a shabby town and called it Manchester. Manchester and the Falls of Niagara! . . . On the Canadian side, a money-seeking party have bought up 400 acres, with the hope of erecting "The City of the Falls;" and still worse, close on the Table Rock,

some party has been busy in erecting a mill dam! The universal voice ought to interfere and prevent them; Niagara does not belong to Canada or America. Such spots should be deemed the property of civilised mankind; and nothing should be allowed to weaken their efficacy on the tastes, the morals, and the enjoyments of all men.

In 1847, an English visitor named George Warburton complained of "the growth of rank bad taste, with equal luxuriance on the English and the American sides—Chinese pagoda, menagerie, camera obscura, museum watch tower, wooden monument and old curiosity shops." Influential Americans such as painter Frederic Church and landscape architect Frederick Law Olmstead deplored the ruin and exploitation of the natural site. In 1878, Lord Dufferin, the governor general of Canada, proposed the idea of an international park to the governor of the state of New York. Then, independently, both Ontario and New York established parks in 1885.

Even after 1885, when the Canadian side came under the control of the Queen Victoria Parks Commission (now the Niagara Parks Commission), hucksterism thrived. After his visit in 1906, English poet Rupert Brooke wrote:

The human race, apt as a child to destroy what it admires, has done its best to surround the Falls with every distraction, incongruity, and vulgarity. Hotels, powerhouses, bridges, trams, picture post-cards, sham legends, stalls, booths, rifle-galleries, and side-shows frame them about. And there are Touts. Niagara is the central home and breeding-place for all the touts of earth. There are touts insinuating, and touts raucous, greasy touts, brazen touts, and upper-class, refined, gentlemanly, take-you-by-the-arm touts; touts who intimidate and touts who wheedle; professionals, amateurs, and *dilettanti*, male and female; touts who would photograph you with your arm around a young lady against a faked background of the sublimest cataract, touts who would bully you into cars, char-à-bancs, elevators or tunnels, or deceive you into a carriage and pair, touts who would sell you picture post-cards, moccasins, sham Indian beadwork, blankets, tee-pees, and crockery; and touts, finally, who have no apparent object in the world, but just purely, simply, merely, incessantly, indefatigably, and ineffugibly—to tout.

In 1827, two local entrepreneurs filled the condemned schooner *Michigan* with a cargo of wild animals and sent it over the Falls.

In 1859, the man known as Blondin carried a small iron stove out over the gorge, lit a fire and cooked an omelet, which he lowered in a dish to passengers on the *Maid of the Mist*.

In 1860, a man named Hunt who called himself Farini carried a washing machine out over the Niagara Gorge, dropped a bucket on a line into the river for water, hauled it up and washed several ladies' handkerchiefs in the washing machine.

A woman named Maria walked across the gorge on a tightrope, blindfolded, in 1876, with peach baskets on her feet.

A woman named Maude died in a barrel on the Whirlpool Rapids in 1901; her dog, also in the barrel, survived.

Even rebellion and diplomatic relations around Niagara Falls were infected by spectacle and the impressario's instinct. In 1837, William Lyon Mackenzie sought refuge in Buffalo after his attempt to overthrow the government of Upper Canada. He received money, arms and considerable popular support from border Americans and set up a provisional government on Navy Island, just above the Falls.

Mackenzie's Proclamation issued from Navy Island promised freedom from the "blighting influence of military despots" and acknowledged American support:

> We have procured the important aid of . . . military men of experience; and the citizens of Buffalo, to their eternal honour be it ever remembered, have proved to us the enduring principles of the revolution of 1776, by supplying us with provisions, money, arms, ammunition, artillery and volunteers; and vast numbers are floating to the standard under which, heaven willing, emancipation will speedily be won for a new and gallant nation, hitherto held in Egyptian thraldom for ever!

Many of Mackenzie's recruits were Americans, the nucleus of the Hunters' Lodges, the secret societies organized in numerous border communities, dedicated to the liberation of the Canadian provinces from British rule. Mackenzie called Navy Island the Canadian Republic and had a flag and some money run up. The American steamboat *Caroline* was chartered to provide supplies from the American side.

At midnight, 29 December 1837, Canadian militia under the command of Colonel Allan McNab seized the *Caroline,* dumped the crew ashore, dragged the boat midstream above the Horseshoe Falls and set it alight.

There is a spectacular painting of this incident, reproduced in George Seibel's *Ontario's Niagara Parks: 100 Years.* The painting, by Nicolino Calyo, shows the *Caroline* as a tall plume of orange and yellow and scarlet in the background, bearing down on the Falls, which glint like hot metal in the firelight. Below the cataract, the water is white, cold, and the mist ascends to mingle with the smoke in the sky. Three gentlemen silhouetted in the foreground on Table Rock wait for the ship to tip over the Falls. Only the darkness and the absence of paying spectators distinguish the scene from old photographs of stunts.

The burning of the *Caroline* brought the United States and Canada to the brink of war. The United States officially struggled to remain neutral; the ubiquitous General Winfield Scott was sent to Buffalo to resolve matters, and he arrested Mackenzie under the Neutrality Act. But the unruly border states spawned the societies that held a convention in Cleveland in September 1838 to plan the invasion of Upper Canada. Raids took place near Kingston and at Windsor. The Canadian ship *Sir Robert Peel* was burned on the St. Lawrence. Tensions were not finally resolved until the Webster-Ashburton Treaty in 1842.

On Good Friday, 1840, the 130-foot-tall pillar of limestone erected on Queenston Heights in memory of General Sir Isaac Brock, the first Brock Monument, was blown to pieces by a charge of gunpowder.

• • •

George Seibel is almost seventy, an upholsterer by trade and a historian by vocation, an asthmatic with boundless energy. His passion is Niagara Falls. His study on the second floor of his house off Lundy's Lane is lined with archival material and an enormous collection of nineteenth-century photographs of Niagara Falls. As a volunteer, he wrote *Ontario's Niagara Parks* for the centenary in 1985 of the establishment of the Canadian parkland on the Niagara River.

George Seibel came to Niagara Falls as a boy in 1925, at "the peak of the rum-running days. When the booze was going to the American side, even the government was co-operating. They had a special railway siding, where things were loaded onto boats with a Customs officer, under bond. The boats were sent out, consigned to Cuba or Peru or wherever, depending how they felt on a given day. Of course the same boats were back over in the morning at the dock again, you see. They were not co-operating with the Americans, because the Americans in a previous time had not co-operated with them. It's the Old Testament, eh, an eye for an eye."

In the early thirties, George's family had a tourist home, when a dollar per person a night was good money. "I used to be sent down to the bridge for customers. They had an area down there they called a bullpen, at the end of the bridge, where every American car that came in had to get a permit. So the people there were sitting ducks, and you would ask if they wanted a room. This was illegal—you were soliciting for rooms, see—and the police would chase you, but I could always run faster than they could.

"Our house was about a block from the liquor store, where people would line up forty or fifty at a time to get a bottle of booze. So I got the idea of telling the Americans we were just a block away from the liquor store, and that worked.

"My dad was an upholsterer, and in those days the automobile seats were all sewn together, you know. So, at a visitor's request, my dad would split open the back of the seat and sew in a bottle of two of booze that nobody could find for them to take back over the border. Oh, there were all sorts of dodges to get liquor across."

There was a small burst of economic activity in Niagara Falls, New York, during the late twenties, and many Canadians went over daily to work in battery plants and chemical plants and to purchase everything from coal to shoes.

"Going over the river was the thing to do in those times. We would walk over to Thom McAn and buy a pair of shoes for three dollars and forty-five cents. I don't think I had a pair of Canadian shoes until I got into the air force.

"There was so much business back and forth. And the movies would be over there a month or six weeks sooner than here." He paused, shaking his head. "You know, I don't remember ever going to the pictures on our side.

"And smuggling, which is what it was, just became part of life. You would tell a Customs officer you had nothing to declare without blinking an eye. We wouldn't steal, you know, but we would steal from the government. This is inherent with anybody who's on the border; it's the people who live inland who get caught, because it's written all over their faces."

Even the Queen Victoria and Niagara Parks Commission employees drifted into smuggling. Their trucks were regularly serviced on the American side, and while they were over there, one of the drivers discovered they could buy very cheaply the souvenir white stone known as Niagara spar jewellery.

George chuckled. "The stone was supposed to come from below the Falls, but it was really imported from Devonshire. One of the hypes was it was congealed mist. But it got to be big business, and they could buy it cheaper on the U.S. side than they could get it wholesale over here. So they started to bring a little bit back every time. Well, they got caught, and then there was a little notice in the newspaper: QUEEN VICTORIA AND NIAGARA FALLS PARKS COMMISSION FINED FIVE THOUSAND DOLLARS FOR SMUGGLING.

"That's how prevalent it was, and we wouldn't think anything of that in Niagara Falls at the time." He paused. "But that's another era, of course, sixty some years ago. I want to make that very clear."

I drove with George Seibel down Ferry Road and Lundy's Lane, where motels beckon with heart-shaped beds for honeymooners, and Turf and Surf signs are blazing at noon. On Drummond Hill, there is a Presbyterian Church and a graveyard.

"Now you're driving right through the battlefield. This was the lane to the Lundy farm. The Americans called it the Battle of Bridgewater, because that was the closest town. People don't realize what happened—let's forget what the causes were—but the fact is that two thousand people were casualties in one evening, on a spot we drive by every day. Half of them British, half of them American. Well, American soldiers are buried there.

"Up to 1860, before the Civil War, the Americans would come on a pilgrimage to Lundy's Lane. After that, they went to Gettysburg."

The Battle of Lundy's Lane took place on a hot July night in 1814. Two (or four) thousand Americans, under General Winfield Scott, and three (or five) thousand Canadians under General Sir Gordon Drummond (accounts differ radically) fought for six hours, in hand-to-hand combat around seven cannon, in total darkness. Blow-by-blow accounts of the battle survive; in the several cessations from fighting, it is reported that "no sound broke upon the stillness of the night, but the groans of the wounded mingling with the distant thunder of the cataract of Niagara." Both sides claimed victory; both sides lost more than seven hundred men.

"Technically the Americans lost," George stated; "they left that battle with two fewer pieces of artillery, and they didn't come back for the second round.

"They still come over, you know. They send Legion people to commemorate the battle, and there is a lot of kidding, eh; we have a lot of fun with it."

As we drove, George Seibel talked about the relative growth of both cities called Niagara Falls.

"They were overdeveloped to start with; they were encroaching on the river, with all sorts of businesses, stores right up to the river bank. Because of our British system, and the British government having kept the road there all along, we had more land available for the park. And we are favoured by nature. We were quasi-wild when they were booming; it was everything for a buck back then, and they don't mind admitting that, eh; everything for a buck. So then the state had to tear down buildings just to make parking lots, and they were left with a wasteland. A hundred years ago, nine out of ten people went to the States when they came to the Falls; now it is almost the reverse.

"Here at Niagara Falls, we're the elephant and they're the mouse in the tourism business, whereas usually it's the other way around. The American Kiwanis Club map stops at the border; they won't even show a road on the Canadian side. I can't understand them."

George Seibel took one of his publications over to the American side to see if he could sell it.

"I took it into the Schrafs Hotel over there, and the man looked at the book and said, 'This is a good book. I like it.' And then he said, 'This is Canadian!' I said, 'Yeah.' He said, 'Get the hell outa here! That's it!'"

On the Canadian skyline, there are the numerous observation towers, and in the centre of town, behind the Maple Leaf Tower, the large span of the ferris wheel. In front of the Maple Leaf Village, in a bed of impatiens, a hideous plastic Saint George stands over the toothy head of a green plastic dragon.

George Seibel barely glanced at the ferris wheel. "You know, nobody here wanted that ferris wheel. The city manager lost his job over it." But the ferris wheel stays, a circular chain of red chairs riding high and empty over the town, flung out shamelessly against the sky.

". . . THE BIGGEST, THE TALLEST, THE FASTEST, THE ZANIEST . . ."

The recorded voice of a barker at the Guinness Museum of World Records blats out endlessly. Grotesque images crowd the windows; on the street, bared and bleeding teeth of vampires and monsters hang over the sidewalk.

". . . THE TOUGHEST RAREST OLDEST YOUNGEST BRIGHTEST . . ."

Nathaniel Hawthorne, in 1834:

> At length my time came to depart. There is a grassy footpath, through the woods, along the summit of the bank, to a point whence a causeway, hewn in the side of the precipice, goes winding down to the Ferry, about half a mile below Table Rock. . . . The solitude of the old wilderness now reigned over the whole vicinity of the falls. My enjoyment became more rapturous because no poet shared it, no wretch devoid of poetry defamed it; but the spot so famous through the world was all my own!

"EXPERIENCE WHAT IT'S LIKE TO BE NINE FEET TALL! COMPARE CLOTHES WORN BY THE WORLD'S TALLEST AND THE WORLD'S SMALLEST WOMAN!"

Harriet Beecher Stowe, in 1834: "I felt as if I could have gone over with the waters; it would be so beautiful a death; there would be no fear in it. I felt the rock tremble under me with a sort of joy. I was so maddened that I could have gone too, if it had gone."

## DETROIT/WINDSOR

Halfway up the Detroit River on the Canadian side, there is a small cemetery between the river and the road. The cemetery is just a little hillock pushed up over the river, the shore casually stacked with broken concrete plates and rock and brush. A twisted grillwork archway over the entrance spells out "wyandotte indian cemetery" against a hot, white summer sky. Heat is intermittently filtered through the oak and maple leaves, but the earth in the cemetery is hard, dry; the grass around the stones, burned to yellow.

The tallest stone is an obelisk in white marble commemorating the life and death of Mondoron, Chief of the Hurons, Joseph White, 1808–85. Another in white bronze honours Phillis, beloved wife of Jos' Warrow. One plot is enclosed with wire fence attached to stone posts carved like tree stumps, ribbed with barklike striations and studded with the knobs of chopped branches. The plaque, dated 1886–87, names Clayton and Robbie and Archie White.

The gravestone of Alexis M. Splitlog lies in three pieces on the ground. He died in 1872, and his monument is a profusion of poetry and images—an anchor, a stone wreath, an elaborate drapery rippling in marble. A few other stones lie scattered and broken, knitted down with weeds and held firm in the ground like steppingstones. There are no flowers.

In the 1820s and 1830s, the Wyandot (also known as the Hurons of Detroit) were fighting for rights to the land of which the cemetery is a tiny remnant. The Wyandot came to the shores of the Detroit River in 1701 to inhabit hunting grounds deserted fifty years earlier during the Iroquois massacre of all other tribes in the area.

Anna Brownell Jameson, English gentlewoman and traveller, covered a great deal of the Great Lakes area, travelling for the most part alone, in the 1830s. She writes of the Wyandot and of the chiefs Warrow and Splitlog. In *Winter Studies and Summer Rambles,* Jameson quotes at length from an 1829 petition, signed by Splitlog, Warrow and others, in which the Wyandot plead for their land with Sir John Colborne, lieutenant governor of Upper Canada. The Wyandot sought first for protection from the claims of the Ottawa, the Chippewa and the Potawatomis, and second for permanent right to these fields, crops, homes. They reminded the British governor of their allegiance during the recent War of 1812; just upstream from this cemetery, on the banks of the River des Canards, the Wyandot Nation and Tecumseh, the great Shawnee chief, fended off the Americans in the first skirmish of the war and then went on to assist General Brock in the capture of Detroit: "Father, when the war-hatchet was sent by our great Father to the Americans, we too raised it against them. Father, we fought your enemies on the very spot we now inherit. The pathway to our doors is red with our blood."

The Wyandot did not lose their land in 1829 to the other tribes. But at the time of Anna Jameson's visit in 1837, their tenure had shrunk to a seven-mile square patch, what she dispassionately refers to as "a stumbling-block in the way of white settlement, diminishing very considerably the value and eligibility of the lands around." The push and shove of white settlement in the subsequent 150 years finally obliterated all but this small hillock, a tiny gap on the coveted river frontage. The Historic Sites and Monument Board of Canada sign at the "wyandotte indian cemetery" merely states: "In the 1840's a number of the Wyandot were moved to a reserve in Kansas while others stayed to help develop this region."

The epitaph of the Wyandot is not written in marble in this little cemetery; it appears as a prophecy in their petition of 1829: "The morning and noonday of our nation has passed away—the evening is fast settling in darkness around us."

This cemetery became a touchstone for me in the Detroit/Windsor area. It seemed to bring the complex, tough and bewildering history of this area into focus, or at least to give it some modest temporal markers. Around the cemetery, the landscape is pastoral. The river is wide here, and brimming, filtered through groups of small drowned islands burdened with weeping willows whose branches trail like skirts in the water. From the Detroit side, a four-storey ferry stuffed with tourists moves briskly downstream to Boblos Island, a vast amusement park owned by the Automobile Club of Michigan. It occupies the Canadian Bois Blanc Island, once a Huron Mission and traditionally the site of annual gift-giving ceremonies, at the end of the Great Sauk Trail.

This northern shoreline of Lake Erie has a tradition of sanctuary. It is an important station on the migration flight path, a destination for wind-battered warblers and bitterns, vireos and Canada geese. In the spring, birders come to count birds at Point Pelee National Park, and in the fall they flock with the geese to the pastures around the homestead of Jack Miner near Kingsville.

It also provided shelter for oppressed people. In 1793, two laws instilled into the boundary line a new significance. Governor John Graves Simcoe effectively ended slavery in Upper Canada with the Upper Canada Abolition Act; in the United States, the first Fugitive Slave Law was passed, whereby slaves who had fled to the free states of the Union could be reclaimed by their Southern masters. In subsequent years, American diplomats would attempt to persuade Britain to enact a reciprocal fugitive slave agreement, specifically to cover the increasing flight of black people to Canada. Britain declined to participate.

In the South, slaves were fed fantastic stories about ice-bound Canada, where "the wild geese were so common . . . they would scratch a man's eyes out. . . ." Children of American abolitionists learned in their antislavery alphabet that

> U is for Upper Canada,
> where the poor slave has found
> rest after all his wanderings,
> For it is British ground.

British ground had not always been safe ground. The Indians of this area sometimes kept black slaves; earlier English settlers both tolerated the tradition and kept slaves of their own. In Malden, in 1863, there was still "the bloody tree" that was used as a whipping post for slaves. But between 1793 and the Emancipation Act of Abraham Lincoln in 1863, it is estimated that more than forty thousand black fugitives found their way to Canada, mostly to the communities on the shore of Lake Erie, like Amherstburg, Sandwich and Windsor. It has been said that without the Underground Railway, there would not have been a Civil War, and there would not have been an Underground Railway without Canada. All this in the context of Britain's official, somewhat murky politics during the Civil War; while small boats crossed Lake Erie laden with refugees, Britain supported the South.

After the Civil War, at least half of the refugees returned to the United States. The hospitality of English Canadians soured; they claimed to have been infected with prejudice by the Americans: "The prejudice against coloured people is growing here. But it is not a British feeling; it does not spring from our people, but *from your people coming over here.* There are many Americans here, and a great deference is paid to their feelings."

There remains a vital black community around Windsor, with strong ties to the black people of Detroit.

Since Detroit was founded on 24 July 1701 by Antoine Laumet de la

Mothe Cadillac, this area has been the setting for a long historical drama about occupation, exploitation, dream and disillusionment. A bard, ten centuries from now, may gather up the scraps of history from this region and make of them an epic poem. An archaeologist will unearth a hoard of icons: the bones of Tecumseh, the grillwork of an Edsel, platinum records of the Supremes, the pillars of a collapsed motorway, fragments of glittering brown glass marked Hiram Walker. One wall of the Detroit Institute of Art may be reassembled from rubble, revealing the glowing colours of Diego Rivera's fantastic mural celebrating work amid the godlike machinery on the assembly line floor.

The evolution of settlement through war, siege, industrialization, rampant development, tribal uprisings, the clash of warships and always, repeatedly, the scourge of fire makes this stretch of placid water and its flat, even shapeless landforms a microcosm of North American history. And the centrepiece, even the soul of the drama, is the stretch of river front that is downtown Detroit.

Where you now emerge from the yellow-tiled belly of the Windsor/Detroit Tunnel, Cadillac in 1701 erected the tidy wooden palisades of his fort. He chose the narrowest point of the river so that he could reach the south bank with cannon and thus inhibit the English infiltration of the fur trade on the upper Great Lakes. His fort was a two-hundred-foot square, set back about forty feet from the original clay bank of the river, where a couple of small jetties made landing possible. All of this foreshore became submerged over time, first beneath a lattice of railway tracks, now beneath a labyrinth of concrete highways, overpasses, underpasses and the levelled and reinforced edges of modern docks. The palisades of modern downtown Detroit are the support grids and track line of the monorail called the Downtown People Mover, a miniature train throwing a cordon around the skyscrapers and defending the city core from the invasion of hostile natives without. The city core is still a fortress.

French settlers occupied both sides of the river until 1760, when Detroit became a British fort. In 1763, Detroit was placed under siege by the Ottawa chief Pontiac for five months. During the American Revolution, Detroit was an important British base. The Revolution was officially terminated by the Treaty of Paris in 1783; Detroit then became American on paper, but it was not until after the signing of Jay's Treaty, in 1794, that the British actually surrendered Detroit. Finally, in 1796, they formally withdrew to the Canadian side, and residents on either side of the river were given one year to choose citizenship.

Population flowed across the river, in both directions. Flanking both modern downtown Detroit and Windsor, there are faint mirror images where there were once villages on either side of the water, sometimes surveyed by the same individual. Were it not for the river, the streets would run into one another. The simple symmetry is still recognizable where you can actually reach the river bank, but it is largely obscured by industrial development.

In 1805, Detroit became the capital of the new territory of Michigan and was completely destroyed by fire. From the ashes of the fort rose a city, a city with ideas of metropolitan grandeur inspired by, if not on the scale of, Washington and Paris. It was the first of several renaissances for Detroit, and the point at which Detroit left Windsor behind.

Windsor was then just "the Ferry," a village huddled over a collection of small docks servicing river traffic to and from Detroit.

Anna Brownell Jameson was fascinated by the difference between Detroit and what was by 1836 called Windsor. She was enchanted by Detroit and condemned the "dolts and blockheads" who, on behalf of Britain, "ignorantly and blindly ceded whole countries," especially this "fine and important place." As she paced up and down the shores of the Detroit River in the summer of 1837, awaiting transportation up Lake Huron, Mrs. Jameson considered what lay before her:

> I hardly know how to convey to you an idea of the difference between the two shores; it will appear to you as incredible as it is to me incomprehensible. Our shore is said to be the most fertile and has been longest settled; but to float between them (as I did today in a little canoe made of a hollow tree, and paddled by a half-breed imp of a boy)—to behold on one side a city, with its towers and spires and animated population, with villas and handsome houses stretching along the shore, and a hundred vessels or more, gigantic steamers, brigs, schooners, crowding the port, loading and unloading; all the bustle, in short, of prosperity and commerce;—and, on the other side, a little straggling hamlet, one schooner, one little wretched steamboat, some windmills, a catholic chapel or two, a supine ignorant peasantry, all the symptoms of apathy, indolence, mistrust, hopelessness!—can I, can anyone, help wondering at the difference and asking whence it arises?

On a stinking hot July day, ten years after the Detroit riots, I was afraid, at first, to go into Detroit. I sat on the Windsor shore in the Piazza Ondine and looked at the Detroit skyline. It is an exceptionally beautiful skyline, or has been until recently; now the striking and particular contours of some of the older buildings are hidden by newer, more conventional window-studded rectangles. It's a skyline that sketches out the history of the American city that perhaps more than any other has formulated the symbols of modern American culture: cars, motorways, the music of Motown, the exuberant buildings erected to celebrate the capitalist dreams of pre-Depression America—the Penobscot, the Sheraton-Cadillac Hotel, the David Stott, the Buhl, the Guardian.

Take, for example, the Guardian Building, built in 1929, called "the cathedral of finance," a red brick art-deco skyscraper edged with pale terra cotta and brightly coloured tiles. Its bold, clean, sharp-angled profile was designed to be seen from a moving vehicle. Nearby, there's the squat, bourgeois shape of the legendary Hudson's Department Store, boarded up, a reminder of the white flight to the suburbs in the 1960s. And, to the east (remember that Windsor is south of Detroit), the smoky glass pillars of the Detroit Renaissance Centre, the symbol of a yet another new Detroit; its round towers reflect the smaller towers of the silent, empty silos in the industrial wasteland at its feet.

Windsor doesn't have any remarkably tall buildings. But it mirrors Detroit in a modest way. The white clusters of the Hiram Walker silos upriver spell out "Canadian Club" across to the Medusa Cement silos in Detroit. The Relax Plaza Hotel on the Windsor waterfront picks up the colour and imagery of the Guardian Building on a much smaller scale. Both the architecture and the history of Windsor are beholden to Detroit. Windsor/Detroit is a clear visual metaphor for Canadian/American relations; our two cultures eyeball one another across the Detroit River as we do nowhere else along the border. In this odd pairing of a vibrant, volatile city and a low-profile lunch-bucket town, you see Canada and the United States at work together daily; close, but distinct, rubbing shoulders industrially and economically, but very different culturally. People in Windsor and along the shores of Lake Erie are clearer than Anglophones elsewhere in Canada about their distinctive identity.

Historically, Windsor has habitually resisted invasion from the United States. Detroit was captured during the War of 1812; in 1838,

Windsor repulsed the forces of the Hunters' Lodges, which were trying to banish the British from North America. After the Battle of Windsor on 4 December 1838, the citizens of Detroit watched from their waterfront as Colonel John Prince hung five Americans on the Windsor shore.

But modern Detroit is formidable, in reputation at least. When I finally tackled the Ambassador Bridge, I locked the doors and rolled up the windows and my hands clenched the steering wheel and sweat poured from my armpits. As you drive over the Ambassador Bridge into Detroit, you see dead trees, deserted houses and crumbling streets, the scars of urban blight. You accelerate into a mob of fast-moving cars that almost jostle one another going seventy miles an hour. The obsession with the automobile has thrown up a fantasia of motorways around the fragile, hollow downtown, over and through a ring of inner-city neighbourhoods blasted with poverty, despair and finally the decay of indifference.

One false move, and I was tossed off the motorway onto a street with no name, its denizens alerted like a pack of stray dogs to the presence of a stranger. My sense of direction was completely skewered by the fact that Detroit is north of Windsor and I couldn't make a mental road map. Off the motorway here, most of the signs are twisted and broken off. I boldly stopped for gas (a perfectly serene transaction, I realized later) and hightailed it back over the bridge.

To Canadians, Detroit symbolizes the dark underbelly of the American dream. The city reels under cycles of unemployment. In the 1960s, the white middle class made a mass exodus to the American minidream—suburbia. In 1967, a mass of factors coalesced: poor housing and education, an unemployed black inner city buckling under a corrupt and largely white police force, a young population bruised internally by Vietnam. The frustration of Detroit's black people boiled over on a hot summer night.

It was 23 July 1967, the 266th anniversary of the founding of Detroit.

The legacy of the 1967 riots is diverse. A renaissance in the city centre, with billion-dollar projects for renovating and building skyscrapers and luxury condominiums. Investment incentives to dazzle entrepreneurs. The gradual transformation of the downtown into a white-collar fortress. In the communities encircling the downtown core, there is a strong sense of neighbourhood and there are vital local initiatives, but these are undercut by increased unemployment, crime and drug wars.

I decided to try the tunnel instead. The American Customs officer leaned on my car, looked me straight in the eye. "How well do you know Detroit?" "Not very well, but . . ." "Do you need a guide?" "Well, I have a map; isn't that good enough?" "I get off duty at four. . . ." I made it on and off the motorways to a quiet street lined with bright, neat houses, in Hamtramck, where I had an appointment with Jeannie Sinclair-Smith.

Jeannie Sinclair-Smith is a thin, lively, middle-aged woman, fair-haired, with bright eyes and a bright laugh. She describes herself as a "born, bred, educated, totally immersed Detroiter." She teaches emotionally and physically impaired adults. Her children are mostly grown; we are meeting in the small Hamtramck bungalow of her son, whose Siamese cat howls passionately throughout our conversation. Jeannie loves Windsor, and Ontario.

"Windsor is an extension of our own city," she said, with great enthusiasm. "We just hop across the water, over it or under it. We use the post office, the parks, the theatres, and of course there is wonderful Point Pelee, where we love to take foreign exchange students."

She laughed suddenly. "Just a couple of months ago, I got into a loud, vociferous argument with a man in the Windsor post office. I was mailing a package to Italy; I discovered years ago that when I sent packages to either Argentina or Italy from the Detroit post office, they would take three weeks or a month to get there, even when I sent them air mail, and sometimes they just wouldn't get there period, even though I paid through the nose for the privilege of sending them. However, when I went to the Windsor post office, I discovered happily that the mail to Italy or Argentina only took eight days, and everything was *always* delivered, totally untouched.

"So this man was complaining and complaining, and finally I couldn't stand it any longer and I just turned around to him and I started telling him, now listen, I pay a dollar each way just to come over here and use the Windsor post office. I proceeded at great length to tell him why, and these people were standing in line with their jaws just *hanging* out!

"And there was one man standing behind the, quote, 'wicket,' and he started applauding, and he said, 'Well, I guess it takes an American to tell you, doesn't it?'

"And I said, well maybe it does, but you people simply don't appreciate what a beautiful thing your post office is. It's just great!"

Jeannie is also enthusiastic about Windsor for shopping. She insisted that I go to Mrs. Shanfield's shop. "That's a fabulous place. You can just wander to your heart's content in there, and it's so homey and fun, and you're not pressured, and yet I swear there's probably not one American who walks out of there without buying something. And I just happen to be crazy about Mrs. Shanfield. She's a darling fantastic personality; she's a piece of Windsor!"

Jeannie Sinclair-Smith sings at weddings, wakes, funerals—show tunes, mostly, but "you name it; I'll do it." Bars, then, and nightclubs? "Oh, no, I'm too old for that. They want somebody with a nice cleavage, and I'm too old for that!"

We talked about the ambivalence Canadians feel about Detroit, and about the fears of some of the people in Windsor. "Do you feel that way about the city?"

"No, no. And I'm a musician, and I run around the city at all kinds of crazy hours. Particularly on weekends; I'll leave a place we have here called the Masonic Temple, which is supposedly in a terrible area, and I'll run out of there at two or three o'clock in the morning in my high heels and my fake eyelashes and all my stage make-up and long gown and fake boobs and all the rest of it, and I have never, ever, I'll say in thirty years, ever had anything untoward happen to me. I have had people come out between houses and help me out of an icy spot, to help me change a tire or something of that sort."

"Do you think any areas are dangerous?"

"Not for me; I'm an adventurous person, and maybe a little loony, too." She laughed, and the Siamese made a small guttural moan.

"I think if you go around with a feeling of fear, then something will happen. This is my city, and I belong here; this belongs to me!"

Midafternoon in Windsor—the sidewalk shimmers. Mink coats pant in the shadowy interiors of thickly carpeted stores. A black woman from Detroit nudges her husband towards a fur shop. They've brought their friends from Los Angeles to shop in Windsor. "We're over here for the money, you know. We can make a killing. And it's safer; the crime rate would be the biggest factor.' Course *downtown* Detroit is safe; Mr. Mayor Coleman Young is gonna make sure of that! You don't have anywhere near the police over here like we do over there." They walked on, arms entwined.

Windsor still trades in the goods long associated with the British Empire—fur, woolens and bone china. The Shanfield-Meyers establishment dominates one intersection. INCREDIBLE SAVINGS ROYAL DOULTON ROYAL ALBERT! HELP WANTED UP TO 70 YEARS YOUNG! read signs in the window in front of figurines with tiny waists and stiff, billowed skirts. I entered and began to move cautiously around china and glass stacked like card houses.

Mrs. Shanfield landed like a fruit fly on my arm.

"If you have anything special in mind, please, lady, let me know. Do you live in Michigan?"

"Uh, yes, yes, I do," I lied. I don't know why, but that seemed like the right answer.

Mrs. Shanfield firmly gripped my elbow. "I think you should look through the whole store just once, then you can say you have seen it all. You know we have a store like no other store. We have china, crystal, silver, stainless, sterling. Collector's items—plates, bells, mugs, eggs. Also diamonds, gold jewellery. Everything." Mrs. Shanfield's voice was delicately encrusted with an accent like rosettes made of bone china.

"We give discounts. For instance. If an item is marked one hundred dollars, on some items we will give you fifty and ten. Which means that for the item that is one hundred dollars, we get forty-five U.S. When we take the forty-five U.S to the bank, we get seventy Canadian. *R-roughly.* So that means we really give you a discount. But when you hear it, it doesn't sound the same. Because if an item is one hundred dollars, we give you forty per cent off, we get sixty dollars from you, and then when we take sixty to the bank, at this time, let me find out how much sixty is today according to the bank rate would be . . . ."

"Jack," she shouted, without a pause (I was backed up against a glittering shelf of Baccarat crystal), "how much would sixty dollars U.S. be today, *roughly?*" Several phones rang. "Jack!"

"She wants to pay in Canadian?" The voice came from behind the Hummel figurines.

"No, no, no; if the lady gives me sixty U.S., how much Canadian do I get, *from the bank?* That's what you need to know," she assured me. I was convinced. "Eighty-two twenty," shouted Jack. "Eighty-two twenty," murmured Mrs. Shanfield, nodding wisely. I was confused but couldn't argue the point. Mrs. Shanfield released me and moved unerringly towards a man in Crown Staffordshire.

. . .

The Honourable Paul Martin, a Liberal cabinet minister for twenty-two years, lives on the eastern side of Windsor in a very large stone house, set at an angle on a big lawn, built in the thirties by rumrunning entrepreneur Harry Low with the profits of Prohibition. Even in his bare feet, with a weakened fractured arm and wearing a white shirt hanging out over what look like gardening trousers, Paul Martin has presence, also a courtesy and frankness unexpected in a politician. He is in his eighties. We drank coffee through the simmering dusk in the screened-in verandah on the back of the house. Smells of cut grass and summer gardens hung in the air.

"We're sorry for the people in Detroit," he said. "When I was a young lawyer here, the Book-Cadillac Hotel was the heart of Detroit. And yes, I still go over to lunch occasionally at the Detroit Athletic Club, one of the finest clubs anywhere. Security guards night and day now, of course. But downtown Detroit is no longer there, all the great theatres and stores, no more. My wife and I never go to Detroit anymore; frankly, we're scared."

Mr. Martin told me about the Canadian consul in Detroit who, early one morning, in one of the best buildings in Detroit, was ordered at gunpoint into the trunk of his own car. (He was agile; knocked over the man and took the gun.) He told me about the young man who went overnight to see a ball game and was killed in a hotel elevator.

"So we're scared of things like that," he said in his soft, persistent voice. "Oh, I go over for lunch, to a ball game maybe, and I go every Saturday to a bookstore in Dearborn, see what's the latest. But I wouldn't go to see a play in the Fox Theatre unless it were lighted, and with lots of security guards.

"But it doesn't make us fearful in our own city. We've strengthened our security on the border and in the police force. But we have a lot of the same abuses. Every one of my neighbours has had a house robbery, but no city in Canada escapes that."

Paul Martin doesn't read the *Detroit Free Press*, as a matter of principle, because, he says, there isn't one word about Canada. He mentally leafed through an album of U.S. presidents, none of whom—he said with more regret than scorn—had any knowledge of Canada; most of them had never been to Canada.

"Why hasn't Detroit had more impact on Windsor?" I asked. "Why isn't Windsor more American minded?"

"There's a strong Anglo-Saxon population around here," said Mr. Martin. "This was where the United Empire Loyalists came to escape from the American Revolution and the American rejection of the British connection. This is the strongest British area in Canada, southwestern Ontario.

"And the rank and file Americans don't try to impose themselves; they just come here to buy things. I've got a friend who runs a china shop, and he is a very wealthy man. The coloured people come over to buy chickens; they take them back by the carload.

"But the strip joints now in Windsor, right on the main street—it sickens you. Now that's because of Detroit; we don't have them elsewhere. Everyone is up in arms."

We walked slowly into the main part of the house. It is spacious, and full of mementos of Martin's distinguished political career. It's a house of accretions, with richly coloured oriental rugs, groupings of crystal, piles of books, a grand piano laden with photos of figures of state, the walls covered with photos and a large painting of a crowd of people, including the Martins and Queen Elizabeth.

In his haste to show me a book in the den, Mr. Martin stumbled and fell against the piano; a loud chord reverberated brilliantly, wavered in the twilight. Mrs. Martin swept down the shining curved staircase, pale and as elegant in her negligee as if it were a ballgown. She shook my hand firmly (how do you do?) and gently scolded her husband for his overexertion.

Darkness closed in suddenly, and I left them, their present small, ordinary and tender in the shadow of their past, grace transcending circumstance.

STOP HERE IF NUDITY OFFENDS YOU! said the sign on the door at Jason's (known as the Windsor Ballet in Detroit), a great big nightclub in downtown Windsor. It's absolutely dark, absolutely crowded, and it's lunchtime. The place is packed with white-collared men, not all of whom drove up in cars with Michigan plates. A cluster of blondes in the entrance turn with one mind to stare deadpanned at me; they wear nothing but tiny leather aprons. Inside, a dense wall of male laughter, thick smoke and bump-and-grind music. A woman with a short silver fringe around her breasts is dancing on a large, low-ceilinged stage. On bollards a cigarette-length from the tables, totally naked women undulate very slowly, as if entranced.

I am barred from entry; was it the dress code?

I went back through the yellow tunnel; I was crisply harassed, for the first and only time along the border, for not having proof of citizenship. My driver's licence was not good enough; the word "deportation" was toyed with briefly, and then I was released into the fortresslike RenCen.

The Renaissance Centre—the RenCen—picks up the light from dawn to dusk, a prism of almost fifty vertical acres of glass reflecting the aspirations of corporate Detroit. Fourteen thousand people work here; it's part of the transformation of Detroit from a blue-collar to a white-collar city. The Westin Hotel hosts conventions of well-heeled middle-class blacks, the Gamma Phi Delta sorority, the Pentecostal church. Its fourteen hundred rooms are often fully booked. From the top of the RenCen, fifty-four floors up, there is a full-circle view of Detroit and Windsor. I rode up the elevator with a man who turned his back on Windsor and said it couldn't be to the south: "Canada's to the nawrth!"

Robert McCabe is the president of Detroit Renaissance, the foundation of businesses and individuals that financed and built the Renaissance Centre. Robert McCabe's office is large, with expensive, glittering surfaces, opulently furnished and high above the street. Mr. McCabe is white haired and energetic, with a big, confident voice and expansive gestures.

"Downtown Detroit was hemorrhaging in 1971. It was my judgement, from the very beginning, that whatever we did, it had to be of such a scale, such a megastructure, that it would really jolt the market. That's exactly what it did.

"Henry Ford II said, we are going to do this as a business community, he said, I'll lead it, but everybody around the table—the bankers and Chrysler and General Motors and K-Mart—all agreed they would put money into it. It was to be a demonstration of the commitment of the private sector to the revitalization of downtown Detroit. There were a lot of naysayers; people said, oh my gosh; 2.2 million square feet; you are going to empty the rest of downtown. It didn't happen. It began the whole renaissance of downtown."

Mr. McCabe does not flinch when I mention Detroit's somewhat malevolent characterization by Canadians.

"We're very, very visible. Detroit is on the cutting edge of American civilization; we put the world on wheels. Probably the easiest time Detroit ever had was when Henry Ford offered workers five dollars a day. But now, we're just a small cog in the big wheel of a world economy. Detroit is used to having economic cycles, but we now face the fact that there are thousands of people who won't be going back to the assembly line. There is heavy unemployment, crime, drugs; we have all of those things. Things don't come easy in Detroit. But, tough as the problems are, there is enormous effort being made here. We're not sitting around here wringing our hands. Detroit is not a glamour town; Detroit is a survivor, a tough survivor."

His large, white-shirted gesture took in the glowing turrets of the RenCen. "The Renaissance Centre raises morale; it has the same drama in modern terms as the buildings put up in Detroit's glory days, the five or six years before the Depression. It's, it's . . ." He briefly searched for words. "I met Isamu Noguchi at the airport one day—he designed the fountain over here, the Dodge fountain, in Hart Plaza, he's an old friend—and we drove into the city, under Cobo Hall, and came up and all of a sudden you could see the Renaissance Centre, and he gasped and said, 'Ohhh, it's the Coq d'Or . . .' It is the Emerald City, it is, well, it was such a blockbuster that people said HEY! something is happening in downtown Detroit. It's for real!"

"But," I said, "what about the deserted neighbourhoods, big empty houses, like those on Brush Street, just north of here; to me it looks so desolate . . ."

Mr. McCabe swept my reservations aside. "If you could have seen Brush Street before," he said, "the area was filled with flop houses; now they are law firms. And then there's the river front; 'Bridge to Bridge,' that's the mayor's concept, from Ambassador Bridge to the Belle Isle Bridge; we're going to make public places, as well as apartments and townhouses. Look—you can see right behind me out my window— we've made a dramatic start on that . . ."

Along the waterfront, derelict warehouse buildings wait to be redeveloped into luxurious condominiums. Loading docks become courtyards, and every open stairwell becomes an atrium. At dusk, the Renaissance pillars cast long, cool shadows over stilled factories. After dark, beside the linear expanse of anachronistic railway tracks, beneath the rusting funnels of an abandoned iron foundry, white limos will cruise to and from nightclubs for the very young.

I descended to the street. There were two black women in the elevator:

"You know the last boy that got killed Sunday?"

"Somebody got killed Sunday?"

"Eighteen years old; someone shot him to death. His mother works with me."

"I didn't know anyone got killed Sunday. It's nothing but bad news."

"I won't even look at the paper anymore. This boy was shot by some thirty-six-year-old lawyer."

"Why?"

"Well, I think this one was drug related."

"I did hear something about that, a lawyer who works for the city, wasn't it?"

"They were fighting over merchandise at five o'clock in the morning . . ."

Only eight minutes by motorway from the guarded towers of the Renaissance Centre is what is known as the Warren-Connor Corridor. Vacant lots, blown-out buildings, boarded-up, run-down city housing, gutted roads, unemployment running at about fifty per cent and one of the highest crime rates in the city. I toured the area with community workers Angela Brown and Jan Johnson. Angela is under thirty, black, eloquent and energetic. Jan is more reflective, white, a little older, and she has an air of having personally survived great adversity. As we drove, I recalled a conversation I had had earlier in the day with the mother of a murdered child.

*My name is Lavinia Hilson; my son was Jeffrey Hilson. At the time of his death, he was eleven years old. His babysitter had let him go to the store to get candy, and on his way back he was seen by two boys and they followed him through the alley, and at the end of the alley they confronted him and asked him for his shirt. When he raised his hands, they just shot him.*

Angela and Jan directed me; we cut back and forth across the industrial strips and the motorways that have turned proper neighbourhoods into isolated, desolate pockets. There were few pedestrians. The grass is high; there are abandoned cars on almost every street and houses being demolished brick by brick in the night. You can buy a small detached bungalow here for five thousand dollars. What's surprising about Detroit's violence is that it happens in these little neighbourhoods. There aren't the high-rise tenements and narrow, crowded streets that I associate with urban crime; there are boulevards, parks and neat little frame and brick houses. Some of those neat little houses are drug houses.

*In one year, forty-three children in Detroit under the age of sixteen were shot to death.*

While the city works hand in glove with the developers downtown ("it's a re-ea-l team effort here," said McCabe), the residential neighbourhoods like Warren-Connor are neglected. "The city is the worst manager, in terms of housing; they just don't do the job," said Angela. Parkside is a low-income housing complex, built in the forties, close to Chandler Park. The city doesn't bother to cut the grass in the park; last year it got to be three feet high. One end of Parkside is deserted, closed down. All these units are boarded up. There's talk of "rehabbing" Parkside, or tearing it down and putting up market-value housing.

Lots of windows are broken out; people have trouble with locks and plumbing. Some people try to keep their place neat; they paint the door, put up curtains. The streets are cracked; there are missing doors on some of the buildings. It's an area of high drug traffic, but very little crime is reported; it's a closed community.

*There was another boy two weeks earlier; they took his gym shoes and shot him, but this was the first time in the neighbourhood a kid so young had got killed.*

*They bought the gun on the street for twenty dollars; that's how much the shirt cost. After they shot him they were going to steal a car, but they said there were too many cops around, so they robbed three more people after that.*

Gun play in the streets is not uncommon. "We know that," said Angela, "but people won't go to the police. They'll tell us, because they know that we're not going to tell the drug dealer, and we're not going to bust the dope house. The police sometimes bust a dope house in Parkside, but it gets set up again in a week, because nobody goes to court. Once you're seen, your unit gets burned or your child gets hurt or something. And it happens . . ."

"Reprisal," said Jan, softly. "Swift and cruel revenge." Seventy-five per cent of the crime is drug related.

*The boys who killed my son were fourteen and fifteen; they showed no remorse, nothing.*

*They're in detention home now until they are nineteen. Then they'll be right back out on the street.*

Back under the river. The heat has yielded to heavy rain falling in sheets, straight into the river, which is invisible; even the Detroit skyline has disappeared. Fronting onto the railway lines on Riverside Drive East in a residential area, surrounded by simple brick houses with porches, there is a sign, dimly lit with a few yellow bulbs:

DANNY'S CANADIAN ROOM TAVERN
25 FRENCH MALE DANCERS

It's a big old rambling club, probably left over from Prohibition days. It has the same surreptitious atmosphere; all the windows are boarded up, and the entrance is through a small side shed, over mouldy carpet, up sagging stairs to a makeshift barrier. The entrance fee is five dollars. A woman stamps my hand and searches my purse but apparently misses my two microphones and Sony Walkman professional tape machine. A big beefy guy (Danny, maybe?) deposits me behind a railing on the outskirts of the action. The club is about half full, women in groups, mostly between twenty-five and fifty. There is something temporary, ugly and contemptuous about the room; it lacks the sumptuous gloss of Jason's. Maybe, like the freak show at the carnival, it won't be here in the morning.

Practically naked men are strolling around, serving drinks. One guy wears only a red leather pouch with $$$$ stamped across it. A current of barely controlled hysteria ripples through the room.

"All right, ladies, put your hands together and welcome— Superjames!" A noisy pause, a surge of mushy music, then Superjames emerges, nude, gleaming ebony, and erect like a bawdy postcard. He flexes, he poses, he executes several deliberate pelvic thrusts, maintaining his erection for about a minute with a string hoisted high under his scrotum. The women scream; a blonde, her face flushed with pleasure and daring, comes to the edge of the waist-high stage with money rolled between her teeth. Superjames, dangling now, kneels before her and takes the money in a kiss.

I walked along the river front, back to the Piazza Ondine. The rain had subsided into a mist curtain, through which the lights of Detroit glowed like a constellation. On the river, the white and red tugboat, the *R. G. Cassidy*, of the Norfolk Southern Railroad, works constantly, night and day. It is prohibited to be in the parks of Windsor after midnight. Fine: fifty dollars. It is prohibited to fish west of a certain sign. There is a three-hundred-dollar penalty for misusing the emergency life preserver. A police cruiser glided silently past me.

From here, the dynamics of Detroit seem curiously remote, so close and yet foreign. The RenCen is a silent modernist chandelier, candles in the wind. The river is black. Downtown Detroit is empty. The grid of motorways that keeps the coiled and heated elements of Detroit insulated from one another also insulates Windsor; I picture a glass, bulletproof shield through which Windsor sees Detroit.

Windsor/Detroit is full of visual metaphors for the differences between two cities, two societies, two nations. But they're only metaphors. The differences remain inexplicable and constant. The *Detroit Free Press* outsells the *Globe and Mail* in Windsor. Its infrequent Canadian content is an editorial on Ontario's inadequate pollution laws or a big spread on Windsor: "Oh Canada's Sin City." Windsor, for its part, frets helplessly about the pollution that will blow freely over the river from a new incinerator in downtown Detroit.

The river carries a certain amount of political freight, but it's placid, gently flowing. In the evening, people walk on the Windsor waterfront, fish down under the Ambassador Bridge, take a bus over to a ball game; "it's a doubleheader and Detroit's gettin' whupped by Cleveland again." They watch the tugs shunting rail barges back and forth across the river, and the dazzling reflection of the Detroit skyline in the water, and don't feel threatened or envious or inhibited by this proximity. The border, an imaginary line on the water, can be interpreted as either a restriction or an opportunity, or both. As a line that joins or a line that divides, or both.

## SAULT STE. MARIE

When Anna Brownell Jameson travelled from Detroit to the Sault in 1837, she travelled up Lake Huron in the steamer *Thomas Jefferson* as far as Mackinac Island and then by a small bateau, rowed by five *voyageurs*, around the eastern shore of the Upper Peninsula, through the islands of the St. Marys River, to the Sault. I am the prisoner of a non-air-conditioned rental car on the I-75, during the hottest week in July. It takes me six soaking hours driving very fast to get to Central Lake, Michigan, a village not far from Grand Traverse Bay in the northern part of the Lower Peninsula, where I spend the night with my grandmother, who is ninety-three. The next day, I travel more slowly to the Straits of Mackinac.

This trip is permeated with memories. As a child, I crossed the border in a fully loaded Buick at Sault Ste. Marie every summer to spend a week or two with my grandparents. It was a matter of family pride to make the journey as fast as possible; we would leave our house east of Kirkland Lake in northern Ontario at 5:30 in the cool June dawn. On the Field cutoff south of Temagami, my little sister would become carsick, and we would stop the car on the dusty gravel road, and she would throw up. West of Sudbury, we would stop beside a lake (always the same lake) and eat soggy egg sandwiches and drink warm chocolate milk, and then the three children would fall asleep again, my mother hoped. We never stopped in the Sault, because in the early days there were two ferries to catch, one at the Sault, and the other across the Straits of Mackinac. We learned at a very early age to remain absolutely silent or to fake sleep as my mother spoke calmly to the border officials.

Then we were in a foreign country, and we were foreigners with strange licence plates. The air was warmer, softer, richer. There were woods instead of the bush, and smooth, straight highways with precise instructions (PASS WITH CARE or DO NOT PASS) and baseball on the radio and roadside attractions like Paul Bunyan and Castle Rock to lure us (rarely) from our mission. We crossed the straits, at first a rough and dramatic journey by ferry, later a heady flight over the airy span of the Mackinac Bridge. At Petoskey we ate enormous hamburgers at a drive-in (also exotic), and then our mother changed our clothes and hard-brushed our hair for the triumphant entry into Central Lake.

Every fall, our grandparents would get into their Dodge or Chrysler and make the drive from Michigan to northern Ontario, bringing Hub-bard squash and sweetcorn and home-canned cherries and Dentyne gum, which I was led to believe was only available in the United States. In the early fifties, they would also bring margarine, in large, glossy white bars with pads of bright orange colour to be added in the electric mixer. The margarine was always smuggled in. My grandparents never reset their mental watches to Ontario time, and they always told us what time it really was, in Michigan.

All of these memories flowed over me as I drove, more than thirty years later, over the still impressive Mackinac Bridge and around the eastern shores of the Upper Peninsula, known locally simply as U.P.

Michilimackinac is no longer a border location, but it reverberates historically as part of the border story. The straits were an important transport route for the Indians and for the fur trade, and the fort on Mackinac Island was regularly a target for occupation by both British and Americans.

The whole area is rich in history, but it hasn't been legitimized or in-tellectualized in any obvious way. It takes the form of crammed gift shops and a sickly, frantic rusticana style of crafts, fake Indian souvenirs and small, commercial museums imbedded behind gift shops. In the book section of a local drugstore (there is nothing as pretentious as a bookstore), I find funny folk histories, *Tales of the U.P.* Somehow they are not real; they are folksy stories rather than true history. They confess to confusion about whether they are true or fictional. So the history and strategic importance are lost under artifice and ambivalence.

The U.P. has the now familiar modest aura that I have come to asso-ciate with border territory. It is ordinary, marginal farming country, in-terspersed with bush—its charm is its small scale. It is unspoiled, not highly populated. There are sweet rural smells in the air, unpainted patchwork barns and houses typical of a scraped-together economy. Un-differentiated bush, poplar and low-lying scrub, swampy land, some birch, patches of cedar, long, straight roads and just a few cars spitting up the rain.

It is nice to be on a road that is smaller than its environs, unlike the I-75, a big, self-important steamroller kind of road, which has impressed itself on the landscape and also created its own landscape. The little roads like M-48 and Old 2, which follows the historic Mackinaw Trail, are of comfortable proportions. They are functional, like the towns.

There are no luxuries except those of simplicity and the genuine friendliness of people. In a restaurant in Rudyard, I am the only stranger, and I don't know how to respond to the question of whether or not to have gravy on the large, steaming homemade Cornish pasty that is politely set down before me.

I drive around the skirt of the peninsula to Drummond Island, separated from the peninsula and the small town of De Tour by a narrow channel. The name has a silent historic irony. Drummond Island became the site of a British fort after the War of 1812 and the Treaty of Ghent, when the British were required to retreat from their fort on Mackinac Island. Drummond Island seemed then to belong logically to the British, and Fort Drummond was maintained and occupied for about ten years.

There is a local unsubstantiated story that when this area came to be surveyed in the big ten-year survey between 1817 and 1827, the American surveyors got the British and Canadian surveyors drunk and steered them around the southern side of Drummond Island and up the eastern coast of that island, where the boundary now lies in False Detour Channel. In fact the main shipping channel is the small channel between DeTour and Drummond Island, which is kept open all year around. After the boundary survey, Fort Drummond was gradually abandoned, and the British shifted farther east, to sites on St. Joseph Island and finally to Penetanguishene.

It is an eight-minute trip across the channel to Drummond Island on a small car ferry. Drummond Island is an odd enclave of ornery individuals with an outpost mentality. The island is completely encircled by little wooden cottages. There are mustard-yellow resorts, where old men wearing glasses and peaked caps sit peering out over sodden, sagging docks perched in the dark and lovely waters of Lake Huron. There are cars with MY LANDS NOT WETLANDS plastered on the back bumpers. There is a huge, wonderful old general store with a waving wooden floor and the smell of something delicious flaring through the smells of wax and old hardware, new T-shirts and ancient, dusty cards. From somewhere, I hear "The Old Rugged Cross" warbled into the open air on an electronic organ, like the call of the mosque at dusk. The air is thick with fine, soft rain.

About seven hundred or eight hundred people live here, some of them descendants of Finnish immigrants brought to the island in the first decade of this century by the feminist entrepreneur Maggie Walz. There is an enormous dolomite quarry slowly chewing up the middle of the island, with its very own majestic road, white and graded, lined with big boulders, leading nowhere; it looks like a ceremonial road out of imperial Rome.

The residents of Drummond Island are not too sure about the location or even the identity of the old British fort. I asked directions in an information centre. The woman looked at me blankly. "The chimleys," she said, "you mean the old chimleys . . ." I drove down several gravel roads, on one-lane wobbly bridges that took me over the big dolomite highway, looking for the "chimleys."

I never found them. The historic site of Fort Drummond has been carved away by the dolomite mining and swallowed up in bush so dense that it is impossible to find the crumbling rubble of old chimneys, or even paths through, except on your belly. I took the eight-minute ferry back to the almost-mainland and drove on north to Sault Ste. Marie.

A grey cloud rimmed the horizon, edged with light diffused behind rain; the cloud was pulled down over the top of the sun like a blanket. Old barns, red and handsome, sat in silhouette on the horizon. There is an air of neat, bare prosperity, a tidy landscape, very Protestant. There are towns like Pickford and Stalwart, where strict ordinances forbid parking on the street during the night.

The main street of Sault Ste. Marie, Michigan, is reminiscent of Niagara Falls, Ontario. Everything of importance faces the St. Marys River, although the main part of the town is now an island because of canals cut through for the power station. There is a row of very plain early-nineteenth-century houses that belonged to important early settlers like Henry Schoolcraft and John Johnston; they display ornate plaques out front but are all boarded up. A great deal of energy has gone into making the main street into the worst possible form of a tourist trap, outside of the pleasantly restrained precincts of a park and the old Fort Brady. The Ojibway Hotel is suitably staid in dun-coloured brick, but then there is the Haunted Depot, Lamplighter Souvenirs, Mocs du Lock and Fudge du Lock and Oldtowne Souvenirs. Tour trains in bright green run on the road, rattling around downtown with bells clanging and a chatty guide telling tall tales. A surfeit of taffy, brittles and ice cream. At Shipwreck Adventure Golf, people mince their way around a miniature course under a sheet of bright blue water. There is an old museum, probably once the railway station; it apparently once contained cars, buggies, Indian relics, stuffed animals, Santa and the Sugarplum Village.

In contrast, on the Canadian side, Sault Ste. Marie appears to have no centre, just a proliferation of one-way streets leading around downtown and to and from the International Bridge.

Almost by accident, I find the natural little park that occupies land between the Soo Canal and the meagre, scanty rapids, which Mrs. Jameson once ran in a canoe made of birch rind. There are only five people there on a summer day, boys fishing or riding their bikes, a family with a picnic. I cross the canal, wander down an unmarked gravel path into the bush, and walk along the Adekanak Channel (named after the once plentiful whitefish), through Scotch thistles, red currants and wild daisies. There is a beaver dam, schools of minnows in brown water, a big duck sitting unperturbed on a pink rock. A narrow retaining wall separates the rapids from the park; kids dangle their feet and dare each other to run along the wall. They climb along the underside of the railway bridge and sit there smoking while a long freight train thunders over top of them.

But these are the impressions of a highway traveller, in whom the towns on both sides are only superficially, briefly interested. The Sault Ste. Maries exist for the locks and the fleets of cargo-bearing ships that pass through here day by day.

In the bookstores, you can buy picture guides to the individual ships that pass through the locks, ships like the *Anangel Sky*, the *Brompton Duchess*, the *Korean Amethyst*, the *Tunisian Reefer*. The guide *Know Your Ships*, for example, boasts SEVEN! colourful pages of stack markings! Complete lists of owners, and ships identified by beam, depth and type—marine agency tender, the long, flat lakers, the self-unloaders. Ships are upbound, to Lake Superior, or downbound to the Seaway, the Far East. It is an entirely legitimate pastime to stand for hours and watch the ships passing through the locks.

Before the first locks were constructed, in 1853, the Sault was a gathering place for native fishermen and and a provision post for fur traders. Across the lively, bubbling surface of the midstream rapids, the Batchawana Band moved in special two-person canoes, one person steering, the other dipping a net on the end of a long pole for the bounty of whitefish. Once the boundary had been settled by Jay's Treaty, and the Territory of Michigan established in 1805, the Americans began to show interest in development and settlement. The Canadian side was slow to follow; a Hudson's Bay agent wrote in 1849:

> The Sault on the American side—for on the British side it consists of a few miserable hovels inhabited by halfbreeds who vegetate on whitefish— is a village of considerable size. The inhabitants are a set of speculating knaves who have been drawn there some years by the expectations of making their fortunes from the pickings of the copper mining business in Lake Superior. . . .

There was competition to build a canal, won by the Americans, who completed contruction of the first set of locks in 1853. The native population was gradually displaced as land was purchased for railways and hydroelectric schemes and the intensely pragmatic character of the communities was established. There are now four large American locks, the MacArthur, the Poe, the Davis and the Sabin, and plans for a new Superlock. The small, old-fashioned Canadian Lock, built in 1895, is temporarily closed, "due to a structural failure."

The impetus to finally construct a canal on the Canadian side of the St. Marys River came partly from a boundary incident. In 1870, the government of Upper Canada wanted to send troops to the Red River community in southern Manitoba, where native and mixed-blood residents under the leadership of Louis Riel had occupied Fort Garry in protest against the transfer of Rupert's Land from the Hudson's Bay Company. The troops could either be sent across American territory, by rail to Minnesota, and then up the Red River, or across Lake Superior and overland to southern Manitoba. To request permission to transport British troops across American soil was first to risk refusal and second to admit that the United States, where annexationist seeds were just taking root, controlled access to the West. The troops came to Sault Ste. Marie in two ships, the *Algoma* and the *Chicora*. The first ship went through the American canal; the second was barred from entry, in unexpected defiance of a long-standing arrangement between Americans and Canadians on the Great Lakes.

The decision to bar the *Chicora* came from the U.S. State Department. It was in part a gesture of sympathy with Louis Riel, who had garnered the support of Americans in Pembina, just south of the 49th parallel. It was also a flare-up of the resentment that still rankled in the United States towards the ambiguous role played by Britain in the American Civil War. During the war, the *Chicora* had been a blockade runner. The *Chicora* was finally allowed to go through the canal empty. The press in Upper Canada fuelled support for a Canadian canal:

> Of all the Governments within the pale of civilization, the Yankee Republic is one of the most uncertain to deal with, and is the most devoid of dignity in its administration. . . . shameless desire to rob us of the north west dictated this policy in preventing the *Chicora* from going through the canal. . . . we should have a canal of our own at Sault Ste. Marie built this season.

The construction of the lock at the Sault is a seldom recognized but important link in Canada's progress towards nationhood.

I travelled through the locks on a two-hour tour. A single ship can now carry a million bushels of grain from the Lakehead, on Lake Superior, to the St. Lawrence; bits of wheat are strewn in its wake like rice at a wedding as it settles into one of the big American locks. On the Canadian side of the river, Algoma Steel is a showcase of industry, employment and pollution. The raw materials of steelmaking sit out in the open beside the water—coal and limestone piles on one side, and iron pellets on other side. Overhead there are tall, blackened cranes and a brisk shuttle service, shovels swinging down into iron ore and sending up clouds of iron dust. Three funnels pour out triple-headed steam. In the morning, the air is clear, the water green and sparkling in a cool breeze, but by midafternoon, the steel plant is releasing different-coloured fogs—brown, black and white—from its funnels, and there is a metallic smell in the air.

But still the fishermen fish. Down by the lovely stone Edison Soo Electric Building on the American side, fishermen tie their boats right beside the tunnels of the seventy-six turbines and wait for the whitefish. Reuben A. Kangas was fishing from the shore with his son, Eric; they drove up in a Chevy pickup laden with rods and nets, and Reuben's latest weapon, the Hummingbird LCR Fishfinder. "Yup, they're here for the whitefish, all right; they're feeding here because of all the flies spawning upstream. Now nobody just eats the whitefish anymore; first they take all the fat off, because of the chemicals just sittin' there in the river."

Reuben used to go up to Wawa for "specs" (speckled trout), and walleye (pickerel to Canadians), but no more, because the licence is too expensive. He fishes all day long, "starting in the morning with a four-pound line and then a lighter line later in the day as it gets brighter." He can find the fish with his electronic fishfinder, but "darned if they won't bite because it tickles them. Can you believe that?"

We turn and watch the water, and the brisk and constant traffic of ships the size of aircraft carriers, the tugs and tiny motorboats. West of Sault Ste. Marie, Lake Superior opens, a formidable, vast sea. It marks the end of the eastern section of the boundary, where a tight web of historical and environmental circumstances unites the people who live close to the border. It is the beginning of the western portion of the boundary, where laying down the line occurred separate from and often before settlement; for the most part, it lies flaccid, invisible and irrelevant to the daily lives of Canadians and Americans.

## A SCAR ON THE BELLY OF THE CONTINENT:
## GROUNDING THE 49TH PARALLEL

The 49th parallel is a twelve-hundred-mile-long figment of our collective imagination.

Over a period of one hundred years, teams of surveyors have painstakingly, repeatedly pinned that fictitious line to the ground, from Lake of the Woods in the east to the Strait of Georgia on the Pacific coast, across muskeg, grassland, desert, mountains and glaciers. Over the same period, small settlements and farms have sprung up along the line. Some have persevered; others have disappeared. On the prairies, cultural vitality is sustained in small, self-contained, deeply religious communities—the Mennonites, the Hutterites, the Ukrainians and Icelanders—who have sown their particular traditions into the soil with little regard for the border, which preceded their immigration. It was simply the line above or below which they settled. Through the mountains, the 49th parallel is no more than a gap in the wilderness, like a thread pulled from a tightly woven rug.

For all its metaphorical weight, the 49th parallel itself has a kind of negative presence, negative in the sense of absence, like the discarded skin of a snake. Its force is counterbalanced all the way along by stronger pulls exerted by cities like Winnipeg and Grand Forks, Vancouver and Seattle.

I did not travel the entire length of the 49th parallel. I made several journeys along parts of it, at different times of the year. I found deserted farms, closed gates, dead-end roads, and heard the marbled godwit whistling in the wind.

* * *

Pembina, North Dakota, is a neglected corner tucked up under the 49th parallel, off Highway 29, north of Grand Forks and south of Winnipeg. There is a little overgrown park at Pembina, with an elaborate layout for an ornamental garden, abandoned; PEMBINA is spelled out in weedy, long-legged marigolds. A small boy climbs on the bars of the modest playground; his mother sits smoking at a picnic table, only half hearing his singsong chatter. Across the street, a man hammers intermittently at a roof. This and the occasional squawk from an unseen raven are the only sounds in Pembina on a fall afternoon. Beside the park, there is a long wooden museum with dusty windows: CLOSED.

The park looks like a graveyard for historical monuments, which are surrounded by yellowing poplars, pale, pinched asters and dandelions gone to seed. There are elaborate, wordy plaques; one details the history of forts here, beginning in 1797, when Charles Baptiste Chabouillez built Fort Pembian. In 1801, a North West Company trading post was built by Alexander Henry on the north side of Pembina, not far from posts for the Hudson's Bay and XY companies. In 1812, the Selkirk settlers erected Fort Darr. A temporary military post was built in 1863 by a Major Hatch, and from 1873 to 1875 the U.S. military occupied Fort Pembina, a mile south of the park.

An 1818 border monument sits in the middle of the park, rusted and dribbled with green paint; it reads, "October 20th 1818, Convention of London." This was the treaty that named the 49th parallel the boundary from Lake of the Woods to the Rocky Mountains. Close by, a large, handsome, square granite monument is deeply carved with noble thoughts:

> MAY GOD BE THE FORTIFICATION
> BETWEEN THESE TWO NATIONS.
> A CHRISTIAN HOME, A SPIRITUAL CHURCH,
> A CLEAN GOVERNMENT
> IS OUR PROSPERITY

It is hard to believe that from here, in the 1860s and 1870s, American annexationists looked hungrily north along the Red River and dreamed of conquest. In 1867, the year that the provinces of Canada West (Ontario) and Canada East (Quebec) and some of the Atlantic colonies became the Dominion of Canada, the American secretary of state in the administration of Abraham Lincoln, William Seward, was buying Alaska and openly urging a broader annexation: "I know that Nature designs that this whole continent, not merely these thirty-six states, shall be sooner or later within the magic circle of the American union." In 1869–70, the British government began the formal procedures for the purchase of the vast territories known as Rupert's Land from the Hudson's Bay Company, while newspapers like the *Nor'Wester* out of Winnipeg and the St. Paul *Daily Press* suggested that most of the settlers in Rupert's Land would probably opt for annexation with the United States.

The stroppy young territories of Minnesota and Dakota carried the vigour of annexationist feeling. People like the freshly appointed U.S. consul in Winnipeg, Oscar Malmros, and the Fenian W. B. O'Donoghue and the lawyer and entrepreneur Enos Stutsman actively campaigned for the U.S. federal government to take over Rupert's Land. It was just another element in the frontier enthusiasm.

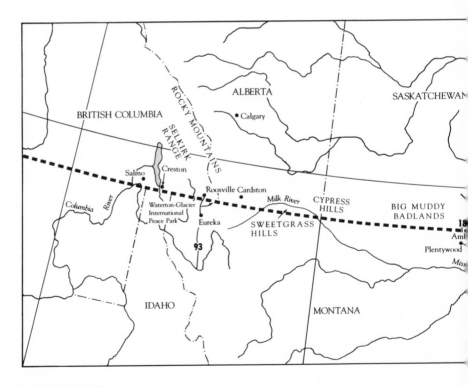

## THE PRAIRIES

I climbed up a grassy bank behind the park to see where the Pembina River flows into the Red River. The Red River flows reluctantly northward, a slow-moving, broad brown stream, a century ago the main route north for settlers, government personnel, surveyors, geologists, land speculators. Small river steamers, like the *Pioneer* and the *Selkirk*, travelled back and forth from Fort Garry, on the edge of the Red River settlement, through Pembina to Georgetown, two hundred miles to the south, often hauling a fully loaded barge alongside, freely burning the timber that grew on the river banks. Pembina was, in the 1860s, a community of close to a thousand people, an assemblage of merchants, farmers and French-speaking Metis, a huddle of log buildings set in mud, around which the prairie sprawled in a vast unguarded circumference.

To Pembina, in 1866, came Enos Stutsman, newly appointed special agent for the U.S. Treasury. Stutsman was a lawyer, a member of the Dakota Territorial Legislature and a frontier entrepreneur. He was articulate, political and unceasing in his quest for both influence and affluence. His fortunes rose and fell as rapidly as the spring flood waters on

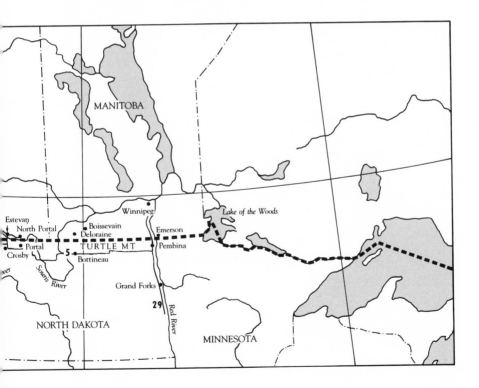

the Red River. For the next four years, Stutsman played a significant role in volatile border politics. His vision of annexation was awakened by his association with western Canada's tragic hero Louis Riel. Stutsman became the hated adversary of William McDougall, posted from Ottawa in 1869 as the governor-designate for the transfer of Rupert's Land from the Hudson's Bay Company to the Dominion of Canada. During the confrontation between Riel and the Canadian government known as the Red River Rebellion, Enos Stutsman held the keys at the port of entry into Canada.

On my way to Pembina, I had spoken to Winnipeg law professor Dale Gibson, who wrote a biography of Stutsman called *Attorney for the Frontier*. As I sat on the river bank, I could hear the dry, light voice of Dale Gibson, and it seemed to become the voice of Stutsman himself. The sound of hammering on the roof stopped. On the river, I imagined a steamboat—the *Pioneer*, perhaps—drawing up to the bank. A plank bridge was set down, and a small, elegant man on short crutches swung briskly over the makeshift bridge and onto the shore.

Enos Stutsman was born without legs. He moved around with surprising rapidity on a six-inch stump, which worked as a pivot between his crutches. He mounted the bank and sat down beside me. We gazed north, down the Red River to the flat, open bend where it curved out of sight.

I asked him how he came to be involved with Louis Riel.

Stutsman smiled and puffed his chest up just a little. Long accustomed to public speaking, he relished a rhetorical flourish even in conversation. "Permit me to suggest with all due modesty," he said, "that my reputation in legal matters opened the door of opportunity for me with the good General Riel. In 1868, I was called upon to defend young Alex McLean of Portage la Prairie, who was charged with the murder of a French half-breed. A delightful challenge for one trained in American law. The young man was acquitted after a jury deliberation of only three minutes. I received a fee of one hundred dollars in gold, and no small amount of personal satisfaction, as it was my first encounter with the Queen's Court. I determined right then to spend more time on the British side of the line, and if Uncle Sam had been ready to purchase or gobble up Red River, well, I would have been delighted to assist in the *easing* of the way.

"Of course it was incumbent upon me, as an American citizen and an official of the Treasury, to convey news of the situation to my president, General Ulysses S. Grant. It was an opportunity for action, you see; the territory of the North West was properly without government, and the profound displeasure of the Metis of Red River suggested to me that annexation was an option they would happily and seriously consider.

"When the Metis settlers realized that they were not to be consulted about the transfer of Rupert's Land, nor to have any part in the formation of government, which I believe was to be an administrative council appointed from Ottawa, they were understandably outraged. This was undemocratic! Being handed over like a flock of sheep, they felt. And there were the government surveyors sniffing around their land, trying to carve it all up according to the English system. So they formed the National Committee of the Metis of Red River; young Riel was the secretary of the committee, but in truth, he was the leader. I was honoured to be of assistance to them in the capacity of legal adviser."

"What kind of legal advice were you required to give? And why didn't they talk to lawyers north of the border?"

Enos Stutsman laughed outright. "In the breadth of the North West Territory, there probably was not another lawyer to be found! And the situation was delicate, very delicate indeed. Land titles, farm boundaries, anti-Papist sentiment—that sort of thing. There happened to be many sympathizers of the Metis insurgents in Pembina, not to mention the interest expressed by the Chippewa of these parts in helping their half-breed brethren. Did that not give Mr. Self-Importance McDougall something to think about!

"Mr. William McDougall, governor-in-waiting, swept into Pembina like a bride with a full entourage of his officials and his family, his cooks and scullions, expecting to get settled in Winnipeg before the transfer of land had taken place. The Metis simply refused to let him in, so here he sat. A king without a kingdom, in Pembina. To his chagrin, he found living quarters almost impossible to come by and the services of our community somewhat less than impartial. It served him right. He was an unpleasant man, vindictive, overbearing. Had the audacity to accuse me, whom he designated the 'prime conspirator,' of tampering with his mail. I once heard him swear he'd have his foot on the neck of the half-breeds who turned him back at the border. When Mr. Riel conveyed to me the importance of denying entry across the boundary to Mr. William McDougall, I was happy to oblige. I kept very close tabs on McDougall and his obstreperous sidekick young Captain Donald Cameron; we called *him* the Penetrator."

"But," I said, "you weren't just Riel's agent in Pembina, were you? Didn't you participate in the Winnipeg conferences with the English-speaking settlers? And what about Riel's proposal for a provisional government, and his well-articulated list of rights, the demands to the Canadian government? It's said that you had a hand in all of that."

Enos Stutsman struggled visibly with a choice between discretion and glory. "I was merely," he said at last, "*merely* an adviser, who enjoyed a liberal share of the confidence of the Red River people. I placed my considerable experience and knowledge of parliamentary process at their disposal. Mr. Riel, you will recall, was a young man of twenty-four at the time. Passionate, committed, he was; wise, he was not."

The demands put together by Louis Riel and his advisers for the Winnipeg Conference on 1 December 1869 were accepted as reasonable by both the French- and English-speaking delegates. But the proviso that McDougall agree to all the demands before setting foot on Canadian soil was essential to Riel and unacceptable to the English settlers. The convention foundered. That same night, Governor-elect McDougall secretly crossed the border to read aloud on Canadian soil his own proclamation claiming jurisdiction of the territory in the name of Queen Victoria. Enos Stutsman wrote the following account, which appeared in the St. Paul *Daily Press* on 21 December 1869:

On the first instance, at the hour of 10 P.M., while the mercury indicated 20 degrees below zero and Old Boreas was on a bender, seven lonely pedestrians, fully armed and equipped, might have been (and were) seen stemming to the blast, and, as best they could, shaping their course in the direction of the oak post marking the international boundary—their brows contracted with the firm resolution to do or die.

This intrepid little band consisted of Governor McDougall and his entire official staff.

His Excellency was armed with the Queen's proclamation, the dominion flag, and two pointer dogs. The fat Attorney-General felt quite secure with an old-fashioned Colt, that had not been discharged for fifteen years, while the Collector of Customs (of a more practical turn of mind), thinking that the aforesaid Boreas would prove the most formidable enemy he should encounter very wisely armed himself with a well charged flask of "forty rod"—hence, while the other members of the party were shivering like frightened puppies—the festive Collector felt as comfortable as could be expected.

On nearing the boundary a skirmish line was advanced—to reconnoiter—and finding all save the firmament, clear, a charge was sounded, and, on double-quick, the brave little band dashed across the line into much coveted territory; whereupon the Dominion flag was unfurled, and, in defiance of the blinding storm and the inky darkness, Mr. McDougall, in the name of that government, assumed formal possesion of the great Northwest Territory. After which the entire command, elated with victory, returned in triumph to their quarters on Uncle Sam's side of the international boundary.

And *thus* was accomplished the conquest of the Northwest Territory.

But McDougall's conquest was limited to his proclamation. He was unaware that the Canadian government had decided to postpone the legal transfer of authority. On 8 December, Louis Riel declared that his provisional government had been in control of the territory since 24 November. He strengthened his own garrison, shut down the *Nor'wester* newspaper, and imprisoned those settlers who did not support him. McDougall and his officials attempted a show of military strength and tried to gain the support of Indian warriors against the Metis, further incurring the wrath of Pembina residents, for whom the Minnesota massacres of 1862 were a fresh memory.

When I reminded Stutsman of his article and subsequent events, he grinned and his face crinkled. "Oh, McDougall decamped soon enough, with his tail between his legs. He gave interviews to all the American papers, of course, told them I was the "head and front of the rebellion," and blamed *me* for arousing and inflaming the passions of the halfbreeds."

"Well?"

A shadow crossed Stutsman's face. "We all may have underestimated the intentions, even the sagacity, of Mr. Riel. We gave him every opportunity to walk into our arms, but he did not. Even went up there myself for a while, and the American residents in Winnipeg put the American flag up over Emmerling's Hotel, half in jest, of course. That old Fenian rascal O'Donoghue was there in the thick of things. But things didn't proceed as we anticipated. And of course, for all of our lobbying and letter-writing campaigns, and pretty constant intelligence reports to Washington—well, I don't know that we had the full support of our own government."

Stutsman soon discovered that the support in the Red River settlement for annexation was softer than he had judged. His relationship with Riel cooled, and his plans to move to Winnipeg and run a newspaper faltered. Stutsman's influence waned, since there was powerful pressure placed on Riel, especially from the Roman Catholic clergy, to negotiate with the Canadian government. The journalist Alexander Begg wrote in his journal:

> Col. Stutsman begins to find his game about played out in the settlement and . . . he has made up his mind to leave for Pembina tomorrow. Poor Americans they have played their hand openly and not too well.
>
> The American flag was lowered and taken down today.

The steamer on the Red River released a blast of steam. Enos Stutsman picked up his crutches and rolled himself up between them, ready to make his way down the bank.

"So you finally had to admit defeat," I said.

Stutsman chuckled. "It was a gamble, you could say, but what's a life without taking chances? I had more to gain than I stood to lose. That was the spirit of things then.

"But for the Red River people—it was a clear victory for them. If they hadn't rebelled, McDougall and his hungry officials would have simply assumed possession, and not one single solitary right of the people would have been respected. Oh, I know there was awkwardness and some real nastiness later on; the Metis were fools to shoot their English prisoner, and Riel never ever recovered from that."

Enos Stutsman moved carefully down the bank to the plank, ascended it to the steamer and then turned and stood at the railing. The boat moved out into the slow tug of the main current and disappeared. Pembina was once again a town fringed with faded marigolds. The vision of the Red River as a vital transportation link, noisy, bustling, laden with steamers churning north and south, filled with curious travellers and smalltime entrepreneurs, faded. Enos Stutsman's final words lingered in the drowsy autumnal air: "But as for the uprising itself? I will tell you this: Never have a handful of people gained so glorious a victory at so small a cost of blood and treasure."

In May 1870, Manitoba became a province of Canada. Louis Riel became an exile in the United States for most of the subsequent years until 1885, when he led the ill-fated rebellion at Batoche, in northern Saskatchewan, and was tried and hung as a traitor.

Enos Stutsman stayed in Pembina, became the first registrar of the United States Land Office, named a street in Pembina after himself and died in 1874, at the age of forty-eight, after an illness.

\* \* \*

Three years after the Red River Rebellion, in 1872, American and British surveyors arrived in Pembina and began to lay the border along the 49th parallel. The vitality of the Red River settlement had been sapped by the shocks of political intrusion from the east; the boundary survey was just another incursion on the traditional settlement patterns of Metis and Indians, people who in many cases had already been displaced by the placement of the international boundary through the Great Lakes. The British survey crew was led by the same Captain Cameron who had drawn the contempt of Enos Stutsman. It also contained a young geologist named George M. Dawson, whose career would bring him several times into the area around the boundary.

George M. Dawson's *Report on the Geology and Resources of the Region in the Vicinity of the Forty-Ninth Parallel,* addressed to Major Cameron, is a great deal more than a catalogue of fossils, plants, animals, birds and technical descriptions of geological formations, although there are large numbers of the last. It is also the beautifully written journal of a lively mind encountering an unknown landscape, a scientist trained in Montreal (where his father was the first principal of McGill University) and at the Royal School of Mines in London, mapping and describing and photographing uncharted seas. In Canada, the uncharted waters were muskeg, reedy swamps and the desertlike space of the prairies.

Dawson's report is silent on his personal struggle with adversity. In the formal portrait of Her Majesty's North American Boundary Commission, fourteen men standing and sitting in discomfort, in frock coats and cravats and hats in what must be blazing sunlight (a dog lies sound asleep at their feet), Dawson is a tiny, erect figure in the back row. His wide-brimmed hat barely scrapes the shoulder of the man next to him, and the photograph does not show his deformed back and shortened spine. As the result of a childhood illness, probably tuberculosis, Dawson's growth was abruptly truncated; he suffered intermittently throughout life from blinding migraines and died at the age of fifty-one. His achievements as a geologist and cartographer-explorer—on the 49th parallel survey (from Lake of the Woods to the Rocky Mountains), and later in the Queen Charlotte Islands, northern British Columbia and the Yukon and Northwest Territories—are remarkable.

The 49th parallel had been negotiated as the boundary between the Red River and the Rocky Mountains in 1818. In the ten years of negotiation preceding that treaty, American President Thomas Jefferson had proposed that the 49th parallel form the boundary except where it happened to intersect the Missouri River; in these places the boundary should be pushed northward to ensure the inclusion of the Missouri watershed in American territory. Jefferson did not, however, subscribe to the corollary to his position, which would have dropped the boundary southwards to include the watershed of the Red River in British territory.

The marking of the 49th parallel is one of the best-documented exercises in the history of the boundary. But it is largely a historical record; few signs of that survey have survived on this flat, laconic land, save for some of the old obelisks and the faintly rutted cart trail across the grasslands. The tall, conical dirt mounds dug up on the original survey to mark the line were easily erased by wind and rain. Here there is no cut line, because there is nothing to cut through. The boundary is obscured by wind-blown dust and waving grasses—just another parallel furrow in a boundless cloth of rectangles. The historical drama is flattened, ploughed under, its main characters ghosts in the ravines of the Milk River, the Souris, the Missouri. The 49th parallel spins along the plains from Pembina, past Pembina Mountain and Turtle Mountain to the Sweetgrass Hills six hundred miles west of Pembina—the untilled, invisible vista, where the wind sweeps up echoes of the first survey in 1872–73.

The documents from this survey include Dawson's geological report, the unpublished report of the British boundary commissioner, Captain Cameron, the *Narrative of the Operations of the British North America Boundary Commission* by Captain Albany Featherstonhaugh of the

deposited by a grounded iceberg, like a shoal made by currents on a shallow river bed.

Lake Metigoshe appears to be the only recreation area for hundreds of miles, and it is thronging with people on a hot June night. It is like the suburbs on the lake front—rows of modest identical bungalows surrounded by boats on trailers and recreational vehicles. The gasoline fumes are almost visible on the lake, and the late, muggy twilight is not hushed but bristling with the noises of Middle America at earnest play. The lake is mercilessly, stupidly overused. There are water-skiers, kids fishing on the docks with their dads in peaked caps, teenagers splitting the dusk on hornetlike hydroplanes, people sitting around drinking beer, listening to the *zzzaaaap!* of bugs being electrocuted.

The next morning, I went to the International Peace Garden, which straddles the border on Turtle Mountain between North Dakota and Manitoba, roughly at the midpoint of North America. The peace garden came into being in 1932; it consists of 2339 acres bisected by the 49th parallel. Right on the boundary, there is the Peace Tower, the Peace Chapel and formal gardens. On the north side, there is the Canadian Natural Drive; on the south side, the United States Cultural Drive. There is only one entrance. The International Peace Garden is completely fortified, surrounded by thick, matted checkerboard wire fencing, joining posts built like chimneys. Odd, on this section of the border especially, where the line of demarcation is for the most part scarcely visible.

The symmetry is exquisite. The eye seeks and finds reference points to the actual boundary line through to the horizons in both directions. Identical plaques echo one another's syntax. The Peace Tower is a stand of four columns, two on either side of the line; the gap between them is mirrored by the narrow rectangular pond in the sunken garden. The symmetry in the formal gardens is maintained right down to the placement of the water sprinklers and flag poles and the perfect matching curves of the flower beds. This careful and elaborate composition is soothing, like a liturgy or a Remembrance Day ceremony or the black and white armies in starting position on a chessboard.

It is also ahistorical, a purely symbolic representation with no reference at all to real events in the history of the border. The 1818 border monument in the International Peace Garden is set in a walkway beside a park bench. Two women behind me paused briefly to glance at it.

"Did we really sign some kind of treaty back in 1818?" "Guess so, eh."
They walked on, into the Peace Chapel, whence wafted the blurred,
wavering tones of prerecorded gospel music.

The Peace Chapel, I read in the brochure, is "part of the wider vision" of the General Grand Chapter, Order of the Eastern Star. It is a
warmly lit, serene space. The sawn limestone walls of the interior are
covered with sixty cleanly engraved quotations, "either spoken or written by great men of peace throughout history." The great men of peace
include St. Paul, Confucius, Sir Francis Drake and Richard Nixon.
Also, one or two women, and several Canadian prime ministers and
American presidents. All of the quotations are in English. Despite the
proximity of the Peace Garden to a town called Boissevain, Manitoba, I
saw no reference anywhere to French Canada, to American blacks or to
the shared native history of both countries. Formal gardens and chapels
do not lend themselves to exposition or ambivalence, but to the enno-
bling simplicity of order, homily and oration.

<table>
<tr><td>WHATEVER YOU DO,<br>ADHERE TO THE UNION.<br>WE ARE A GREAT<br>COUNTRY, AND SHALL<br>BECOME ONE OF THE<br>GREATEST IF WE PRESERVE<br>IT; WE SHALL SINK INTO<br>INSIGNIFICANCE AND<br>ADVERSITY IF WE SUFFER<br>IT TO BE BROKEN.<br><br>*Sir John A. Macdonald*<br>*Father of Confederation*</td><td>OUR GOAL IS NOT THE<br>VICTORY OF MIGHT, BUT<br>THE VINDICATION OF<br>RIGHT; NOT PEACE AT THE<br>EXPENSE OF FREEDOM, BUT<br>BOTH PEACE AND<br>FREEDOM, HERE IN THIS<br>HEMISPHERE AND<br>AROUND THE WORLD.<br>GOD WILLING THAT GOAL<br>WILL BE REACHED.<br><br>*John F. Kennedy*</td></tr>
</table>

The sponsorship of various picnic areas and buildings in the International Peace Garden is a litany of small-town charities, service clubs and
arcane secret societies: the Sovereign Grand Lodge of Oddfellows, the
Rebekahs, the Imperial Order of the Daughters of the Empire, the National Homemakers, the Knights of Columbus, the Royal Canadian
Legion, the Grand Lodge of Masons from North Dakota and Manitoba,

even the North Dakota Homemakers Extension Council and Ducks Unlimited.

The North Dakota side of the park consists largely of reclaimed agricultural land and an artificial lake built by the Civilian Conservation Corps. It is a succession of low-profile buildings, organized around group activities—sports, camping, music. There is a floral clock, by Bulova, and a tablet containing the Ten Commandments, dedicated by Charleton Heston because he played Moses in the movie *The Ten Commandments.*

The Manitoba side of the garden is a drive through 1451 acres of barely contoured wilderness. A small lake ringed with cattails hums with buzzing flies and dragonflies and big fat bees and the yellow and black flicker of alfalfa sulfur butterflies. Paper birch and bur oak and fluttery aspen are mirrored in dark, clear water. Red-winged blackbirds nod on lightly swinging branches, warbling their clear carillon tune to one another. Yellow-headed blackbirds perch like solitary beacons and laugh harshly. The air is laden with heat and fragrance, a murmuring bird song and the sweet smell of green.

I drove from Turtle Mountain to the edge of the Big Muddy Badlands in Saskatchewan and Montana, crisscrossing the border. Actually, you can't crisscross very often; the routes are a rigid grid of right-angle county roads, with long, long stretches of nothingness between junctions. Infrequent signs on either side of the line point to another country beyond a field or down a tarred road. I rarely saw people, only other vehicles with dusted-up windows, presumably carrying bodies as steeped in sweat as my own. The signs of community are few, spread over vast distances: abandoned grain elevators, boarded-up houses, dirt tracks dwindling to nothing, as if they had forgotten their destinations. All the tiny towns by-passed by the highways. Centres like Minot and Bottineau and Crosby in North Dakota, and Deloraine, Manitoba, and Estevan, Saskatchewan, are discrete cells of populace and marginal prosperity, reservoirs in a land sometimes as barren as the Sahara.

In Deloraine, there was a parade. Sturdy people on well-rounded horses bearing the flags of Canada, the United States and Manitoba were followed by a walking band solemnly playing "Sweet Georgia Brown." Then came Brownies with orange and white pom-poms on their bicycles, the carpet bowlers in green, the Elks on a float swathed in white and deep purple. The parade was long; the streets were lined from one end of town to the other. People ate ice cream from Dixie cups, and there was an air of modest contentment in Deloraine.

"Now you can buy a midway bracelet for only six dollars!" From Bottineau, on the car radio, came news of the Bottineau County Fair, minute by minute, all afternoon. "We've been having both the pig scramble *and* the pig-dressing contests this afternoon; first place went to April Johnson. . . . Third place to Lorne and Lathan Orkey, and Ryan Bernstein. First place in the pig scramble went to Angela Sibelius and Sara Shwankey. Don't forget, folks, the demolition derby starts at five o'clock tomorrow. . . ."

Close to the border crossing on Saskatchewan Highway 8, which becomes "No. Dak." 28, I stopped beside a marshy pond, bridged by the road. It was covered with wading birds, black-bellied plovers, snipes, sandpipers making a persistent high-pitched sound. Several red-winged blackbirds perched on bowed dark green rushes on the fringes of the pond. Where the pond narrowed, big, fat dark brown cattle stood up to their knees in the water, groaning rhythmically.

A hot wind was blowing. The clouds were piled in tall dark drifts shifting around the lower sky, and the oil rigs, small, brightly coloured mechanical dwarfs, danced their relentless tarantella on the horizon. *Cladunk-cladunk-cladunk.* Not far away, in a small refinery, a single bright pink flame burned like a large match.

I drove down a rutted road running parallel to the boundary until I saw a cast-iron 1908 boundary monument in a field. It was hardly visible. I walked across to look at it; it was hot to the touch and caked with bird droppings. There was not another one to be seen in either direction. Only the cattle and the oil rigs nodding side by side in the same field.

I asked the American Immigration officer about the boundary. He was very old, and his face was as lined and rutted as the fields. He knew nothing about the boundary, beyond the two concrete markers on either side of the road, which delineated his responsibilities. "That's all what I know," he said. I drove on west, straight into the eye of the sun.

North Portal, Saskatchewan, and Portal, North Dakota, are randomly arranged along a railway. As many as four trains run through here a day, past the 1903 brick Grandview Hotel (grand view of the railway), square faced and boarded over, and the Portal State Bank, a tiny brick building with an elaborate Grecian façade done in concrete. Pierre's Place is the bar in Portal, richly decorated with flowing neon signs and blinking clocks and oversized, gleaming whiskey bottles reflecting the light. Dorothy serves beer and cheese balls, gizzards and drummies. In the corner, men in their dotage wearing peaked caps and glasses play cards. They talk in monosyllabic calm about the drought.

Outside, it is ninety-five degrees, and the silence is profound and hot. My dust rolls out behind me in a mushroom-coloured veil. Sometimes an activity cracks the lethargy of the land: irrigation, fertilizing, seeding, little men on big machines raising clouds of dust as startling as forest fires. Elsewhere fields look simply dead—not unsown, or lying fallow, or harvested—but dead. In the little towns I detour through at random, there are always the same two or three structures that leave an impression: the church, the bar, the forlorn grain elevators like discarded temples.

South of Estevan lie the lumpy trails of the coal-mining drag line, like sleeping dragons rolling and stretching and breaking through the surface. George M. Dawson found extensive lignite deposits during the 1873 boundary survey, and since the 1890s coal has been mined around the Souris River. Now 17,000 tons of that coal is burned each day in the Boundary Dam Power Station, which dominates the skyline.

Where there are valleys here, there are groves of aspen huddled close to the ground. But above ground level, along the road, there are few trees, just mounds of the caked, lumpy, pale soil. Near Estevan, I saw a sign beside the road, with an arrow pointing down a dusty side road: SEED GROWER. The sign showed a male figure holding a large shallow bowl on his hip; from his outstretched hand, perfect round seeds dropped in a straight line to the ground. The wind battered and mocked the sign, in the rubbly texture of a landscape almost Biblical in its desolation. I drove down the road for several miles, past the drag line pulled up in a ditch, past coal-blackened fields and idle trucks. I could not find the seed man.

From south of the border, the four tall stacks of the Boundary Dam Power Station poured out white smoke that very quickly became black. The smoke seemed to sketch an enigmatic message, like runes in the sky. Giant pylons swing across a long, open plateau in their seven-league boots, bearing a row of power lines in a long sweep north to south.

I drove north on a narrow gravel road that took me finally into the yard of an abandoned property on the border. When I stepped out of the car, I was battened against the door by a hot, hot wind, a solid sheet of air rushing parallel to the ground from the west. It picked up a hawk like a piece of ash from a chimney, then tossed it away again on an updraft.

The wind, and time, had flattened the fences and the outbuildings so that only a wonky, twisted roof or two stood on the ground over piles of grey weatherboards. On the long west side of the house, only one small window peeked out up under the roof; these houses do not care to witness their own destruction. There was an old International truck, grounded on a rusting wheelbase, stripped of its movable parts, last licensed in 1959. The fields around the house lay in the grip of random clumps of weed, furrows dried into lumpy waves sucked completely dry, soon to crumble into fine grains of dust. The earth, too, would someday abandon the land.

As I drove on, a pair of long-billed curlews flew parallel to the car, dipping in the wind, swooping into the trenches of earth, then wheeling skyward.

I am drawn off the road by Ambrose, North Dakota; the sun reflects off white buildings and a delicate church spire. It is a mirage of prosperity. Where the centre of the town should be, there is only an open space burnt dry, where tiny prairie dogs play like squirrels. There are houses so empty you can see right through them. A yield sign sags above a grass-covered road. Rusted-out machinery slumbers in empty paddocks. Grain elevators loom like ghosts beside the railway tracks. Only the Ambrose saloon showed signs of occupation; it is a low-slung, vinyl-panelled prefab beside the prairie dog playground.

The bar was full. Men with red faces and loud voices demanded four cases of beer from a reluctant bartender. Beside me, a morose old man methodically sipped hard liquor.

His family came here in 1905, he said, from Wisconsin, but they were originally from Norway. He grew up on a farm half a mile from the border.

"Our closest neighbours were just across the line," he said. "Germans. Catholic, of course, but that didn't make any difference. They were our neighbours.

"Used to be, back in the twenties and thirties, if you had a crippled horse and your neighbour had a good horse, you just swapped back and forth. And no one would've called it smuggling back then. It was just bein' neighbourly."

He drank, looked me straight in the eye. "You a journalist? You're askin' questions. No one asks questions unless they're from some newspaper."

The noise level intensified. A new group of people had pushed through the small door. They were young middle-aged, laughing, smoking.

"Now those are Canadians. They come over here all the time to drink."

"But do you still have friends, neighbours, across the line?" I asked.

"Not anymore. That's all gone. Most of the people are gone from around here, mostly to Crosby. Ambrose used to have about seven hundred people. There's only about eighty, mebee ninety, left now. And over there, they go their way; we go ours. Nobody's doin' too good these days."

"What about the oil?" I asked. "There seems to be quite a bit of activity, with all those little oil rigs all over the place."

"Oh, sure, but who owns the mineral rights? Just think about that. When people had to give up their land in the Depression, they gave up the mineral rights, too. Well, then they might have got the land back, but the bank or the finance company would hang on to the mineral rights, see. So that's a real mess, all that. Most people don't own the mineral rights on their own land."

We sat in silence. He was still thinking about the border.

"All this Reagan and Mulroney talk about neighbours," he finally blurted, "that's just politicians' PR. Just bullshit. If you tried to do something really neighbourly . . ."

His sentence dwindled into the bottom of his glass. He pushed it across the bar and stood up to leave.

"Enjoy your visit," he said, and walked out.

Beside one of the few occupied houses in Ambrose, an old, old man walked up and down the rows of his small vegetable garden. He was terribly crippled. He used his hoe as a walking stick, taking a deep bow to the earth at every step.

Just below the border crossing at Ambrose, there is a small, crumpled sign tacked to a short post. It bears the image of a rust-coloured longhorn steer. It reads:

THE END OF THE LOST TRAIL

GOING UP THE

TEXAS CHISHOLM TRAIL

1867

I drove on westward. I am at sea on the prairie, aware of the curvature of the earth. The land rolls out and away from you, and around the edges it disappears into the sky. The sky outweighs the land. I feel small, and earthbound.

What is it that makes a horizon? Here the horizon is made of intermittent interruptions, far, far away on the linear plane, eruptions on the surface, pop-up grain elevators, buildings clustered as if magnetized onto selected squares of the board. The tall, thin verticals—radio transmitters and telephone poles, holding a fragile web of wires off the ground—barely intrude. But the horizon itself is simply that point at which the land is overtaken by the sky and beaten into a thin line of nothingness. I have the sense of being in a circle, a bug in the centre of an inverted bowl on a large plate. Today the bowl is Wedgewood porcelain, with white and silvery clouds attenuated across the pale blue translucent surface of the sky.

Then, as I approached the Big Muddy Badlands, there were no clouds, only a solid blue desert sky. No trees. Shaven patches of a green that is almost lurid, bright runs of hope abruptly ending. Mottled hawks lurking in bald fields. White cattle, bone thin, stood in a white saucer where once there was water. They licked the alkaline dust. Calcined ashes. Tumbleweed drifted across the road like discarded crinolines.

From the diaries of surveyors and engineers, an ephemeral fragment of history:

September, 1873. Prairie fire in the great Coteau marking the Missouri watershed. We've all lost hair and beards. Sometimes we lie face down and hope the fire will race over us. All our oxen were badly singed. The only place to avoid the fire is in the swamps. I took a hundred head of horses and mules around the burned-out areas through to the swamp.

Everywhere, nothing but black, scorched ground dotted with white buffalo bones. There will be nothing for the stock to eat when we come back this way in two months' time.

\* \* \*

The Waterton-Glacier International Peace Park straddles the boundary as one million acres of mountainous wilderness in Alberta, Montana and British Columbia. These are, in fact, two separately administered national parks, identified as biosphere reserves by UNESCO. Razorback summits, hanging valleys, gouged-out bellies called glacial cirques and deep icy lakes—the landscape asserts an authority untouched by human treaties. But the vista is diligently cleared and maintained by the International Boundary Commission and despised by rangers and wardens as an open wound on the pristine forest. And the conventions of Customs and Immigration inspections are honoured even here.

West of Waterton-Glacier, Roosville, British Columbia, sits in the Rocky Mountain Trench, the flat plateau between two mountain ranges. It consists of a Gulf station and restaurant, a Canada Customs building and a substantial chain fence. The nearest Montana town is Eureka, nine miles south, but there is a bar on the American side about as close to the border as it could be. U.S. Highway 93, one of the longest highways in the world ("It's still 93 way down in central America," said the U.S. Customs officer), trickles to a stop just north of here. The closest border crossings are 250 miles by road to the east, on the other side of the Waterton Lakes parks, and 117 miles driving westward, at Eastport, Idaho. The pull of the highways is away from and around the borderlands.

The territory on the Canadian side is the reserve of the Tobacco Plains Band, about 10,000 acres, in a plot three miles wide and six miles long, butting right up to the 49th parallel. About eighty people live here. It is clearly indifferent land, flat, dusty, edged in scrubby bush.

In the band community centre, a solid shining log building, I met Elizabeth Gravelle. She is a soft-spoken, thoughtful woman who in the early sixties was elected chief of the Tobacco Plains Band, one of the first British Columbian women to be elected chief. She is still a council member. Handsome, serious, a grandmother.

"I always say you can tell when you're coming to a reservation. No matter where I travel, when the land starts getting poor, I say to myself, that's the Indian reservation. Because look at all the good land all through the valley, and we got this here. It's just dry land. We don't even have a mountain on the reserve. And it's not really ours; it's Her Majesty the Queen's. She kindly is letting us use *her* land." Her ironic tone was softened by a small laugh.

"And they keep taking the land. They put in highways and power lines all over the reserve, but they never give us more. They say it's government to government."

Elizabeth Gravelle grew up off the reserve, coming to visit relatives when she was a child, spending the last years of her childhood in a mission school. Her parents weren't registered, because her grandmother lost her status through marriage to a non-Indian. Elizabeth gained it back through her own marriage.

The date of the establishment of the reserve is suppressed in the communal memory; there is residual bitterness about the settlement. "I guess the chief—it was Chief David back then—he never did sign. He wanted from where he sat at the border up the mountain that way, and way back, and he wanted across the river, too. So instead, they just gave this little piece here, and the people that were there to survey, with the documents and everything, they pulled out in the middle of the night, and the chiefs claim they never signed any papers with them."

"Do you think of yourselves as Canadians?"

She shrugged, and shook her head slightly. "We're natives of this country, and we should be allowed to be what we were, what our forefathers were. They were just one nation. And if they wanted to winter over here, okay, they were here. Or if they wanted to go south, there was nobody to say, hey, you can't do that. I think that's the way it should be.

"We shouldn't be classified as Canadian or American. We are the same people; we're all Kootenays. They come here, and we go there. There are Tobacco Plains people in Montana and some in Idaho; we're known as Tobacco Plains Number Two." There was a pause, the silence dinted faintly by the grinding gears of lumber trucks on the road as they approached the border crossing.

"They grew tobacco down in Montana, but it must have been way, way back, because even the old people I talked to down there never saw the tobacco; they just saw the old furrows in the land.

"Before they put the border in, a lot of them were really into farming over there. They were homesteaders; they had cattle and everything. Even a little store. Then they were told if they didn't come back here, they would lose out and end up with nothing." She laughed drily. "Which they did anyways.

"One fellow sold his ranch for a couple hundred pounds of potatoes. They could have just stayed there; they didn't have to move. It was just a trick to get them on the reserve, I think, because they were promised, you know, land of their own. They didn't know it was reserve land, that they couldn't ever own.

"Anyways, they were told the border wasn't for them. That they could still go back and forth. They were trusting. They couldn't read or write. That was their understanding, that they were told that the border wasn't going to be for them.

"Even when I was a child, there was no fence there. You could just go anywhere. And there was no Customs building. But then later there used to be a Customs man; he just pitched a tent right in the middle of the prairie there. There was no fence, but I guess that was when he first started stopping Indians from goin' across. I guess I was about five . . ."

The Tobacco Plains Band asked the Department of Indian Affairs for the right to open a duty-free shop on the reservation. The band was turned down. Proposals for other other projects—a mulch plant and one for reforestation—were unsuccessful. "What we wanted to do was start all these projects, so everyone on the reserve would have jobs, and get them off the social assistance programs. There's a lot of young people wonder what they're even existing for."

And no one, she said, has ever thought to apply for a job at the Customs.

* * *

It's 7:00 A.M., on the 49th parallel, about eighty miles west of Roosville, just east of the Columbia River. I am sitting beside a small green circular lake in the shadow of Snowy Top Mountain, waiting for Carl Gustafson, chief of the International Boundary Commission survey team. There is no sun here, though it has risen. We got up at 3:30 A.M., left the motel at Salmo in darkness and came up the back wall of the Selkirk Range on a logging road. The road is maintained, roughly speaking, by the B.C. Forest Service. It is a series of gouged-out trenches decorated with large boulders and shredded sheets of bark and uprooted trees. Carl Gustafson is obscurely embarrassed by the condition of the logging road; the Canadians compare "their" logging roads with those of the Americans, just over the border, and they feel like poor cousins. We also regularly catch sight of the B.C. Hydro power lines, around which an enormous and ugly swath has been cut like a wound on the land. Unclaimed timber litters the hillside.

By comparison, the cut line of the boundary is a model of tidiness and containment. It stretches up the hills on either side of the lake, perfectly straight, a narrow, cleared, precise strip, twenty feet wide. The surveyors work the line as if they were laying out formal gardens; everything is measured, and even trees and stumps to be removed are individually marked. The monuments here are set on every peak, and between them are pickets to show where work is to be done. At the end of the day, the sure, practised eye of Carl Gustafson will sweep over the day's work and pronounce it perfect or not quite good enough.

Even the birds are quiet in the cool, shadowy morning forest. The survey team members will soon shatter the silence with their chain saws; they work fast and hard for the full morning and quit sawing at one o'clock, because of the fire hazard. Already they are far ahead of me, bounding up the vertical slope like young animals. They carry their chain saws, swinging from one hand, and pack fuel and lunch and two-way radios on their backs.

Carl Gustafson arrives; he had gone briefly in the other direction to check a monument. We begin the climb above the lake. We climb straight up the vista, through seeping streams, bear lilies, loose shale. It takes us several hours. Ahead on the trail, the young men lope eagerly, springing from rock to rock. The shale clatters like plates around us. The edges of rock become razor sharp and our choice of foothold increasingly limited.

"We have a saying in the boundary commission," Carl said. "A summer on the line makes men out of young men."

Carl has been with the International Boundary Commission for twenty-five years. He is a lean, bearded, laconic man from Georgeville on Lake Memphrémagog, cousin of the Canadian poet Ralph Gustafson. Carl doesn't drink, doesn't smoke and prefers his food without salt. He is content in solitude, or in the company of working men. He drives his men from three in the morning until six at night, all summer long, but he seems to be a kindly boss, not without a sense of humour and self-awareness, which flicker through occasionally in his speech or in the glint in his eye. He loves fieldwork and in the fall prolongs his return to home and office as long as possible. He speaks with tenderness about his children and instills a profound respect for the wilderness in his survey teams.

Carl does not make decisions quickly; he examines a situation at length before pronouncing briefly on it. He is patient, deliberate. He takes one problem at a time and doesn't seek a theoretical framework. When he finally speaks, his voice is a soft drawl, with pauses. He is reluctant to refer casually to figures, because he is bound by ideals of precision and accuracy. The incidental and unheralded heroism in his work—well, he might tell you the stories, but mostly they are buried in his mind. The straightness of the vista is his life.

We leave behind the underbrush and trees, spindly fir mostly, and climb a rock face that curves out over our heads and narrows to a small, sharp point. On top is a silver-coloured monument, beside which two people can stand—one in Canada, the other in the United States.

Snowy Top Mountain, in the Selkirk Range, is about 9800 feet above sea level, the third highest peak on the 49th parallel, on the boundary between British Columbia and the Panhandle of Idaho. From here we can see almost fifty miles to the east, a little less to the west, in both directions a rippling series of bony ridges, the scanty upper fringes of forest, countless peaks and a distant hazy horizon. The cut line is as clean as a fault line, an opening that looks swept, marked only with the fingerlike shadows of individual trees. A pause, bisecting the wilderness.

This is Monument 196. About five feet tall, cast bronze, painted silver, set in a concrete base two feet square.

"These monuments were installed between 1903 and 1907," said Carl, "and this one had to be packed up here by mule. It would've been necessary to pack up a bag of cement, as well as the monument. In those early days, you used to carry the cement in canvas containers. I've seen some of those old canvas cement bags along the Alaska/Yukon boundary, up near the snow line. The gravel they would have gathered locally, but it would've been quite an effort just to get the boundary monument up here and cement for the base.

"The original demarcation of the line began here in 1857, eleven years after the Oregon Treaty. Work was completed in 1862, and then from 1903 to 1907, the line was marked more completely and more permanently and precisely with these bronze boundary obelisks. The cut line was cleared out then for the full length from the Strait of Georgia right to where the trees stop on the prairies, near Cardston, Alberta."

The International Boundary Commission was last through here in 1958. There are no signs of human trespass; only caribou and porcupine cross the border up here.

"Is this really the forty-ninth parallel, exactly?" I asked.

There was a brief silence. "Well, I'd have to refer to some technical data to tell you about this particular monument. But as the forty-ninth parallel is presently defined, it appears that only one of these monuments, which number about a thousand, is on the line as it would be defined to one-inch accuracy. At present, there are several monuments that are approximately twelve seconds of latitude away from the forty-ninth parallel, and that would amount to twelve hundred feet in distance. Those are in the vicinity of the Sweetgrass Hills between Alberta and Montana.

"Then at the Pacific coast, at Point Roberts there, the boundary markers are approximately eight hundred feet off. And if it favours the Canadians at Three Buttes, it favours the Americans at the coast. So I guess you could say it evens out in the end."

"Why isn't it right on the parallel?"

Carl thought a bit. Below us on the scree leading up to the ridge, we could hear the boys sawing up a big log stump. "Well, what we prefer to say," he said at last, "is that the original surveys were done the very best that they could have been done, at that time. But there were some secondary effects from the local variation of gravity, which were not taken into account. They were aware that they had these deflections of the vertical, as they're called, but they were unwilling to take the time to determine the mean parallel and to take out these deflections.

"At that time, transportation was very difficult in the area, and there were some hostilities with the Indians on the American side. So I think it was probably in the right interest to leave the boundary as it was established and get on with other jobs at hand."

Carl picks up a large ax and heads down to give some instruction to his men. I stand beside the monument, looking west. The line on the ground looks completely arbitrary, cutting at right angles to the natural north/south flow of the land and transforming landscape into a map. I strain for a glimpse of the valley of the Columbia River, the true divide if there must be one, between the land to the north and the land to the south.

# 5

## 54-40 OR FIGHT:
## THE PACIFIC NORTHWEST

I sat on the bank of the Columbia River near Bossburg, Washington. Bossburg is a tiny hamlet snared by forked roads and the railway. A cluster of mailboxes clings to a single wooden post amid a scattering of tumbling-down houses and outbuildings. North of here at Waneta (I hear "Juanita"), British Columbia, the Canadian side seems feverishly populated by comparison, a bright necklace of Spanish bungalows and elaborate rock gardens on a small ridge. In Bossburg on an August Friday around noon, I saw only a black mongrel dog on an overgrown driveway. It growled halfheartedly as I drove past on the road to the river.

Down on the river bank, the only sound comes from passing motorboats, about one an hour moving in graceful arcs across the silky green surface. The fir and cedar forest is pungent, sweet, and the hum of individual flies stings the hush. Birds are listless in the midday heat. The Columbia here is called the Franklin Roosevelt, and south of here is Kettle Falls, then Grand Coulee Dam and the Big Bend, then the river pours south across Washington State, is joined by the Yakima and the Snake, becomes three quarters of the length of the boundary between Washington and Oregon and finally reaches the Pacific. At half a dozen points in its course, the natural flow of the Columbia is channelled into some of the world's largest hydroelectric power schemes.

But this section of the river is placid, lakelike, an adagio, where the force of the currents is submerged but for the random lace edge of an eddy, or a straight streak of fast water stretched like naked muscle over a curve. North of here at the border, where the Columbia is joined by the

Pend Oreille, the waters are in messy noisy turmoil, muddied and foaming and rushing past in a terrible haste. In its various moods and rhythms over almost thirteen hundred miles, the Columbia is like a symphony coaxed out of the impassive, rigid terrain.

The force of the landscape is palpable, a series of long, powerful mountain ridges thrown in loose, sharp north/south crescents: the southern edges of the Rockies; the Lewis, Bitterroot and Monashee ranges; the Selkirks and the Cascades, through which rivers, even those as broad and powerful as the Columbia, have to find the weak spots. The ridges seem to be a race of dormant, primitive creatures with bared razorback skeletons. They are impenetrable and fearsome even when fossilized as rock and trapped in the remnants of glaciers. To fly across this landscape is to acknowledge the victory of permanent nature over transient society, which is not to say that this landscape cannot be destroyed. It has not, however, been tamed, and the international boundary line is here as absurd as graffiti scratched on a rock face.

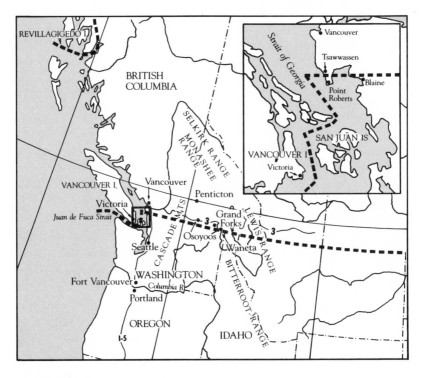

## THE PACIFIC NORTHWEST

All modes of transport and habitation hug the shores of the river, in the northeastern corner of Washington State, at least. The terrain is tough and hard; roadside signs south and west of Bossburg advertise land for five hundred dollars an acre, dry. Dirt that isn't irrigated around here just dries up and blows away. Communities dwindle. Most little towns on both sides of the border have a shapeless presence—a silent railway siding, a shrunken sawdust pile, sometimes little more than a huddle of recreational vehicles tethered to the earth. There isn't the patina of civilization; there are few graveyards. Small signs acknowledge the passing of history, the building of the railway, the sweep and trample of prospectors, the invisible site of a trading post. Lumber trucks and tourists roll through, oblivious to monuments.

The water of the Columbia is very green, reflecting the darker green of the hills and the clean, light-coloured bones of a limestone cliff face on the other side. A thin road is sketched along the far river bank; a single vehicle, a half-ton truck, raises a small lateral spiral of dust that dwindles into nothingness. The reflection flows right across the river, wavering only slightly in the green mirror, a transparent ruffle of foliage above the glassy pull of the current. It seems that I should be able to reach out and touch the tops of the trees in the water.

The river is wide enough to feel like a physical barrier, and I might be standing on this shore looking across into another country. The Columbia River has the stature, the dignity, the weight of a natural boundary like the St. Lawrence and the Saint John rivers. The great explorers, David Thompson, Meriwether Lewis and William Clark, raced to follow its course to the Pacific Ocean in the early years of the last century; its importance to North American trade and settlement was both real and symbolic. When David Thompson, on behalf of the North West Company, reached the mouth of the Columbia in 1811, he found it occupied by the Americans and their Fort Astoria. In the War of 1812, the British took Fort Astoria, and the positioning of forces for the ultimate possession of the coveted Columbia and its drainage area began. In fact, the hills and the limestone outcrop on the other side of the river might well have been Canadian.

Our modern visual sense of the west coast is conditioned by the presence of the 49th parallel. It seems perfectly logical that this line of latitude should extend right through to the Pacific Ocean as the international boundary, neatly bisecting the continent. But the treaty of 1818

named the 49th parallel the boundary only as far as the Rocky Mountains, leaving the Oregon Territory to be occupied jointly by the Americans and the British. The Oregon Territory was a large and comprehen-
sive tract of land, extending as far north as latitude 54°40', above which
at that time was Russian Alaska, and as far south as the 42nd parallel, to
the Spanish territory then known as Mexico. In the minds of people
travelling to the West in the 1830s, the Oregon Territory was just that,
a geographically distinct unit stretching from the Rocky Mountains to
the Pacific Ocean. Contemporary accounts not only assume the geographical coherence of the territory but present elaborate arguments for
the claims of either Britain or the United States for official and final
possession.

In 1843, the American traveller Thomas J. Farnham reviewed the
claims of explorers, Spanish and British, and the history of treaties and
the incipient patterns of settlement in the Oregon Territory and con-
cluded that the Spaniards had explored the coast 184 years before the
English (in the person of Captain Cook); that the British had abandoned rights of possession by default after a series of treaties with Spain;
that the United States had acquired all rights of possession from the
Spanish; that furthermore, the Americans had been the first to discover
and explore the Columbia River and so had rights of occupancy; that
the Americans also had been the first to navigate around the Queen
Charlotte Islands south of Alaska, and that therefore "Oregon Territory, for all these reasons and many others which will be found in the
energy with which if necessary, our citizens will defend it, is the rightful
property of the United States."

Whatever the intentions of the treaty makers in 1818 in establishing
joint possession of the land west of the Rockies, there seems little doubt
that both nations used the subsequent period, with varying degrees of
conviction and specific policy, to consolidate their respective claims on
the largely unoccupied territory. The main battle for possession of the
Oregon Territory was fought on its southernmost corner, close to the
mouth of the Columbia River, where Portland, Oregon, and Vancouver, Washington, are now joined by long-spanned bridges over the
Columbia. Fort Astoria was abandoned by the British; Fort Vancouver,
on the north bank of the Columbia, was established as a Hudson's Bay
trading post in 1825. At the opening ceremony, Hudson's Bay Governor
George Simpson named the post in honour of George Vancouver to

"identify our Soil and Trade with his discovery of the River and the Coast on behalf of Great Britain." Simpson's declaration was undoubtedly motivated by a murky blend of patriotism and politics; the Columbia was actually discovered by the American trader Robert Gray.

The post rapidly became the centre of a settlement of fur traders, Indians and mixed bloods, many of whom were current or retired employees of the Hudson's Bay Company, which was, by the early 1840s, evolving from a fur-trading empire into a more broadly based international company. The fort's chief factor, John McLoughlin, was also in charge of forts as distant as Fort Simpson (just below Alaska) and an agency in the Sandwich Islands (now Hawaii). Fort Vancouver was the base for the company's final fur-trading fling; by 1870, the Hudson's Bay Company had completely relinquished its hold on the West to the British government.

But in 1838, John McLoughlin imagined the Oregon Territory as fertile ground for extensive British settlement. One hundred and fifteen people were brought to Oregon from Red River, but no communities flourished. At the same time, an increasingly antagonistic relationship developed between the Hudson's Bay Company and the aggressive, independent American fur traders. Meanwhile, a slow but steady flow of American missionaries and entrepreneurs moved into the territory.

The Oregon Trail attracted Americans to the open West in a way that could not be matched by the bureaucratic Hudson's Bay Company. As early as 1821, the U.S. Congress had advocated settlement and occupation of the Oregon Territory and beyond, as far north as the 60th parallel. In the early 1830s, a Methodist community formed on the south banks of the Columbia River, not far upstream from Fort Vancouver. By 1842, the Americans had lowered their sights from the 60th parallel to 54-40 and had begun to settle in larger numbers around the Columbia River. American politicians saw their population "rolling towards the shores of the Pacific with an impetus greater than we realize"; a trickle of curious and hardy immigrants had officially become a flood of Americans and then evolved into a full-scale settlement policy.

By 1843, the American settlers in the Oregon Territory were demanding annexation with the United States; in 1844, Democratic presidential candidate James Polk won an election with his slogan "54-40 or Fight." Polk wrote, "Our title to the country of the Oregon is clear and unquestionable, and already our people are preparing to perfect that title by occupying it with their wives and children . . . increasing to many millions, establishing the blessings of self-government in valleys of which the rivers flow to the Pacific." The white population of Oregon was about six thousand by 1846. In the lands around Fort Vancouver, meanwhile, according to McLoughlin, "British feeling is dying away. . . . Englishmen are either afraid or ashamed to own their own country." American newspapers wrote excitedly of war, and Britain began the slow mustering of its navy.

But in 1846, after protracted diplomatic discussion, Britain in a sense lost interest in distant colonial adventures. The Americans lowered their sights even further, to the 49th parallel, which was then extended to the Strait of Georgia as the boundary line. A treaty was signed in June 1846, known in Canada as the Oregon Treaty and in the United States as the first Treaty of Washington. Britain lost the Columbia River and kept Vancouver Island. The United States turned its attention southwards and declared war on Mexico.

There are historians who argue that Britain need not have lost the territory between the 49th parallel and the Columbia River, that even the redoubtable Daniel Webster was open to persuasion on the British claim to that land, as long as the Columbia remained a shared waterway. But the pattern for British/American negotiations was set and would be picked up again some fifty years later in the Alaska boundary dispute.

John McLoughlin left Fort Vancouver, crossed the Columbia to live in Oregon City and became an American citizen. Today he is known as the father of Oregon. The Hudson's Bay Company made Fort Victoria on Vancouver Island its western administrative headquarters, and in 1849 the American army occupied the old fort, calling it Camp Columbia. The Hudson's Bay Company finally sold the site to the army in 1860, and in 1866 the fur-trading post burned to the ground.

Fort Vancouver is now a national park, restored to its 1840s condition. It is a quaint anachronism between an interstate highway, an airport and a famous river. It is three hundred miles south of the 49th parallel, 150 years from our current political reality, five hours of fast driving from Blaine, Washington, and Zero Avenue in Langley, British Columbia.

\* \* \*

Point Roberts is 4.9 square miles of American land, part of Whatcom County, Washington. From the state of Washington, it can only be reached by driving north into Canada at Blaine and south again at Tsawwassen. At the time of the boundary settlement in 1846, Point Roberts was described as a "bleak spit or promontory," useless, except possibly as a smuggling depot. The British declared it was "of not the slightest value to the United States" and suggested that their own boundary commissioner attempt to "relieve the American government from the inconvenient appendage of a patch of ground of little value."

But the definition of the boundary in 1846 had not been sufficiently precise; its route through the Strait of Juan de Fuca had been loosely designated as passing through the "middle of the channel which separates the continent from Vancouver Island." This description obscured the complexity of the strait, where there are three distinct channels running north/south and an irregular archipelago of beautiful wooded islands. Both the Americans and the British, in the shape of the Hudson's Bay Company, claimed the large San Juan Island. In 1859, an American settler shot a British pig on San Juan Island, highlighting the need for arbitrated settlement.

San Juan Island is a pastoral island, where old stands of timber frame dark ponds, where fat, pale cattle graze on bleached grass and small horses nuzzle one another beside the road. Yachts ride the fierce, tugging tidal currents that swing around the island; minke and orca whales abound just offshore in Haro Strait.

The island was jointly occupied for 12 years by British and American troops, between 1860 and 1872, while its ownership was in doubt. The British sent over a regiment of Royal Marines from their post on what was then known as Vancouver's Island, well south of San Juan Island. They created what is called English Camp on the northwestern side of the island, above Garrison Bay, around enormous braided maple trees now more than 350 years old. On a sheltered bluff, they built gracious quarters, even elaborate birdhouses; they planted formal gardens on the verdant green meadow and entertained the local settlers at picnics and balls.

On the exposed southern banks of the island, the Americans sketched out a redoubt and roughly assembled a sprawling camp. Their quarters were apparently cold and poorly constructed; there was misery—an un-

usually high incidence of alcoholism and suicide. The siege was otherwise good-natured, even friendly.

The San Juan Island dispute became part of a parcel of disagreements
between Britain and the United States, with Canada as a handicapped
little monkey in the middle. The Americans declared Point Roberts a
military reserve. General Winfield Scott, who fought the War of 1812
in Niagara and who helped avert the Aroostook War in Maine and New
Brunswick in the 1830s, was brought to the west coast to maintain order.

The disputed issues included fishing rights for the Americans in Canadian waters, American access to the St. Lawrence canals, tariffs on
Canadian products, retribution for the Fenian raids and British support
for the South during the Civil War, implicit in the outfitting of the
Confederate ship the *Alabama*. American senators proposed that Britain
pay the United States $2 billion, or alternatively, give up Canada as a
mortgage. Canada was represented in the protracted negotiations by
Prime Minister John A. Macdonald, but only as part of the British team
and an irritant to both major powers. The settlement in 1871, known as
the Treaty of Washington, included a series of arbitrations. The *Alabama* cost the British $15.5 million; the Americans won twelve years of
fishing rights in exchange for $5.5 million and no tariff on Canadian
fish in the American market. The British compensated the Canadians
for the Fenian raids. Kaiser Wilhelm of Germany was selected to ar-
bitrate on the San Juan Island boundary dispute, and he pinned the tail
on the American position, the westernmost and largest channel.

Any sense of victory is curiously muted on San Juan Island; it may be
the pacifist temperament of the island, or the fact that the city of Victoria is very visible across Haro Strait. The stark contrast between the
British and American regiments is entrenched in the mythology of the
Pig War, interpreted in what have become two small national parks.
The American Camp is a bleak, wind-swept prairie that looks as if it
should have been a battlefield; there is not a single building, just a scattering of modest, woeful plaques. The English Camp is still dotted with
neat, white buildings; boys play football on the lush grass, and a handsome white-haired volunteer patrols in the red-jacketed woolen uniform
of the Royal Marines. On the sheltering wooded hillside, the sweet fragrance of cedar and wild rose is cut by the briny scent rising from the

mud flats exposed at low tide, where families with babies and large dogs and long-handled shovels dig for clams.

But here also ennui took its toll; the two armies never met in battle, and the pig was the only official casualty. On the small mountain above the English Camp, there is a little cemetery where lie the bodies of seven young Englishmen commemorated by five plain plaques; there were three drownings and one accidental shooting.

By 1873, the boundary had been surveyed to the coast, and Point Roberts became what it is still today, a small collection of determined, eccentric individuals, their houses buried in stands of pine or facing out on long, pebbled beaches, people who treasure their isolation. It is still possible to view Point Roberts as a bleak promontory. Seals caper on its western coast. In the sheltered and shallow curve of Boundary Bay, blue heron graze in ignorance of territorial regulations. They wheel in slow and considered arrogance over the boundary monuments caked with the droppings of seagulls.

The Point Roberts border is a ditch, running parallel to Roosevelt Road. On the eastern end, at Boundary Bay, a range tower flaunts an orange square high over a beach where people stroll, often back and forth across the border. In 1861, the massive obelisk that marks the end of the 49th parallel was set on the edge of the western cliff, more than 150 feet above the shore. It is one of the largest monuments on the entire boundary; in its small, shaded clearing, between wild apple trees on the American side and an extravagant cliffhanging condominium on the Canadian side, it has an ironic grandeur, which celebrates not so much the political determination of the boundary as the dogged deter-mination of the surveyors and commissioners who put the line in place. The names of the commissioners, Prevost, Richards, Hawkins and Campbell, are carved deep into the stone. The obelisk is believed to sit on four small coins and to contain the bones of a British soldier.

You drive along Roosevelt Road, and on the American side there is a deep woods, rich with the colour and smell of decaying leaves. On the north side, you see the backs of comfortable Canadian retirement homes. Their gardens spill over into the trench, which the residents think of as no man's land; pumpkins ripen dangerously near the ditch, and blackberry canes obscure the line of demarcation.

John Baker was born and raised at Point Roberts. "Been a commercial fisherman all my life," he says. He lives on a secluded hillside, right in the middle of the peninsula, with views of downtown Vancouver in Canada and Mount Baker in the United States. His grandparents homesteaded the same property at the turn of the century. It is now the site of a large, sharply contoured modern house with many windows. John Baker escorted me into his living room. He is a big man, the same tough, cool breed of man as the earlier John Baker of the Aroostook War in Maine and New Brunswick. But his mother was Danish; his father was Icelandic.

The Point Roberts cemetery, on a quiet road not far from the eastern bluffs, is inhabited by Icelandic and Danish families; the Thorsteinsons, Johannsens, Goodmans, Eversens, Svensons, Samuelsons; there is an almost identical cemetery full of Icelanders at Pembina, North Dakota, also just a mile or so south of the 49th parallel. The Icelandic immigrants first came to Canada, to Victoria, and then moved on to Point Roberts for the cheap land. They built farms, worked in the fish canneries, caught salmon in the notorious omnivorous fish traps, which almost destroyed the fish stocks until they were banned in the 1930s. The Icelanders are still a vigorous presence on the Point.

From the beginning, the Point has been eyed acquisitively by Canadians; in the 1890s, the release of military reserve land to settlers resulted in "a stampede of adventurers from the British side, who flocked to the Point for the purpose of securing a forty on which to speculate." The Canadians are still flocking to Point Roberts, to summer cottages, cheap gas and an excellent wine store. And the post office. "Your service is terrible," according to John Baker.

I asked John Baker about the population. "Ballpark, two hundred registered voters on the Point, so say four hundred and fifty U.S. citizens. In the summertime, twenty-five hundred, three thousand Canadians here, permanent. Permanent for six months of the year, that is. They own eighty-five to ninety per cent of Point Roberts. But when they get sick, zing! Back across the line for B.C. Medical. As far as growth at Point Roberts, B.C. Medical and the border control that, and they always will."

Despite the isolated access to the Point and its smallness, there is not a sense of intimacy along this stretch of border. Canadians whose lots back onto it appear to treat it as an extended lower garden. But the American Customs officials perform their duties as if they were sitting at the gateway to Washington, D.C. The bureaucracy is incongruous, beside the trench.

"There's walkways made right across it," said John Baker, "and they jog back and forth, and they're breakin' the law. Kids cut through, packin' beer through there steady."

"When I was here awhile ago," I said, "there were some war games or something going on in the woods on the American side; I could hear gunfire, and down a little dirt road I found a lot of trucks parked. What's that all about?"

John Baker snorted. "What they're doing is shooting those paint darts they use to mark trees. You see them walking around with big bruises on their arms; it's a macho trip. I'm against that. You know, they want to play for real, go join up."

"But who's doing it; is it Canadians?"

"Ninety-nine point nine per cent Canadians."

We sat in silence briefly, on the long, long sofa looking east. A clock chimed as discreetly as a covered cough, a comment on the incongruous notion of Canadians playing war on American turf, a tiny crack in Canadian decorum on the edge of the Pacific Ocean.

"Do you think there is any remote possibility that Point Roberts would become part of Canada?" I asked.

John Baker laughed. "It's come up a few times, and people really get up in arms. But the way it's getting now—the younger people, you know, they don't really care, but, boy I'm telling you, the *older* people . . ."

"We're Americans, and this is ours. Go back to Fifty-four Forty or Fight. We should have had the Fraser as well."

I couldn't resist the bait. "Or, conversely," I suggested, "*we* should have had the Columbia!"

"Try taking it," said John Baker.

* * *

"With all due respect to my American cousins," said Paddy Green, "when they weren't ripping off the Mexicans, they were ripping off the Canadians; whether on the east coast or on the land north of the Columbia River and the San Juan Islands. They have a very long history of taking what belongs to someone else."

Prince Rupert, British Columbia, sits in the coastal waters just south

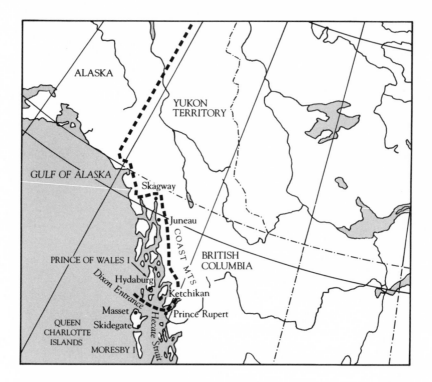

## THE ALASKA PANHANDLE

of the 54-40 line, at the base of the Alaska Panhandle. I flew there from Vancouver, over the slumbering, snow-drifted peaks of the Coast Mountains.

Paddy Green is a very big man with a ruddy, serious face; he spoke on behalf of several solemn fishermen clothed mostly in rubber, who nodded in silent agreement. We were sitting upstairs, on a rainy afternoon, at the Prince Rupert Fishermen's Co-operative Association. The waters in front of the yellow pragmatic co-op building were very quiet—fishing boats at rest by the floats, a single raven scavenging for fish, not one seagull. The rain and the mist and the flat water were a grey continuum. In places a small drowned island became briefly visible, then disappeared like a mythical sea creature. Prince Rupert itself is an island; the mountains push right up to the edge of the land mass of coastal British Columbia. To build an airport, Prince Rupert had to look to another island, slightly farther out in Hecate Strait.

In the plant below us, a room full of processors were cheerfully filleting cod. They were almost all women, immigrant Asian and native, in hats, scarves and rubber gloves, sitting on tall stools beside a conveyor belt at stations bearing their names. With sharp filleting knives, under running water, they slashed the fish, crudely, swiftly, one fillet off each side. The fillets were then skinned on a belt, graded by weight and frozen.

Prince Rupert is fishing; fishing is Prince Rupert. The official population of just under seventeen thousand swells to more than twenty thousand in the fishing season. Fishermen, otherwise mild-mannered, good-natured and phlegmatic people, react visibly to talk about the boundary. Their blood bubbles at the mere thought of the A-B line, the tracing of the 54-40 line of latitude over the waters of Dixon Entrance. It is still "54-40 or Fight." The same would seem to be true in Masset, on the northern fringe of the Queen Charolotte Islands, and in Ketchikan, Alaska, on the southwestern side of Revillagigedo Island, some ninety miles northwest of Prince Rupert, across Dixon Entrance. The border has some electricity here, which I have not encountered since Grand Manan Island on the east coast.

The United States bought Alaska from the Russians in 1867—coincidentally, in the same year the Dominion of Canada was created, as an entity separate from Britain. The Alaska Purchase was a contentious decision; the American sense of Manifest Destiny had ebbed somewhat, or did not extend northwards with the same urgency that it had spread westward. Alaska was sold by the Russians to the Americans on terms identical to those negotiated between Britain and Russia in 1825; the same curious boundaries applied. By 1871, all territories touching Alaska had become part of the Dominion of Canada.

The inclusion of the Panhandle, which still irks west coast Canadians, was part of the original agreement between Britain and Russia; that long fringe of coastal mountains, running down more than half of what is now British Columbia and known as a lisière, was set aside for the Russians in the 1825 treaty as a form of security for their string of settlements on the Alexander archipelago. The British/Russian agreement defined the Panhandle by a line of demarcation running from summit to summit in the mountain range running parallel to the coast. As is typical of boundary treaty language, the mountain range and the precise dimensions of the lisière were not specified.

The boundary running north from the Panhandle to the "Frozen

Ocean" (the Beaufort Sea) was also defined in 1825, as a form of protection for the British fur-trading forts; during the British/Russian negotiations, that line was shunted westward from the 135th meridian to its current location along the 141st meridian, putting what would become the Klondike gold fields in British territory. During the period of Russian/British occupation, the Hudson's Bay Company surreptitiously contravened the agreement by constructing the fur-trading post Fort Yukon on Russian territory in 1847, at the important junction of the Yukon and Porcupine rivers. The transgression was not discovered until the Canadians and the Americans formally surveyed the 141st meridian.

When both Canadians and Americans began looking speculatively to the north in the 1880s, thinking of exploration and settlement, the real location of the boundaries became important. The North at that time was unmapped, a vast network of rivers in a glacial landscape, a scattering of trading forts, a land known intimately by the Tlingit, the Chilkat and the Han native bands. Between 1869 and 1890, both the Canadians and the Americans sent surveying parties to locate the 141st meridian on the ground. In 1876, an incident on the Stikine River with an American prisoner in Canadian custody caused both governments to consider the precise location of the boundary in the southern portion of the Panhandle. Several overtures were made by the Americans to the Canadians for opening discussions; various independent and wildly different interpretations of the boundary line were proposed. The Canadians sent an agent to surreptitiously observe the Americans surveying in the Portland Canal. Then, in 1892, the two governments agreed to a joint survey of the Panhandle.

It became clear almost immediately that the definition of the Panhandle boundary would require interpretation, negotiation, perhaps even subterfuge. The 1825 Russian/British Treaty, by which the Americans and Canadians were also bound, stated that the Panhandle boundary "shall be formed by a line parallel to the windings of the coast, and which shall never exceed the distance of 10 marine leagues [about 33 miles] therefrom." But which channel was the Portland Canal? And what was meant in the 1825 treaty by "the summit of the mountain," and "the coast," in a coastline of long, narrow canals, cutting deeply inland?

" 'While sailing upon the coast, the boundary shall be the tops of the mountains,' " Paddy Green quoted grandly, and with some licence.

"You have to remember they were in sailing ships then. And they weren't up in all the little inlets and canals; they were in the broad sounds in the southeast, and the mountains were whatever they saw from the ships."

By the 1890s, gold was drawing prospectors and merchants to Alaska and the Yukon Territory. Most of the first speculators were American, and they came north up the waters of the Panhandle to Skagway. There was confusion about where the boundary was. In 1897–98, Customs officials and the Mounted Police took up positions on the landscape. Both the Canadian and American governments happily collected customs duties in the mountain passes and conducted surveys of the terrain.

Paddy Green shifted in his chair and gestured in the direction of a map on the wall. "American surveyors climbed up to the tops of the mountains, and what did they find? They found opportunity, because what did they see? They saw more mountains. Here was a God-given opportunity for Manifest Destiny.

"I was talking one time to Wiggs O'Neil, an early person up here who was on the original Canadian boundary survey, when they were verifying the original Russian stone cairns. When they got up into the mountains, he told me, they found empty bags of Portland cement where the Americans had gone in a few years before and created their own "Russian" stone cairns. And that was generally known around here; that was just how they operated in those days."

In 1902, the Americans accused the Canadians of destroying Russian boundary monuments.

In 1903, President Roosevelt instigated the Alaska Boundary Tribunal, which was to consist of three Americans and three British or Canadian "impartial jurists of repute" and was to adhere to a very strict timetable, issuing a report within seven months. The tribunal consisted of the Americans Senator Henry Cabot Lodge, Secretary of War Elihu Root and an ex-senator, George Turner ("political hacks," snorted Paddy Green); the British lord chief justice, Lord Alverstone, and two Canadians, Toronto lawyer Allen Aylesworth and Sir Louis Jetté, the lieutenant governor of Quebec and former member of the Quebec Supreme Court.

Of all the international boundary disputes, the one arbitrated by the Alaska Boundary Tribunal is the best known, and the one that makes Canadians most uncomfortable about negotiations with the United

States. The reasons for this are primarily in the process itelf, not the re-
sults, which would not have been significantly different had the Canadians achieved their objectives; there would still have been a Panhandle. The defeat was symbolic. Subsequent revelations of the degree
of interference by President Roosevelt, the Americans' flagrant courting
of Britain's Lord Alverstone and the Canadians' miserable sense of isolation and injustice are almost the stuff of drama.

President Roosevelt merely tolerated the tribunal as a way of doing
things with Britain in a dignified manner. He thought that the Canadian demand for access to tidewater inlets on the Panhandle was as absurd as the idea that Canadians might suddenly annex the island of
Nantucket, south of Cape Cod. He made it known that were the tribunal decision not to be satisfactory, he would not only refuse arbitration
but would feel that he had "the authority to run the line as we claim it."

Lord Alverstone seems to have struggled in the general direction of
careful impartiality. But in the final hours of negotiations, he reversed
his previous written opinion on the assignment to Canada of two small
islands in the Portland Canal. The loss of approximately seven square
miles of land was interpreted by the Canadians as the final indignity in a
prearranged scenario. The Canadian members of the tribunal refused to
sign the official tribunal award. Giving the two islands to the United
States (which put a kink in the boundary in its seaward course down the
Portland Canal) was seen by Canadian Prime Minister Wilfrid Laurier as
"one of those concessions which have made British diplomacy odious to
Canadian people."

"The Boer War was going on," said Paddy Green, "and Britain got its
tail twisted politically by the Americans, and Canada quite frankly got
screwed. Any further adjustment of that line is out of the question. We
are the offended party; anyone who now suggests that the A-B line
should be moved is totally warped."

The A-B line is the 54-40 line, running west from the end of the Portland Canal to Cape Muzon on Dall Island. It was the final line to be
drawn between American and Canadian territory, and it is the source of
continuing disagreement between the two countries. The A-B line is an
unusual water boundary line in that it actually touches the shores of
Alaska at Cape Chacon and Cape Muzon, allowing the Americans virtually no territorial waters. As national territorial water limits have been

extended from three miles to twelve miles to two hundred miles, so has territorial nationalism been extended, on both sides of the border. And, as on the east coast, the boundary issue is a fishing issue; at stake are the rich salmon, halibut and cod grounds of Dixon Entrance.

It is the Americans who want to reopen negotiations on this part of the boundary. They are now taking the position that the A-B line, cutting across Dixon Entrance, was never intended to be an official boundary line, but merely a line of land allocation, separating the land masses of the two countries. They would like to see what they call a "fisheries conservation line," dividing Dixon Entrance in half, as the boundary between American and Canadian waters. In fact, the official American charts for the water of Dixon Entrance do not even show the A-B line; they show the fisheries conservation or midway line. Canadians are skeptical about American intentions; several years ago, the Americans offered a number of oil leases in the waters of Dixon Entrance below the A-B line. Fishermen of both nations in recent years have found themselves caught in a tangled skein of boundary enforcement.

"Oh, the Canadian side is rather gentle out there," said Paddy Green. "They'll grab someone and bring them in. But when a Canadian boat is seized in a disputed area, the American authorities more or less blackmail them. They send armed men aboard the boat, handcuff the Canadians, strip them, put them in orange coveralls and haul them away to Ketchikan. They say, 'If you plead guilty, we'll give you your boat back and fine you X amount. If you plead not guilty, your boat will be charged in Juneau, you'll be charged here, you won't see daylight for six months and you'll never get your boat back.' *That's* been the climate around here," he said with the wave of a hand, and the other fishermen nodded silently.

I spoke on the telephone to Bruce Wallace and Mike Jewitt, two Alaskan fishermen working out of Ketchikan.

"Nobody," said Bruce Wallace, "likes to see a big steel vessel, one hundred feet in length, rising up and dropping down twenty feet off your stern, in a four- or five-foot surge. Those Canadian enforcement vessels get right up and push our trawlers. Physically putting you back up over the A-B line, or attempting to board you. They would crush the stern of a trawl vessel if they made a mistake, and that's what has been going on out there. Gunboat diplomacy, we call it."

Mike Jewitt "trawls Muzon more than most people." He starts the season longlining for black cod and then halibut. Then he goes trawling, and in the fall fishes prawns with pots.

"About six years ago, some overzealous American Coast Guard skipper on a cutter boarded a Canadian longliner for fishing what he assumed to be too close. I don't think the Canadian was too close; he was in this disputed area where the Canadians and Americans have fished side by side for a while.

"Shortly thereafter, when we were trawling down there, we had a Canadian gunboat harassing us and telling us to get inside the A-B line. See, actually, we can't hardly go outside Cape Muzon before we are over the A-B line and in what the Canadians consider to be Canadian waters. We also had our American Coast Guard on the scene, flying around in a helicopter dropping little sandbags with messages in them telling us to get back inside the cape."

Both countries agreed to a policy of "flag state enforcement," whereby American patrol boats deal with American fishermen, Canadian with Canadian fishermen. But the Canadian position is that this protocol agreement *only* applies to "traditional" fisheries. And the Canadians and Americans do not agree on what constitutes "traditional" fisheries; to the Canadians, only ground fisheries are traditional in Dixon Entrance, and therefore they claim the right to apprehend Alaskan salmon trawlers working south of the A-B line.

"The Canadians are fishing more gear than we are," said Mike Jewitt. "They're keeping smaller fish, and we're fishing on the same stocks. I wouldn't be a bit surprised if a lot of the fish they catch originate in Alaska. It's the inequality of it all that grates the American fishermen. When we travel down from Alaska in Canadian waters, we have to have our gear off the boat, and here are these Canadian trawlers that can fish right on our beach; they can go in the harbour at night with their leads and gear all hooked up. The Canadian laws prevent us from doing that.

"Our American Coast Guard have been telling us to take a line of passive resistance, and telling us, write your congressman. I told our Coast Guard, hey, it's not feasible to write your congressman in the middle of your season when it only lasts a few months.

"It's getting to the point where we are down to being like kids. But that Canadian gunboat is not going to board me."

The quarrel over the boundaries of the fishing grounds is compounded by the issue of fish quotas according to spawning grounds. Again the Canadian fishermen are militant; they point to the Panhandle as an irritant because of the rivers that rise in British Columbia and flow out to sea through the Panhandle, like the Stikine, one of the largest spawning grounds in the province, they say. Fisheries officials talk about schemes for identifying fish by the waters they spawn in. I imagine salmon racing up streams with Canadian and American flags in their gills, or a breeding and colouration process that imprints the appropriate logo on their bellies.

So far, Canada has shown no inclination to even talk about the A-B line.

"No Canadian government would *dare* give up Canadian territory," said Paddy Green, in the very soft voice of a very big man.

* * *

Taking the ferry to the Queen Charlotte Islands, across Hecate Strait from Prince Rupert, is an all-day journey. At first, the rail line forms the shore; through the mist, I see bald eagles and a black mountain of coal, the bright green struts of the container port and the ship *Korean Morning* from Panama. Beyond a scattering of low islands, the open sea stretches into a distant horizon. Then there is only the ferry and flat, blue-black waters around the ribbon of foam; no land is visible.

But the archipelago known as the Queen Charlottes is a magnetic force beyond the horizon. It was the first land along the Pacific coast of North America to be sighted and recorded by Europeans, the Spaniards, in 1774, who named the islands Sierra de San Christoval. In August 1787, the islands were named again by Captain George Dixon, after his ship, the *Queen Charlotte.* In 1789, American Captain Robert Gray named the group Washington's Island, thinking the islands were one land mass.

> One of the old tricks of the colonizers is to change the name of the land; Haidaguay is the name of these islands.

The border, the arbitrary limits of the A-B line staked out across Dixon Entrance, cuts against the grain of a civilization that long preceded European intrusion. Defenders of the Canadian position on the A-B line suggest that one of Canada's strongest arguments is the notion of historical waters. The Haida disagree. The Haida have never agreed to become part of Canada or the United States; they describe a conspiracy of legislation over the period of European occupation to strip them of their traditions and distinct identity and to divide their ancestral lands and waters.

The tables in the ferry bar are covered with Haida images; Shark, Raven, Woman Who Was Taken Away by a Whale. The Haida of Masset and Skidegate take the ferry to Prince Rupert to go to the dentist, to buy food and oolichan oil. I was travelling with Michael Nicoll of the Council of the Haida Nation. He offered me dried seaweed and oolichan oil, a bargain in Prince Rupert at twenty-five dollars for a half-gallon yellow bucket. The black, crunchy, salty snack dipped in fish grease is the Haida equivalent of tacos or pappadums or potato chips. Like many Haida, Michael Nicoll travels easily between his aboriginal and white cultures. He is a stocky, fair young man in a suit, sandals and Haidaguay red sweatshirt.

"The Haida presence in the area has been constant here for at least three hundred years," said Michael Nicoll, "preceding the appearance of Spanish, Russian, American and British adventurers. There are stories about the Great Flood and the survival of our people, so perhaps we have been here for thousands of years."

The territory of the Haida Nation extends southwesterly from the 56th parallel, including all of Dixon Entrance and half of Hecate Strait. The boundary lines have been agreed to by the Haida and the Heiltsuk or Bella Bella, the Tsimshian and the Nootka peoples.

"Our boundaries are not used as weapons" said Michael, staring out to sea. "We have no grief or grievance with the other aboriginal people of this area. We refer to this boundary as an interlocking boundary, not overlapping; Canada says we have an overlapping boundary and calls that a problem, but it's the federal government of Canada's problem, not ours.

"In 1979 a couple of lads travelled from Masset to Hydaburg on Prince of Wales Island to deliver an invitation to a feast. They travelled directly, about seven and a half hours, without seeking permission from either Canadian or American authorities. Because it was clear in their minds that this was very much Haida territory and to seek permission would have been inappropriate."

I listened to the soft, flat voices of Haida women, talking about their families. Violet, forty-seven, in pin curls, is thin and hardened; she was born in the forties, when there were only about four hundred Haida. Now there are about twelve hundred, but "the kids today don't even know how to gut a fish," she lamented. Talk of wicked stepmothers and lost children and the price of food; I dozed in the cold, pearly light, until the archipelago rose from the foam to embrace the ship.

Skidegate and Queen Charlotte City on Graham Island are on the strait facing Morseby Island. Small islands sit in mirror-clear water, little more than groves of trees on rocky platforms, their shoulders exposed at low tide. Settlements are perched on the thin shoreline strip between the black water and the primeval forest. They are facing a series of open graveyards of clearcut logging on Moresby, where discarded trees like white bones litter hillside after hillside, and the scraped land looks pink and angry, like a freshly picked scab. Ravens and eagles flock in high trees and on the piers and rocks at the water's edge, where they vastly outnumber the seagulls; Raven and Eagle are also the two matriarchal lineages of the Haida Nation.

Conventions don't apply here; even gas stations don't look ordinary, and all the places seem to be called Gracie's or Marg's or Lucy's, just that and no more. White settlement, in Queen Charlotte City and up at Masset, on the north end of the island, is a clutter of machinery, eccentric houses and tough, plain-speaking people, one of those places that is a series of crude but not unpleasant shocks to the system. In no way can it be said that the Queen Charlottes pander to mainland, urban sensibilities. Breakfast at Marg's is served on oilcloth-covered tables; there are church basement chairs, a can of Carnation milk with a punctured hole on the table and the largest pancakes imaginable. At Gracie's Place, where I stayed, the porch is overflowing with plants and toys and cats and gadgets, and there is a microwave sitting beside the wood stove.

The housing ranges from ornate, cathedral-style structures with gables and slatted cedar balconies to low bungalows constructed from slabs of siding with plastic-covered windows. A caravan has come to rest beside the road, with a cedar-shake wing attached to it. A lean-to made of stumps and boards is slung around behind.

The brief tenure of white settlement is recorded in roadside debris: A Gremlin, a Grainger, a Galaxie 500. A Cougar, completely bashed in, as if it just fell off the road and died there. A very old fishing boat, with a long, narrow hull, lying on its side, beside the road; a rusted-out red Ford Fairlane convertible; a truck overgrown with bush. (When I say rusted out, I mean sitting on blocks or simply wheel-less, the doors and hood ripped off, engine bits removed, the roof hammered in.)

In a parody of Haida culture, there are chain-saw totem poles in empty pastures, roughly hewn, painted brown—a bear, a fish, a man with a chain saw over his shoulder.

Beyond Queen Charlotte City, there is a small graveyard beside the water. The concrete gravestones are flat, slightly convex, with a pebbled facing, from 1910. Wooden crosses that have broken off the stones lie on the ground in beds of cow parsley. A stillborn child's grave is marked with a piece of varnished cedar.

Michael took me to see Guujaaw, whose potlatch name means "drum." Guujaaw is a musician, a member of the council, a carver. Guujaaw is both deeply serious and mischievous. He is very handsome, with black eyes, a fine braid, a hard, lean body. He has renounced his Canadian citizenship and carries a Haidaguay passport. We go to the council house at Skidegate Mission, and then to a workshop to look at Guujaaw's latest work—a small totem pole.

Skidegate Mission, around the eastern curve of the harbour, is a Haida village. There is a neat gravel beach, facing a large island, then a rash of bungalows on stilts, painted dull green and rust, or white with light green roofs. All the small creeks have names. The power poles at Skidegate line up around the bay the way the totem poles used to. When the surveyor George M. Dawson came to Skidegate in 1878, he photographed the shoreline, where more than three dozen memorial poles, mortuary poles and house frontal poles stood shoulder to shoulder. The images in these photographs are so powerful that they become superimposed on the present; in some way they still exist.

We went to the beach at Balanced Rock, climbing down a wooded cliff to the water's edge. The tide was out, and the smell of the sea sharp and stinging. Smoke from village fires hung close to the water like mosquito netting. The sky was streaked with pink filaments of cloud and held a moon as fragile as a nail clipping. Guujaaw and Michael leapt like boys across the slate platters strewn on the beach. They gave me wild asparagus and soft green spruce tips to eat. They came upon a hollowed-out log, grey, weathered, tossed up on the beach, and grabbing sticks, they beat a pulse on the log that was now a drum, and Guujaaw began to sing, kneeling beside the log. They hid the log; that was why we had come there, they said.

We went back to Guujaaw's house, where he cooked rice and gow, herring roe scraped from a bed of spruce boughs, served with dried seaweed and grease—oolichan oil. The herring roe was salted, white, with a texture of crunchy bubbles. We talked about the Queen Charlotte Islands, Canada and the Haida people.

"How should you be regarded?" I asked.

"We are under colonial domination," said Guujaaw, simply. "A priority should be given to the original people. In 1983, we formally filed a dispute with the United Nations, when Canada became signatory to the international law of the sea.

"Canada has no grounds to claim this land or these waters; in fact, there is no reason why we shouldn't make a treaty with the Americans."

I drove north to Masset, where I stayed with David Phillips, a great cook, an imaginative hustler with a social conscience. He is a loose-framed man with a pleasant light baritone voice, whose passions are gardening, antiques and New Wave music. And the Queen Charlottes. Through the big branches of a magnificent copper beech tree, I could see the lights from the small fishing boats, a hundred years away from Vancouver.

David Phillips said with some emphasis, "The A-B line is not a fisheries issue; it a military issue. If all the smoke is cleared away and the mirrors put to rest, that's what this is really all about."

Rumours filter through the Queen Charlottes about a Trident submarine base in the waters of Alaska and the American government's desire for free and silent passage of nuclear ships and submarines through the waters of Hecate Strait. But apart from such matters, David Phillips takes an open-minded approach to the subject of the boundary.

"Fifty years ago," he said, "people could just whip up there to Alaska, go back and forth really easily. Now there is a barrier; you have to go through so much process just to get there. The Charlottes could be the breadbasket for this whole region; we could have a dairy, a fruit industry, if we could have a little transportation network so that we could share goods and services. Those people up there are prisoners to a system they have no control over. That's the future—bioregional control.

"Let's be creative about our border; let's not be so hard-edged and nineteenth century about it. We need each other."

At the band office in Skidegate, I talked to Miles Richardson, president of the Council of the Haida Nation.

"In the discussion on the A-B line," he said, "they are excluding our interests as the aboriginal sovereign authority. We know that's wrong. In our view of the world, these are still the territories of the Haida Nation, in that we have never ceded or given up these territories to any other nation on earth. In protecting our interests, we look at the fishing resources, the subsea resources like the oil, and the coastal-zone fish and bird habitats. Our interests in the absence of a treaty are focussed on protecting what is crucial to our nation.

"Our relationship to the land and sea has kept us in touch with our past and our vision of the future. Everyone gathers food, gets out on the land, and consequently, through severe challenges, we survive today. The basis of our existence and our relationship to Canada or the United States is how we formalize our relationship with our lands and seas, because that's what gives us our identity, not political relationships. Although history has shown that those political relationships are necessary if we are going to coexist peacefully."

Miles Richardson is also a big man with a very soft voice. "And that's what we desire."

I sat on the bank of the Yakoun River, which tugs at the heart of Graham Island, Haidaguay. The water is the colour of light amber, so still the deadheads are reflected, so clear they throw a shadow. The forest is thickly padded with its own decay, trunks lying like totems where they have fallen, light filtered and deflected into single rays. There is a burden of bird song. The slightest change in light or air dramatically alters the scene, so delicate is the balance of elements. A passing cloud cools like a sigh. When the sun comes out, the landscape is lit from above and below, the water glows, clouds confront their mirrored images, and light catches the moss-hung, shaggy trees.

The Haida are the guardians of their land, these islands. The notion of guardianship is an element sorely missing in our border negotiations, disputes and treaties. We have concerned ourselves with defining the limits of separate jurisdiction, but not the realm of shared responsibility, except for what passes over the line in either direction. The landscape itself has become merely the convenient surface upon which to draw the lines, its inherent integrity obscured under a latticework of mathematically determined reference points, the fine point work of legal argument and a web of political imperatives.

Here, and on the Panhandle, and along the 141st meridian between the Yukon and Alaska, the international boundary is for the most part a silent abstraction, the pride of surveyors and geologists and cartographers.

# 6

## "REGRET MY WORK COMPLETED":
## THE 141ST MERIDIAN

Late August, driving from Whitehorse to Dawson City through tapestries of muted colour. The sun turns the road into a hard bright sheen, but everyone drives at least seventy-five miles per hour. The road is the only manmade object on the landscape, except for scattered gas stations and cafés. It seems that everyone stops at every stop, just to break the monotony of driving. By the time I get to Dawson City, I feel a kinship with the handful of other travellers—the man in an old Chevrolet with no back window, the white-haired Alaskan couple in a sleek, burgundy-coloured jeep—we have been overtaking each other all the way up. I have picked up a couple of German students, and in the next few days I will run into them constantly. The possibilities for independent, unobserved activities are few once you head up this highway; there are only so many hotels and campgrounds, so many activities, so many crossroads, so few people. There is so little traffic that gluttonous magpies and ravens can scarcely be bothered to move away from their highway dinners; they hop a few steps towards the ditch when a car approaches. The long black and white tail feathers of the magpies drag disdainfully along the gravel shoulders. I swerved to avoid hitting a bloated raven staggering away from the half-devoured guts of a smaller bird in the middle of the road.

You can go all the way to Inuvik, in the Northwest Territories, on this road, and it seems like a fine idea on a bright late-summer afternoon; I feel as if I am driving across the top curve of the globe towards the North Pole. The air is translucent, and you can see into the depths of cloud formations hundreds of miles away, clouds massed like big

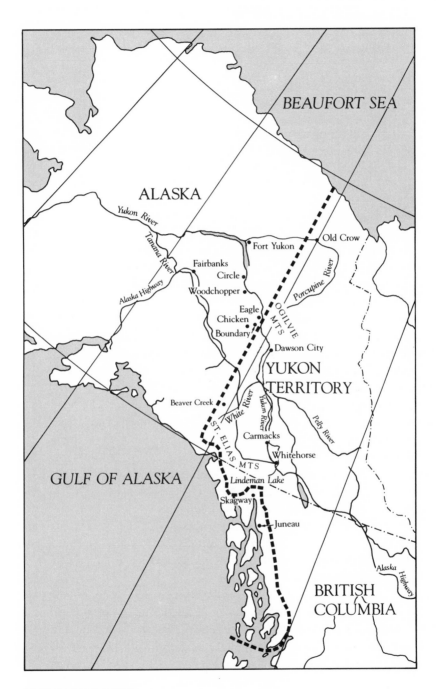

**YUKON/ALASKA**

clumps of white flowers, suspended in thin air. Fringing the hilltops are black spruce, stunted, dwindling to points—not a forest at all, but a stubble of matchsticks. Quivering aspens catch the light, throwing back flashes of light green and yellow; on some hillsides, it is already fall. On hills of gravel and sand, there are blond sedge grasses rippled with light and wind.

In late afternoon, on this road, the journey to Dawson is effortless, requiring only a driver's concentration for five or six hours. An image breaks through from my memory; it is a photograph, in black and white, a long, crooked black line of men crawling like ants up a snowdrifted mountain pass, grotesque under the weight of their idiosyncratic possessions, slouching towards Dawson City. I am travelling parallel to the Yukon River, which sometimes is visible and sometimes not; I cross the river at Carmacks and imagine below me a fleet of crudely built rafts, bearing camp stoves and tools and sacks of waterlogged flour and rice, also in black and white.

The Klondike gold rush is the mental framework for this journey around the northernmost portion of the international boundary. Here history is not obscured by settlement. There is nothing on the road to distract my mind from the image of my destination: Dawson City. Dawson City is and always has been a mirage, on a river bend under the dark, cold shoulder of a hill called the Dome. For two years, 1897–98, the mirage became a delirious dream for people whose real lives were bleak and shrunken by a depression. The gold rushes drifted into the collective imagination like the wanton succubi of Mephistopheles and pulled thousands of people out of cities and villages from all over the world. They were drawn, as if hypnotized, through Seattle ("more wicked than Sodom") and Skagway ("the most outrageously lawless quarter I ever struck") to Hell, the journey to the Klondike.

Equal parts greed, curiosity, determination and hysteria drove men and women up the glaciated mountain passes, through mosquito-thickened swamps, across frozen, unyielding valleys of mud, down cold, wind-swept lakes and unforgiving rivers to Dawson. They carried loads of up to eight hundred pounds on their backs and visions of solid gold boulders in their heads. Acts of heroism, courage and kindness during this mass odyssey are fleeting gleams in the chronicle of folly, brutality and obsession. Two images from Pierre Berton's *Klondike* are irrepressible: a dead man with a hole in his back just sitting beside the trail; the head and tail of a horse thrown to either side of the path, its body, still warm, beaten into the ground by men on foot. In the annals of humanity's capacity for overextension in adversity, the Klondike gold rush seems to have been the inverse of war, drawing out common frailties and conspiracies of selfishness instead of valour and compassion. Contemporary accounts are more daunting than medieval moralities.

It could take more than ninety days for a prospector to haul his equipment over White Pass, travelling back and forth a thousand miles to cover forty-five miles. Berton states that horses rarely survived the trip:

> A quarter of a mile from the Canadian border, each owner performed a grisly rite. He carefully unloaded his pack animal and then smoothed a blanket over its back to conceal the running sores that most horses suffered at the hands of amateurs. The Mounted Police would shoot a sore or injured horse on sight if he was brought into Canada.

For the prospectors, the Customs outpost was a significant obstacle. The Mounted Police perched themselves in tiny makeshift huts under Union Jacks at the tops of both White and Chilkoot passes. They were armed with machine guns. They demanded cash and proof that the prospectors were bringing with them a year's supply of food, three pounds for each day.

The journey down the Yukon was unpredictable and dangerous; one party imagined it would take four hours to cross Bennett Lake; it took four days. The Chilkoot Pass is only thirty-two miles long, from Skagway to Lake Bennett, British Columbia, which is where most of the prospectors built their boats or assembled collapsible canoes for the journey downstream to Dawson. The route over the pass has become a national park, and it follows the prospectors' trail, still littered with torn boots, rusted tools and the skeletons of boats lying broken-backed on the loose rock.

Tourism was an instant secondary industry. Flotillas of curious journalists, retired geologists and hardy, genteel women swept through Alaska and the Yukon. Their legacy, now mouldering in public libraries, is a collection of stunning photographs, hand-drawn maps and ornate prose, weaving an elaborate skein of equally unbelievable facts and fictions in fat, gilded guidebooks. The Yukon and Alaska were to the early twentieth-century imagination what the Alps were to the eighteenth century, an awesome repository of all that was savage and glorious in Nature. The gold rush was only one element; others were the itinerant and mysterious native population (all "witchcraft and barbarism"), the legacy of the fur trade, bones of ancient mammoths, remnants of Russian habitation, and the glaciers. Travel writers found transcendence in icebergs, which, wrote Charles Hallock in *Our New Alaska*, were "sentient and expressive, with that sort of poetical light termed '*spirituelle.*'" They described phantom cities (one that was identical to Bristol, England,) caught in the sheer blue depths of glaciers, cities of twenty thousand inhabitants, with "beautifully formed spires, apparently three or four hundred feet high." They responded emotionally, unreservedly, to the Yukon River as the bloodstream of the North.

The early guidebooks convey a curious blend of national pride and bewilderment about the separate identities of Alaska and the Yukon. Charlotte Cameron, 1920s English author of *Cheechako in Alaska and the Yukon,* deliberately included the Yukon in her itinerary as an act of patriotism. Mary Lee Davis, in *Uncle Sam's Attic,* worried at great length about why it is necessary to enter Alaska through Canadian territory. *Our Northern Domain* (American titles consistently celebrated possession), published in 1910 by Dana Estes of Boston, lamented the "foolish and unfortunate business of marking an imaginary boundary between Alaska and the Dominion."

Between 1867 and the end of the century, both the American and the Canadian governments made sporadic attempts to locate the boundaries on the ground and at the same time to explore and map their northern territories. In 1869, the Americans travelled up the Yukon River from Norton Sound, formally established the approximate location of the 141st meridian and requested the removal of the Hudson's Bay Fort Yukon (at the junction of the Porcupine and Yukon rivers) from American territory. In 1883, Lieutenant Frederick Schwatka of the U.S. Navy rafted thirteen hundred miles down the Yukon River from Lindeman Lake to the mouth of the Tanana River, where he transferred to a schooner for the remaining seven hundred miles to the coast. Canadian surveyors George M. Dawson, William Ogilvie and R. G. McConnell completed the Yukon Expedition in 1887–88, a surveying and mapping exercise and geological study extending from the Stikine River to the mouth of the Mackenzie River.

Schwatka's journey was that of a maverick, daring and almost clandestine, only partly official. He christened things as he went along, oblivious to the names they already had. His 1885 account, *Along Alaska's Great River*, reveals a man in a hurry, reluctant to waste even half a day on astronomical surveying, rapidly propelling his raft towards the sea.

> That day's drift gave us forty-seven and a half miles, and all our scores were good while passing the ramparts, the delays from sand, mud and gravel bars being very small.
>
> Believing that I was now in close proximity to the British boundary, as shown by our dead reckoning . . . I reluctantly determined on giving a day to astronomical observations—reluctantly because every day was of vital importance in reaching St. Michael's, near the mouth of the river, in time to reach any outgoing vessels for the United States; for if too late to catch them, we should have to spend a dismal and profitless year at that place. That day, however, proved so tempestuous, and the prospect so uninviting, that after getting a couple of poor "sights" for longitude, I ordered camp broken, and we got away shortly after eleven o'clock.

Dawson and Ogilvie, in contrast, were models of caution and exactitude. Ogilvie's journals describe geological features, encounters with Indians and his work determining the boundary in the winter of 1896 in the style of an anatomy textbook:

> I have produced the boundary line about five miles north of where it crosses the Yukon River, which is as far as I thought needful at present. I have also produced it about seven miles south, and about the end of February will resume work, and run it as far as Sixty Mile Creek. In connection with this I have occupied six photograph stations and developed all the plates exposed, which have turned out satisfactorily. . . . Up to date, our lowest temperature has been 63 degrees below zero. . . . No mail from outside since September.

Location of the boundary became a more urgent matter during the Klondike gold rush, not only because of the location of the claims themselves, but also because of the inordinate movement of people and goods across an uncontrolled landscape, a situation begging for law, order and taxation. The temperamental differences between two cultures were best illustrated by the respective characters of Skagway and Dawson City. Skagway was infamously riotous and lawless, run by the notorious Soapy Smith, who was eventually killed in a barroom brawl. Dawson City was decorous by comparison, strictly controlled by a full detachment of the North-West Mounted Police and stamped from the beginning with regulation, officialdom, bureaucracy.

The formal delineation of the Canada/U.S. boundary in the North did not take place until the Alaska Boundary Tribunal was created in 1903. Between 1904 and 1920, American and Canadian surveyors marked the line of compromise on the ground. It is the most intractable section of the Canada/U.S. border. On the Panhandle, a third of the boundary lies forever beneath ice and snow, stretched across peaks of fifteen thousand feet. The surveyors approached the mountains from the coast, up wild rivers, through cottonwood forests, across glacier and quagmire. There were no power boats or helicopters, only canoes. There were floods, mudslides, avalanches, deaths. And on the 141st meridian, muskeg and tundra, moss in thick veils over deep chasms, swamps under a fog of mosquitoes.

Cultural differences between the two places persist. Although the majority of people moving through Alaska and the Yukon are that most benign and respectable breed, the retired tourist, and although both Alaska and the Yukon have imposed their particular forms of order on society and the economy, there remains, around the fringes of Alaskan settlement, an edge, a more finely honed misanthropy than is likely to be found in the Yukon Territory. For Canadians, the Yukon is part of our collective self-image as Northerners; there is a simple logic in our fantasies, extending from the 49th parallel in the south right through to the Arctic. It is similar to the nineteenth-century American dream of Manifest Destiny, except that it does not for the most part express itself in settlement, or even in exploration. It derives from our first exposure as schoolchildren to big red maps of the Dominion of Canada, which indelibly printed in our minds a sense of nationhood extending unimpeded to the North Pole. There are no barriers between the rest of Canada and our northern territories.

In contrast, Alaskans have a sharp sense of themselves as being apart from the rest of their country, which they call the Lower Forty-Eight. There are regular calls for independence, a loathing for the federal bureaucracy and a beleaguered sense of being a misunderstood, different society (not so much a society as a far-flung penal colony of irascible in-dividuals). Alaska is an island for intolerant Americans, especially in those communites remote from urban centres or close to the Canadian border.

But the character of Alaska is also coloured by its original role in the completion of the American nation; it was a purchase, an investment, and its history has always been linked to its productivity and the ex-ploitation of its resources. Thus, in 1910, the unnamed author of *Our Northern Domain* wrote:

> It is certainly a romance of history, that this once despised land . . . should, within less than twenty years, have added to the resources of the world in gold, one hundred and forty-two millions, and nearly forty mil-lions in seal skins; while the grand total from furs, fisheries, and minerals, from 1868 to 1908, amounted to three hundred and twenty-seven mil-lion, five hundred and fifty-three thousand, six hundred and thirty-seven dollars. . . ."

The romance of productivity. Alaska became a state in 1958 and was at that time given twenty-five years in which to set aside 103 million acres for settlement. But in 1971, the discovery of a new resource, oil, and the subsequent desire for a pipeline changed the rules. The sudden economic challenge roused both the environmentalists and the residents of Alaska; 44 million acres were given to the natives in the Alaska Na-tive Claims Settlement, and 80 million acres were designated for federal wildlife and recreational reserves. The Alaskan homesteader, with only 250 million acres left in which to roam, felt trapped. Miners, suddenly subjected to arbitrary and changing systems of permits, regulations and controls, both environmental and bureaucratic, felt wronged.

\* \* \*

Not until you are just outside Dawson do you see much rock; here there are dramatic changes in the landscape, both natural and manmade. Just south of Dawson, the road follows the clear waters of the Klondike be-fore they rush into the Yukon and are folded into the flowing mocha-coloured silt. Quite suddenly, there is the turmoil of detritus from placer mining, piled hills of loose rock, the landscape literally overturned in the search for gold. Mostly you can't see the river for the debris from dredging done in the midsixties; rock and gravel have been pushed into long ridges along the road, piled higher than the car, so it seems that I am driving through a roofless tunnel, or into a sandbox belonging to a giant child. The scale of the recent search for gold was much grander than it was in the late 1800s; the tools became bigger over time.

After five and a half hours of painted landscape, there is a sense of anticipation as you get close to Dawson. The few strung-out houses, even a field with hay stacked into blocks, seem dynamic. The airport runway is a cleared grassy strip. Beneath a broad rounded bluff, the Yukon and Klondike rivers collide and join for the long race north and west to the Bering Strait. Then Dawson City, the phantom city on the river bank.

It began as a collection of canvas and tin shacks, floated on a swamp. Now the town is buttressed from the river by a high gravel walkway, which is in fact a dike constructed after a flood in 1979. It's again like something in a sandbox; a smoothed-down version of the ribbed rubble to the south. The town is a surreal pastiche of restoration and disintegration. For exactly one year—1898—it was truly a city. Even by 1909 the glory of Dawson City was a blurred memory, something for an old-timer to insist upon: "She was a hummer, I tell you. This burg was the speediest town on earth."

Dawson City is a town inhabited by ghosts. In *Klondike*, Pierre Berton estimates that 100,000 people set out for the Klondike; 30,000 or 40,000 of them made it; half of those looked for gold, and only 4000 found any. I try to imagine Dawson City crowded with people, be it 30,000, or 40,000, here where 1200 people now live year round; I look at the river and imagine boats jostling each other to land, the big river stern-wheelers, ten of them lined up together, and the makeshift wooden low-lying variations on a raft that men constructed to come down the Yukon. Now there is one stern-wheeler, the *Keno*, permanently high and dry, for tourists to look at. There is a miniature paddlesteamer for miniature trips on the Yukon. And there are a few outboard motorboats tied up to a modest dock.

Dawson City is officially a national park, but it is also a working mining town; hence its schizophrenic nature. Parks Canada is trying to re-create historically accurate buildings, right down to the insulation, from what look like stage sets abandoned in dirt, tussock and rubble. The streets are wide and muddy; boardwalks break off in the middle of nowhere. The names of former theatres and music halls on Front Street ring out like bells—there were the Orpheum, the Monte Carlo, the Arctic, the Aurora—but they are long gone; on Front Street now there are pastel imitation Victoriana stores with fake pane lines sketched out on their bow windows, selling pastel designer leisure wear emblazoned with "The Land of the Midnight Sun."

On Second Avenue, a storefront window is a museum case on the street; on display, empty gloves and top hats, limp leather pokes for carrying gold and the hollow bodices of dresses. Through the glass I try to invoke the presence of full-bosomed, flirtatious entrepreneurial women and lean, leathery men bristling with wealth and whiskers. Their names are passwords into the mythology of Dawson City: Big Alex McDonald (the King of the Klondike), Charley Anderson (Lucky Swede), Swiftwater Bill Gates, Klondike Kate and Belinda Mulroney, Skookum Jim and Tagish Charley, One-Eyed Riley and Nigger Jim. Pseudonyms and nicknames; even in the brief flare of reality, make-believe prevailed.

Inside a large wooden corner building that was once a bank, there are enormous photographs, black and white, blown up to life-size, a time caught in mercury but not mercurial. Is there a button to push to make them come to life? There are the interiors of the saloons, chandeliers and champagne and velvet draperies and glowing polished bars. Out on the street, the Red Feather Saloon still stands, barely; it is a naked, low and sunken shell, buckling at the knees, held up by a strut and a promise; "future project of Parks Canada."

"Nothing rowdy or exuberant survives," wrote T. A. Rickard wistfully in 1909; "a stroll through Dawson gives an impression of respectability compelled by impoverishment, of the temperance that succeeds dissipation, of the bust after the boom. . . . Dawson looks like a stout man who has grown very thin and yet wears the cloths made for him in his adipose days."

On Fourth Street, in the middle of town in a clump of trees, stands a very old log cabin with a corrugated tin roof, a miniature rusted-out backhoe curled up beside it.

Here there is a sense of children's theatre, of boys playing in sandboxes and girls dressed up in ball gowns on a movie set; people in costume day and night, trying to fit themselves into the pictures of the past, forcing an illusion to come to life for the busloads of passive tourists, who get their assignments from the Tourist Information Centre and set off down the carefully marked, well-worn historical path.

But beneath the play lie a bedrock entrepreneurial shrewdness and a thin vein of desperation. There are the official tourist attractions, the Palace Theatre and Diamond Tooth Gerties' saloon and the Eldorado Hotel, but there is also a clumsily labelled "beer parlour" where the cheap and serious drinking goes on, as well as ugly prefabs set higgledy-piggledy on the cross streets, a bakery and video arcade united, strip housing built to resemble recreational vehicles, and thin black dogs and aimless teenagers wandering on the streets. Mary's Rooms offers accommodation for thirty-nine dollars a night in a flat, one-storey building that looks like a corridor between rows of single rooms. Dawson is reminiscent of hundreds of marginal mining towns right across the continent. Except here nothing can be knocked down. Rickard observed in 1909 that "a Carnegie library, enclosed in tin-plate, simulating stone, serves as an ugly monument to a great rebater desirous of notoriety." The library still stands.

Still, the mining goes on up the Bonanza Creek road; the shapeless, muddy creek twists between huge piles of rubble, under gouged-out hillsides. Underbrush grows on the debris; it will become bush in time. It's all secondary growth; the hills were all ripped bare in the first gold rush and after that, three or four times. A clutter of old machinery, rusted buckets, a dismembered plough make mute testimony. Beside one claim currently being reworked, the old backhoe buckets have been filled with white and purple petunias. Here, the rocks that were spit out by the sluicing machines are as big as your head, there, no bigger than the end of your thumb. I drove up the gravel road, stopping at KMA, the Kiss My Ass claim now being mined by Gene and Kathy Fowler, retired Alaskans with EASY on their licence plates and a back-pocket mining operation run out of the expanded recreational vehicle they live in beside the road.

I climbed up the mud slope to watch two bulldozers waddling down into a deep, rounded hollow, scooping up muck and bringing it up the hillside; then the muck is picked up by a shovel, thrown into a sluicing machine and hosed down by an operator. The claim is like an open bowl, under a hillside fringed with aspen, and in the bowl the cats push around gobs of wet sludge. Gene Fowler joined me and shouted out over the sound of the bulldozers.

"This was solid cliff, once, and the old river came right through here, where the hole is now. We have come down one hundred and fifty feet into where the old-timers worked, right into their timbers and shafts. They went four feet into bedrock; we get down to eight feet. And you turn up all sorts of things—a frozen dog, a St. Christopher medal on a chain, boots and of course all the old timber from the stopes. We've got two runs coming off the sluicing machine down the hill to the jig. We're actually working nine claims."

Gene Fowler is a short, tough-looking man; he was a contractor in Anchorage who retired and came here looking for gold in 1980. His wife, Kathy, does afternoon shift on the sluicing machine. We had coffee at a long table inside the grounded RV; it has a big wooden porch, and showers and toilets built off the back for the several labourers who work for the Fowlers.

They refine the gold to dust, or granular form, and then pour the bars. Kathy put a spice jar on the table; it was filled with cinnamon-coloured crumbs and was very heavy. "This is how we take it out of the box, just like this. When we want to pour bars, we borrow a little furnace, about the size of a kid's wagon, and pour it right here beside the porch." Gene brought out a bar, pale, glowing gold, the size of a large bar of Ivory soap. Silky to the touch. "How much is this worth?"

"This grade is seventy-eight per cent pure; it takes one hundred and two ounces of fine grade to make a bar this size. It's worth, oh, about thirty-six thousand dollars U.S."

"Why did you come to the Klondike?"

Gene laughed. "Oh, we met a man, came over to visit and then we came back. Lots have the gold fever and come over here and end up staying too long."

"Are you making money?"

"Hell, no; we've spent six hundred thousand taking out four hundred thousand. But one day last year, we took out three hundred and twelve ounces—that's one hundred thousand dollars U.S.—in twenty-two hours. My health is bad; if they buy me out, I'll leave next year. It's a fun game, but it's always a dream."

> You come to get rich (damned good reason);
> You feel like an exile at first;
> You hate it like hell for a season,
> And then you are worse than the worst.

> It grips you like some kinds of sinning;
> It twists you from foe to a friend;
> It seems it's been since the beginning;
> It seems it will be to the end.

Eighth Street leans right up against the hill in Dawson City; here is the cabin of poet Robert Service, enclosed with a sapling fence. The cabin consists of two small rooms under five beams, on a sloping grassy section surrounded by willow, alder and birch. It has been a tourist attraction since the 1920s and looks exactly as it did in contemporary photographs. Here Service, a Scottish bank clerk, tapped out the primary rhythms and barroom tales that have come to stand for the mythology of the Yukon, a mythology so simple it is still relevant in its original setting.

There is even a Robert Service. A handful of tourists gather on a dew-drenched bench in midmorning, still cold under the shadow of the hill rising directly behind the cabin. Robert Service, in an impeccable waistcoat and brown velvet jacket, brings a rocking chair out onto the grass and tells his story; he is and is not the character in this biographical sketch enlivened by readings from the poetry. His triumphs are the images in the poetry, better spoken than read; they hang like smoke in the clear air:

> There's gold, and it's haunting and haunting;
> It's luring me on as of old;
> Yet it isn't the gold that I'm wantin'
> So much as just finding the gold.
> It's the great, big, broad land 'way up yonder,
> It's the forests where silence has lease;
> It's the beauty that fills me with wonder,
> It's the silence that fills me with peace.

We are a funny group, retired Americans under blankets snapping photographs, young, earnest students from Germany, a few wholesome families at the end of a long camping holiday who will soon turn south for September and reality.

At one end of Eighth Street, a rusting archway frames the Yukon Order of Pioneers cemetery. Iron railings mark plots, like bedsteads, and the bush is barely restrained by white pickets. The grave markers are colourless wooden slabs leaning on grey stone or lying on the hillside in patches of wild strawberries and mushrooms:

IN LOVING MEMORY OF LILLIE
WIFE OF CHARLES DRUGAN
DIED JULY 12, 1919

HARRY SPENCER, DIED 1898 AT 36

And on the same road, the unmarked graves of discarded houses. Shards of tarpaper hang on the faded frameworks, and in the roofless living rooms lie shreds of canvas, charred wood and the springs of an old sofa; burlap-backed oilpaper in an art-deco pattern clings to the outside wall.

At night, the sun is still up at 10:30. The game and the make-believe can go on, and we don't have to go to bed. The obliteration of night is a licence for cautious revelry and self-conscious gambling. There is a nightly performance at the Palace Theatre; from there, the tourists go directly to Diamond Tooth Gertie's, to date the only licensed gambling operation in Canada. This is government-regulated gambling, where straight-backed young women in starched shirts neatly scrape the felt, stack the chips, spin the wheel, collect the money; they could be on the assembly line of a tomato-canning plant in southwestern Ontario. You can buy fruit juice and muffins in the saloon. Dawson from its brief year of glory has always had the reputation for virtue. The North-West Mounted Police under Sam Steele were strict in how they ran the town; there was gambling, prostitution and bootlegging, but "no cheating is allowed and none is tried."

Diamond Tooth Gertie's is a large, noisy room with a stage, reminiscent of a high-school auditorium. Toothy, full-faced young women pump and bellow their way through songs like "Frankie and Johnnie"; their cancans are no better and no worse than you would see at any hotel from Whitehorse to New Orleans. People drink beer and stroll from game to game or else hunker down at one table all night long, oblivious to the carnival around them. All the tables are full, local regulars rooted in among the retired tourists. I saw Gene Fowler, playing Texas five-card in a darkened corner. I watched one elderly native woman; she sat motionless through half an hour of roulette, then finally threw out a tightly wadded ten-dollar bill from her hand and bought into the game.

In the slow fade to twilight, I walked down to the river front. The lilac-coloured river was sliding past blue fringed hills, under long horizontal clouds, banked grey on the apricot scrim. In the clear, cool air the sounds mingled: out-of-tune pianos and applause from the music hall; raw and raucous singing from the casino, untrained voices wavering, the flutter of the wheel, like a distorted heartbeat, and chips clicking on the smooth, green felt beds. Below me, the ferry made its brief crossing, but there is nowhere to go but the campsite until morning when the border reopens.

In winter, Dawson the dream/memory shuts down; the top-of-the-world highway closes; the sound is switched off, and the river is frozen in its tracks. Some people hibernate, but others get out and go where it is warm, for at least part of the time.

From somewhere up near Eighth Street, the long, luxurious howl of a dog or a wolf is loosed on the pale evening sky, the echo clinging to the last shreds of light.

* * *

In the morning, I was the first car across the top-of-the-world highway to the border, breaking ground. To the north, the even ripple of the Ogilvie Mountains; to the southwest, the sensuous folds of purple hills, peeling away from the hard sand road. A long line of mist was rising from the Yukon River, like an outpouring of breath. The river has enormous potency, rolling like a live creature through the centre of this country for two thousand miles. High above, on the highway, it does feel like the top of the world, as close as you can get to flying. But, again, the trees, with all the light in the world, are scrubby, stunted willows and dwarf black spruce, underbrush that has never matured into a forest. The gift of light in summer in the North is some terrible compromise between two warring gods, the price being its brevity, a gleam caught in the parentheses of darkness pressing in on either side of summer.

The names up here are like bits of brown paper stuck onto exotic and original landforms: Dawson, Ogilvie, Fortymile, Sixtymile; Eagle and

Chicken and Circle. No poetic outreachings; men named places after the first thing that came into their heads, which might be the man they were travelling with. Dawson is George M. Dawson, the geologist and surveyor, whose name turns up in the prairie boundary survey, on the Queen Charlottes, where he wrote detailed accounts of the Haida, and here in the Yukon, where in 1887–88 he and William Ogilvie travelled and mapped the complete landscape. Ogilvie located the 141st meridian on the Yukon River and was resident surveyor in Dawson during the gold rush, scrupulously and dispassionately identifying claims as if they were simple plots of land, unmoved by greed for what lay below his instruments.

A red-bellied crossbill flip-flopped across the road, a small sign of life. Here on the last frontier, where the land is wide open, you can only cross the border between 9:00 A.M. and 9:00 P.M. There is scarcely a building between Dawson and the border sixty-five miles away, except for an occasional log cabin, abandoned, with a grassy roof. There are rare outbursts of rock heaved up through the loose shale and gravel soil. The rock is barely covered and glows red from the close-knit cranberry scrub. Horsetail grasses have a purplish lustre, as if stained by fireweed and cranberry. Fragments of snow fence with double rows of pickets rise unexpectedly on some exposed hillsides, arresting the eye like modernist works of art.

Vehicles waver like mirages on the curves ahead, then disappear for so long that you are startled to suddenly see them again. This is not a sociable setting; people don't wave when you meet them on the road, and the pale, lumpy side roads must lead somewhere, but they don't have signposts, are only for local, knowing use. A billboard announces the caribou hunting season dates, from 1 August to 30 September; limit— one bull caribou only.

Close to the border there are no trees, only a flat red leaf like a rash on the shale, and bare-naked hills, where bits of fireweed catch a grip in the gravel and faint tracks roll off across the hills at right angles to the roads. Both customs houses have addresses; the Canadian house is apparently on Little Gold Creek, the American log cabin on Poker Creek, both high above even a trickle of water. Between them, a cut line, neatly defined by small white cones, barely visible at the tops of the grey quartzite ridges undulating north and south.

POKER CREEK, ALASKA, MOST NORTHERLY

LAND BORDER PORT IN THE U.S.A.

ELEVATION 4127 FT,

POP. 4.

The American border officials put a barrier across the road at nine o'clock in the evening. Then they send five-thousand-dollar fines to the people who go through illegally. "We see them come through; we don't have a lot to do around here at night, so we do a lot of staying up late. The word is out in the area local now, so they've stopped doing it."

They patrol "just what we can see from here; we have control, but not many people are immigrating from Canada up here. Sure, it's possible to walk, and they've had walk-arounds down at Alcan. But people get lost and driven insane by the mosquitoes. It gets real cold at night; the ground is rocky with moss on top of it, so it's like walking on pillows. If you go down out there, no one will ever find you."

The American officials were happy to talk; the Canadian offical was officious and coy, not about to be trapped into an interview, and self-important about his main job, assessing the duty on mining machinery. At the height of summer, about 120 vehicles move through here in either direction. It has now dwindled to half that.

I cross into Alaska, again into open, uninhabited terrain, the silence of landscape. I am forty-three miles from Chicken and seventy-nine miles from Eagle, the only communities even close to the border. Along the 141st meridian, what passes for civilization is dispersed into far-flung pockets of settlement. Yet there is a sense of community; it just takes in an unbelievable amount of territory.

At Boundary Lodge (tour buses welcome), an enormous American flag slaps the empty air, over a scattering of old machinery, dewheeled motor homes, rusted-out buses and the rear ends of trailers. A row of painted white one-room shacks with corrugated iron roofs and a restaurant in a log cabin constitute the lodge. Action Jackson's Bar is a landmark; the man himself is now dead, but his imprint is vivid and lingering. The outside of the bar is decorated with racks of horns and a sign: NO GUNS OR SHEATH KNIVES ALLOWED IN BAR. There are outhouses for pointers and setters; I figure out which I am and wash my hands in a white enamel bowl of water. While waiting for someone or something, or to give myself some meagre validity, I eat caribou sausage in the restaurant. In the bar, I can't bring myself to order a beer at nine in the morning, so I have a Coke. The bar is low and dark with old paint, yellowed varnish and smoke-blackened wood. Crude little cartoons and postcards ("We flashed the customs man!") are stuck to the walls. Behind the bar, a sign:

ACTION JACKSON'S

MATCHED SET 44 VIRGINIAN DRAGOON

MAGNUM

RAFFEL

$10 PER CHANCE

The man on the stool beside me wears a thick knitted cap and heavy overalls and is reputed to have been a crack pilot; I heard in Dawson that he once almost died of cold and since then has never been able to get warm. He is drinking bourbon. Three or four old young men, wrinkled early, features obscured by hats and beards and hair, slow to speak, miners and would-be miners and has-been miners, wander in and out of the bar, skirting around the first drink of the day. Outside, beside a pickup truck with a cracked windshield and a rifle in the back window, a man with shoulder-length hair, a felt peaked hat and knee-high boots plays with a shotgun. His face is white with a hangover.

The men decided I should go and see Danny Draper to talk about the mining. You'll have to drive through the river, they said. I took one of the unmarked sandy roads, straight down to the bottom of a valley, where a river about six feet wide was flowing across the road; no way of telling how deep. Just downstream I saw a man—large, bearded, in khaki—kneeling to wash his clothes in the water. I called to him for advice; he said I would have no problem driving through the river, so I did. I felt the water slop over the wheelbase of my rented car, the tires seeking traction in the mud, slowing and swerving, but I knew I would be chicken not to try.

I drove up over another ridge and down again on a hairpin dirt road, dodging potholes and boulders. Then a smattering of temporary buildings and trailers, and mining equipment at rest in midclimb, it seemed. It was a Saturday morning, and the mining camp spread over a hillside was deserted, except for Danny Draper. He came down from his trailer, a can of beer in his hand. He is grizzly, I guess in his late sixties, his body sinewy, eyes bright, speech precise through a big grin and a haphazard arrangement of teeth. He wore a T-shirt and a Yukon Order of Pioneers peaked cap. He took me into the cook shed, made of plywood with no floor, where his certificate of membership in the Yukon Order of Pioneers is the only decoration. "Do unto others as you would be done by" is inscribed on the rainbow that joins the prospector on one side with the pile of gold on the other; "Daniel D. Draper, arrived on the waters of the Yukon, 1960."

I saw a hodge-podge of machinery, shacks, trailers, cats abandoned halfway up a hill, pieces of dredges, engines I couldn't identify. We began to walk briskly around the camp.

"There are restrictions on buildings; you cannot put permanent buildings on mining claims. See, here, all my hand tools, compressors, vices. I have to keep everything exposed." He showed me a shed full of tools and equipment. "This set of sockets is my pride and joy; look at this five-gallon bucket, full of them, one-inch drive, heavy duty for the big cats, just one costs two hundred and thirty-eight dollars. A torque wrench costs three thousand dollars. But in winter I leave it all here; it's a big area, but we know who strangers are. The local people on this side of the highway are honest with each other; honesty is the one thing we demand." We walked down a small wooded slope.

"Refrigerator, generator, and here's the Turk Creek laundromat." (An old wringer washing machine and a couple of tubs.) Danny pulled on a line of rope. "A bear chasing a crippled moose through here pulled this clothesline right down in the spring." Another small shack: "There's the heat barrel, and the shower; I fixed it up with a mirror, raised and carpeted the floor, and see, it's even got mixing valves. My men deserve it."

There is an outhouse made of poplar poles, built to the specifications of a woman who comes in to cook. An ice house, also built out of poles, insulated inside and out, containing three bins, eight by four by two, lined with heavy black plastic. "In the fall, I pump water up from the creek, open the door and leave, and when I come back in the spring I've got three big chunks of ice, enough to last us all season."

The season is one hundred days. Six days a week, ten hours a day for Danny and his crew, although he does not work the dirt anymore himself.

"If they can't make their yearly wage in one hundred days, then I'm working poor ground. My men do not turn worthless dirt. I have a gift for locating the veins, the pockets, the alluvial fans, and I have my instruments and I have my laboratory for checking the dirt.

"You see, there is a key to this if you follow it."

He knelt on the hard bank of the stream, a stick in hand to illustrate his point. The silica sand dries like concrete, so his sketch was faint.

"I realized this many years ago when I was studying geology and mineralogy, and I didn't go to college to do it. I'm a self-taught man." His voice dropped, and I had to lean in to hear him.

"The sun rises in the east; it sets in the west, and the equator is the centre of gravity. Right here we are thirty-two-degree magnetic north deviations. Now, everywhere I have found my gold in this whole complete country—I've done Mount Jordeen, I've done the Tyonek, I've done the Sixtymile, over in the Klondike—every time you will find these veins running a true thirty-two degrees, northeast/southwest. And every time you find a vein you will find water, moving underground into one of these pockets and coming up against the high wall."

He pointed to the ridge on the other side of the stream. I saw only a modest hillside, covered with bush and the gutted tracks of bulldozers. Danny Draper saw a cross-section, a three-dimensional geological map stripped of foliage. I saw a flat landscape painting; he saw a dynamic process, the movement of rock bearing gold over seasons and centuries.

"This whole valley is alive; these mountains, they cry and they cry." He laughed. "When they stop crying, I'm going to start crying!" He pointed with his beer can. "You see that cut up there on the hill, by that green row of brush? Now that whole thing is a producer, and down below there is a little pocket. So what I am going to do is go up there with my little cat, knock off the vegetation so the sun can hit the dirt and thaw the permafrost. Then I'm going to lay down a whole row of logs, here at the bottom—that's what they call a ground sluice. And when the dirt erodes, that gold put there by Mother Nature will follow the water and lodge in the logs. Then once a year, I'll go clean up the logs." His pleasure was as warming as sunshine.

The rock forming the hills consists of granite, quartzite, barite and sandstone. Like all the old-timers, Danny Draper can identify the creek from which a handful of gold dust has come by its colour. Sandstone means copper, which has a green colour. The gold from a sandstone creek has a green tint to it when you first get it out.

"Now, over there on Cherry Creek is granite, with a heavy iron content, and the gold there has a red tinge to it. Poker Creek is loaded with iron ore, and over there the gold turns out almost black. So you got to be able to recognize all these different things."

Danny pushed aside some brush and showed me the old sluice box, a coffin-sized rectangle of thick boards, grey, but still usable. "This got me started; it still looks pretty good! I was working alone, and if I got eight yards a day I was doing real good.

"I love this valley; it's been my pride and joy for many years. I've just started this particular stream with the big equipment, but that was where I started many years ago with my little sluice box. Some places you have to mine with dredges, trammels, sluice boxes, hydraulics—got to know all different methods to handle your property properly. The good Lord was good enough to give it to us, and you must respect it for that reason. The placer miners, now, they're just dirt movers. They're not miners."

"Do you feel like one of the original gold rush miners?" I asked. I had to run a little to keep up to him.

"Well, they sure set a pattern," Danny said. "And they knew something, and I had to find out what it was. So I had an old prospector, by the name of Ramblin' Sam Gamblin', a good friend, and I used to go out prospecting with him every year. He tipped me off to a lot of things, and that's what allowed me to be the way I am today."

We walked on down the path, towards the flat of the valley.

"This here is Cherry Creek; this is going to have to be a dragline show because there is so much water."

He stopped suddenly and crouched, pointing to a faint imprint on the ground. "Now right here, see this track; see that one hoof how it's crook like that? That's the moose with the crooked toe that tore down the clothesline; I've seen her twice this year. Usually the bears get her calf. Here's our garden here." He pointed to a row of small, pale lettuces.

Beside Cherry Creek, we paused. He brought a harmonica out of his pocket and played a chorus of "When Irish Eyes Are Smiling." His laughing eyes held mine as he played. The faltering notes shivered in the breeze, against a background of water bubbling over gravel. Then we walked back up the hill, through the camp and down to a stream bed on the other side.

"Now, this here is a precision ten-inch dredge, powered with a Volkswagen engine. The stream doesn't look like much, but then you put the dam in to control the water table. You see the water coming in over there?" There was a slow, dark trickle of water seeping from the bush. "*This* is what I mean by the mountains crying. So I built a dam across here, make a water pocket in here, put the dredge in, and I can keep two men busy all day every day, just sucking out this little bitty pocket. Three veins converge here, and every year we get our spring runoff that brings the gold down from up above. This machine has been in this hole for three years."

The water is thick, creamy with mud. Every day, Danny is required by a recent law to do turbidity tests on the site.

"The only time we have to take the turbidity tests are when we are in actual production. We have a big vial, shaped like a cone. You go out to the tail end of your holding ponds once a day, fill that vial and let it settle for exactly one hour. We are allowed exactly two milligrams of sedimentary deposits, and if we go over that, we have to change our recoveries, maybe add more dams; there are places here where I have as many as nine dams to hold everything. I recycle all of my waters."

All of these waters flow finally into the Yukon, which for the fifteen hundred miles of its length below the White River is laden with moving silt. I remembered the journal of Frederick Schwatka, who recorded the force with which the waters of the White River at its mouth shot right across the clear blue Yukon and mingled with them instantly; from then on, "all fishing with hook and line ceases."

"This is what bothers me," said Danny, with only mild irritation, "they will never clean up the Yukon. But there was an article in the Fairbanks *Daily News Miner* that said that the Fairbanks drinking water did not match the turbidity tests that the miners are required to meet out here. Now all of the clear waters, like Fortymile, and South Fork, they've made wild and scenic, and that's good. But the environmentalists are eating up the smalltime miners around here, and unless you get big, you won't survive."

Danny Draper's operation is comparatively big, but its impact is limited by what a handful of men can do in a hundred-day season with a couple of bulldozers and dredges. The scars made here are shallow, and they will heal. The deep structures of the land are unaffected. There is superficially, at least, a balance between the extent of Danny Draper's operation and its yield. He has worked the same small, hidden valley, nestled up against the boundary, for almost a quarter of a century.

"The people who are doing all the complaining could never even survive up here. It takes a breed of men, and women, to survive up here. A certain kind of people cannot tolerate the cities and the society and responsibilities, and that's why they come up here."

Danny Draper is scrupulous in his attention to regulation and correct process. His connection with his claim is intimate, immediate, like that of a farmer or a gardener. If this country were to be mined by large international corporations, instead of people like Danny Draper, the effect on the environment would be massive, uncontrollable and probably disastrous. Danny Draper measures his own impact on the environment in simple tangibles.

"When I first came here, I would pick fish up out of my sluice box, and they wouldn't be much over five or six inches long and not much bigger round than my thumb. And since we have been muddying the waters, where it used to be you would have one fish in each hole all the way along this stream here, now you get five or six fish out of each hole, twelve or fourteen inches long and as much as two pound. We are disturbing food for them.

"As far as vegetation is concerned, you see all this scrub brush, the size of these trees?" He made a gesture of contempt with his beer can. They're just nubbles, hardly anything to them. Trash trees. But as we go along, and up here by my camp—you see the trees with the beautiful green foliage, growing like the dickens? So consequently, I believe that by disturbing the land as we are, we're improving the environment, and the ecology, and the economy of the whole nine yards."

We sat on a worn leather bus seat in front of the cookhouse. Danny sucked on his beer.

"The Canadians have one of the finest mining laws I have ever seen," he said, "but the Americans change theirs from one day to the next. The Canadians have a set pattern, tell you how to do it, and they will protect you, because they are trying to uphold the mining industry. The Americans are trying to destroy the mining industry. Consequently, I would much rather be working on the Canadian side."

We sat for several minutes, in silence. When I first arrived at the camp, it looked like a dump. Just a carved-out heap of vehicles and trailers scattered around, makeshift huts with plastic over top and nothing on the ground and rivers spilling their guts out over the land. When Danny Draper first talked about being backed up against the wall, I wondered what in the hell he was talking about. Then he took me into the stream bed and described how the gold runs, how he sees the mountains crying. Now I too can see the wall, and the camp has become a place of order, history and beauty.

By noon, at Action Jackson's, the serious drinking has begun.

In the early afternoon, I drove up the Taylor Highway to Eagle, on the Yukon River. It's tough driving, sliding around a narrow, lumpy, dusty, gutted, potted road, littered with loose rock. I can only travel thirty miles an hour through here. A seven-mile descent took me to Fortymile River at the bottom of a valley; it's a clear, dark amber colour, a glittering braided stream, with white rocks rounding up above the water. When I climb again, the terrain seems to be getting sharper. The road is thrown like long loose lassos around the hills, not tightly wound like the roads are in Europe. All the bridges are one lane, and they are all under construction.

It is difficult to harness this spare, aloof landscape to the historic battles for territory that have been fought in Alaska in the past quarter of a century. The territorial imperative up here is exercised almost entirely theoretically by the bureaucracy, not on the ground. There is nothing, nothing, nothing for thousands of square miles. Historically, nobody has pushed anyone out of the way. Direct confrontations between natives and whites were never fought up here. Even now the claims being made on the land are often abstract, governments carving up maps in the time-honoured way. There are paper skirmishes between smalltime homesteaders and the Alaskan government. Settlement of native land claims is in the lily-white hands of lawyers, not warriors.

Apart from the regular clusters of construction vehicles and huts, the land is quiet and empty. The fireweed is getting ready to fly, loading up with white seedlings, ready to propagate like crazy. Close to Eagle, the vegetation thickens into dense bush, with stands of birch and poplar. A bright pink exposed mountain comes into view, a sheer, crumbling cliff face. On top, an American flag. Signs of self-conscious civilization, different from the defiantly haphazard style that is normal in Alaska; here there is a speed zone, and several solitary joggers along the roadside.

EAGLE POPULATION 120+
INCORPORATED FEB 9, 1901.
WELCOME

For about twenty-five years, Eagle was an important transportation and communications centre. A single wire telegraph system was built from Valdez, in southwestern Alaska, to Eagle, with log cabin maintenance stations every twenty miles. The army became resident in the rough form of Fort Egbert. In 1905, the Norwegian explorer Roald Amundsen walked into Eagle, more than four hundred miles from his icebound ship, to dispatch his telegram announcing the discovery of the Northwest Passage.

Eagle reeks of suburban prosperity, with sturdy log cabins on neatly squared streets and avenues. Lawns and sedate gardens brim with nasturtiums, and parsley grows in log window boxes. There are tiny domestic tractors and artfully shaped woodpiles. It is a conservative activist community, where the struggles between homesteaders and government, between environmentalists and miners, were bitterly fought in the 1970s. The heat seems to have gone out of the community now, leaving a legacy of outraged signs in black paint on boarded-up barns:

NATIONAL PARK SERVICE EMPLOYEES
AND ANYONE ELSE ADVOCATING A DICTATORSHIP,
INCLUDING THOSE WHO LOCALLY SUPPORT NATIONAL PARK
SERVICE ACTIVITIES UNDER THE ANTIQUITIES ACT
ARE NOT WELCOME HERE.

There is a fire-hall, with a bell on top, and an old courthouse, white frame, with green trim and upper and lower balconies. A library, a tiny customs house and a large, gleaming globe and elaborate copper-etched monument to Amundsen: "When his life's work was accomplished, he returned to the Arctic and found an unknown grave under the clean sky of the ice world. . . ."

On the bank of the Yukon River, a red-cheeked, wholesome young man was building a handsome structure, a huge house, restaurant and motel in highly varnished wood. Land in the village costs five thousand dollars for a fifty-foot-by-one-hundred-foot lot, so many people are buying acreage on adjacent native lands, from people on the reserve

about three miles upstream. The natives are being taken advantage of
hand over fist, the man said, mostly by lawyers.

More stern, cranky graffiti in confused, oratorical syntax:

> THEY HUMBLE THEIR MINDS, ADMIT ERROR,
>
> BECOME LOYAL,
>
> FOUND MERCY

Eagle is virtuous, complacent and dry. American writer John McPhee
came here off and on for several years in the midseventies while writing
his book *Coming Into the Country*. He found "a community deeply com-
pressed in its own isolation, where a cup of sugar can go off like a
grenade." Just beneath the surface serenity, McPhee unpicked a society
deeply etched with the "countless crosshatching of cabin-fever feuds."

The town sits on an open curve on the Yukon, one hundred miles
downstream from Dawson. The river slides lazily by, at about six or eight
miles an hour. There is a flat island in front of the town. The raw pink
hill, called Eagle Bluff, makes a jagged descent to the river and is perhaps the bluff where the caribou killed themselves. Above the island,
the cut line through the trees marking the boundary is barely visible.

The 141st meridian boundary is 647 miles long, from Mount St. Elias
in the south, at the top of the Panhandle, to Demarcation Point on the
Beaufort Sea in the north. The marking of this boundary took seven seasons, between 1906 and 1913. There are only two access points between
here and the sea—the Yukon River and, farther north, the Porcupine
River. South of the Yukon River, for 225 miles, all the supplies were
carried on the backs of horses. There were no roads, just knee-deep
mud, tundra and swamp, for a travelling speed of 2 miles an hour. In the
season of 1908, the surveying parties located the main points on the
boundary over 85 miles and cut 40 miles of vista. In the 1909 season,
the American party walked 300 miles before they started work. In 1911,
the surveying party identified and controlled a smallpox epidemic
among the Indians of the Porcupine, in the course of carrying out their
surveying tasks.

The tasks seem elaborate, tedious and almost impossible to complete
successfully on this varied and unyielding terrain. The boundary line
cuts directly across the grain of the land. Around the narrow, unswerv-
ing line of the boundary itself, the surveyors laid an intricate imaginary

triangulation net, a series of points from which they could make confirming and interacting calculations. Some of the stations they built in order to make their calculation were as far as thirty miles from the boundary line. As elsewhere, they methodically cleared the vista, leaving a shaven track across the tundra.

The surveying teams sometimes travelled with as many as 166 pack horses. They set 190 thirty-inch intervisible monuments and 11 tall bronze obelisks between the Arctic coast and the St. Elias Mountains at the top of the Panhandle. Each obelisk required eighteen hundred pounds of materials, including tools, and three hundred pounds of water. The American chief of party, Thomas Riggs, Jr., recalled in a 1909 *National Geographic* article:

> In the interior, the difficulties of work are changed. Long wooded stretches, interrupted by barren ridges, take the place of glaciers and craggy mountains. In place of snow fields there are heartbreaking "nigger-head" swamps to be crossed. . . . Supplies have to be ferried across the rivers on log rafts while the horses swim. Clouds of poisonous mosquitoes and gnats arise from every pool and clump of moss, driving horses and men to distraction.

During the 1913 boundary survey, another gold rush brought prospectors and surveyors into contact. From Dawson City, there was a stampede south and west to the Chisana gold strike; part of the route followed the boundary line. The map handed out in Dawson City seriously underestimated the distance, and consequently, as Riggs recorded in his Season's Report,

> the stampeders who had outfitted for a five days trip were considerably damaged by the time they struck our camp. Every stampeder seemed to think that a government outfit was being run for their especial benefit, and hardly a day passed without our having from one to twenty men in camp demanding all manner of assistance. We would try to conceal the camp by getting well off into the woods, but to no avail. As soon as the cook tent was pitched, we would be besieged by a bunch of hungry miners. As soon as the fry pan was on the stove, we would not have been surprised to see stampeders coming down a tree, where they had been laying in wait.

. . .There were men without enough clothing to cover them decently, without shoes or bedding, but all were hurrying to the new Eldorado, anxious to be among the first to stake.

. . . There are many who started from Dawson who will never be heard of again.

Surveyors are a phlegmatic breed, not given to introspection, with little sense that their work is in any way imbued with the heroic. Thomas Riggs, who led the American surveyors for eight years, kept a journal himself, but noted of his coworkers, ". . . if you were to ask Raeburn, Gilmore, Ryus, Guerin, or Baldwin to relate some adventure they would not be able to recall one little one, for like Percy, the Machination Man of the Sunday supplements, 'Of imagination they have nix.'. . . It is simply their life."

In *The Boundary Hunters,* Canadian writer Lewis Green, himself a surveyor and geologist, plots the entire survey of the Alaska/Yukon border. Beneath a grid of complex technical terms and procedures, Green evokes the stoical, antiheroic character of the surveyors and the utterly focussed determination with which they completed their assignments. Comparisons with Klondike gold seekers are inevitable; the surveyors emerge as both compassionate and punctilious, driven by a formidable sense of duty. From the 1910 Season Report of Riggs:

> The trip out was a nightmare. The horses were failing fast as the sustenance had departed from the frozen grass. Hardly a day passed that some horse did not play out and have to be shot. . . . A third of the horses were in the "hospital train", the men were all carrying packs, every extra ounce had been abandoned and, had it not been for the oat caches along the way, not a horse would have survived. As it was Raeburn and I would bring up the rear and shoot the horses as they fell out of the train. The tenderfeet were disheartened and afraid. Four days out of the Yukon I was forced to send in for assistance.

Of men, a sparse record of madness and early death: "a cry and a dark shape hurtling through a thousand feet to a glacier below. . . . Two are in pauper asylums for the insane."

In July 1912, American boundary surveyor Thomas Riggs and Canadian J. D. Craig reached the Arctic coast:

"Seeing" conditions at the coast were bad, and delayed projection and triangulation greatly. The air seemed to be in a state of continual disturbance. . . . Haze was very persistent, and mirages were frequent, beautiful and at times awe-inspiring. On one occasion, when moving camp along the coast, one of the pack-trains made a detour of several miles to avoid an imaginary lake. . . . The sun at midnight . . . assumed most fantastic shapes, but its rays, even at noon-day, seemed to be powerless to counteract the piercing effects of the prevailing and northeast winds.

They set Monument 1 in the tundra, two hundred feet from the Arctic shore, and went for a brief swim in the sea. There is a photograph of the two men beneath their flags, to which are appended the pennants of Princeton and Queens universities. Their final reports record their experience and the feelings, seldom expressed, of those who work on the line:

July 18, 1912. The Arctic Coast. It was with a rather lost feeling that we arrived at the shore of the Arctic Ocean and saw the practical completion of the work on which we had been engaged for so many years.

. . . the years spent in the survey of the 141st Meridian, even with all their hardships and almost unsurmountable difficulties, have resulted in being the happiest years of my life.

On 31 August 1913, when Riggs reached the tiny village of McCarthy, Alaska, after his final inspection of the line, he sent the following telegram:

REGRET MY WORK COMPLETED.

The line he left behind, the longest surveyed straight line in the world, is a barely visible series of small white cones perched in the hollowed peaks.

The line of monuments placed between 1906 and 1913 is scrupulously maintained by the International Boundary Commission. It has claimed the passion of surveyors like Carl Gustafson, who seems to know the boundary inch by inch, monument by monument, and who, like his predecessors, knows the epiphany of survival:

"I guess one of the closest calls I might have had was in the Grizzly

Range, up on the 141st meridian, up near the Beaufort Sea. The two young men with me were in extremely good condition, and they were giving me a tough run for my money. The helicopter had dropped us off well below the summit because of the poor weather, and we were making our way up in somewhat of a competitive fashion. The other two had gotten a little bit ahead of me when I saw a good way of getting around them.

"But at a certain point I was confronted with a break in the ledge of the ridge I was following, and I had to step across a span of about six feet to get to a continuation of the ledge on the other side. The ridge itself was what we call a narrow razorback, almost vertical on the two sides, and it was the steepest side that I was following. It just seemed to go almost vertically downwards for several thousand feet.

"In trying to get from one side of this ledge to the other, I found a lump on the wall of rock there about the size and shape of a goose egg, and I reached out with my right foot for this to negotiate the break between the ledges. But when I dropped most of my weight onto this little projection of rock, I found it wasn't large enough to sustain my weight, and I didn't have any kind of grip with my hands on the sides. So while I tried to get a better grip on the rock with my foot, I found that instead of improving it, my foot was slipping away beneath me, at such a rate that I only had seconds to act, or I'd be on my way down.

"In the most peculiar way, it felt then that instead of your wishing to save yourself, it was just natural to have an end, and you were quite relaxed about it coming. It just felt as though I was about to float off in a nice, warm, furry ether, and that was the most easy and natural thing at the moment. But my mind told me I would really rather not do that.

"So without really thinking, I instinctively made a move, and it was in the right direction. My left foot behind me was quite a bit higher, but I found I was able to get my weight back on the ledge I was leaving and I regained my footing.

"Somewhat shaken, I should say.

"So I always remember the Grizzly Range, on the 141st meridian, with that little goose-egg projection of rock, and just nothing below it."

\* \* \*

The 141st Meridian is crossed by the highway at only two points, at Boundary and farther south near Beaver Creek. It is a kind of homing line for prospectors and miners like Danny Draper, and its defining destination remains Dawson City. Beyond Dawson to the north, the road stops at Eagle; beyond, there are small outposts like Woodchopper, Alaska, on the Yukon River, and Old Crow, on the Yukon side of the line on the Porcupine River, reached by river or by air. The vista is the domain of caribou, grizzlies, eagles, mosquitoes.

There is a russet hue on the hillsides now, and gold, dark green and mauve. In the foreground, yellow and dusty shrubbery, a few hapless black spruce staggering across the reddish hills, more hills and a couple of peaks that look shaven on top. In the distance, ridges of mountains folding backwards towards the Arctic. The road is a sand colour here, sometimes white, then dark grey, clinging to the edges of cliffs that fall into rivers far below. There are lemon-coloured poppies waving on rocks you have to squeeze around. Where the contours are tight, you simply hope that the odds are against anyone's coming the other way.

On a branch of a black spruce curved over the road, a gyrfalcon watches me, unperturbed by my proximity. Its big white chest supports a small-looking head that seems to swivel around alert eyes. Its huge wings are at rest in a bed of speckled black and white body feathers.

I cross over O'Brien Creek and follow Fortymile, looking in the shadows of the buffy cliffs for bear or caribou. All the rivers and streams go through incredible contortions until they find the Yukon. I recall from John McPhee's splendid book an image of the forest of logs and uprooted trees that floats down the Yukon with the spring breakup, firewood for the coastal Inuit from forests that they may not even be able to imagine. The silent gift of the river; the river holds the country together, even now when it is no longer the lifeline. Despite the thin network of roads, the invisible Alaska pipeline, the meagre patches that pass for airfields, it is the Yukon River that has shaped history and commanded settlement, in the same way that the St. Lawrence and the Mississippi once did. But in the Yukon and Alaska, the subsequent episode in the movement towards a more complex (not necessarily more mature) social organization has not taken place. There is no perceptible move away from the river and its tributaries, no significant settlement elsewhere. The roads here have not replaced the river as the gathering points for people; the roads are simply shortcuts to the communities on the rivers.

There is a melancholy sharpness in the air. It is only the last week of August, but the smell of winter is in the air; mentally, the country is closing. In Eagle, they say that in winter the town is not snowed in, but outsiders are snowed out.

The drive down from Eagle to the junction with the Alaska Highway is like a descent through a suburb of Hell. The scenery becomes bleak and blank until it is no longer scenery. Mining is a mocking roadside attendant, a spirit both past and present. A chain of crude dams and pipes and settling ponds at Jack Wade is temporarily unused, awaiting reanimation. The enormous old dredge called Wade Number One looms up like a beached shipwreck. It supports a structure as big as a two-storey house, with a central tower that rivals the height of telephone poles, holding rusted, stretched-out wires. It has been shot full of holes, like all the road signs, and left to die, to bury itself in undergrowth on the river bed.

Lost Chicken Hill, and Lost Chicken Creek, and then Chicken. Population, 11, and on the map. A row of shacks, a country store, liquor store, saloon and café, each with a rack of antlers tacked up over the door. There are gas tanks and a gang of pickup trucks pulled into a circle like a wagon train. It's 10:15 at night, and all eleven residents seem to be in the bar belting back rounds of elaborate cocktails. It looks like a quarantine camp for frontier hippies with long hair and red eyes, one of whom affably detaches himself from a bar stool to sell the crazed female tourist ten dollars' worth of gas. Whereas Eagle has an elevated idea of itself, Chicken looks like a chicken coop. It has taken the barnyard chicken as its symbol, not the small, pretty ptarmigan after which it was named. On billboards, there are bright yellow cartoon chickens. I imagine chickens scratching around in the dirt, looking for kernels of gold. Eagle has its lofty bluff, green grass and park, and high-flying symbol. Chicken has a saloon and the ability to supply a three-piece band for a barbecue up at Action Jackson's the following day.

I drive on, both manic and depressed. I look off to the left and see the hills caught in a fire of light, catching the last angles of the sun, vividly outlined, then softening to a rich raspberry colour. The trees have become smaller and smaller on this drive south; the black spruce are no more than rigid black feathers poking out of thin soil.

On the car radio, a dissonant choir plaintively sings a long and tuneless song; the words, "Jesus, Jesus," come and go as waves of comprehensible sound in a bed of static and a chorus in the Inuit language. This is the only signal strong enough to find me on the Taylor Highway, at 11:00 on a Saturday night. The scale of isolation here is immeasurable.

About once every half hour, a vehicle appears from the other direction. No one is going my way.

Now I can see nothing; I am driving in a rough dirt tunnel. Big birds swoop across the road in front of the car. They are silent, colourless, ghosts that hover just above the beam of my headlights. Marsh hawks. They seem to rush at me like bats and then slide up skyward, and I duck involuntarily inside the car. The bare bones of a sunset linger in the black sky at 11:30 at night. The road skitters across the empty landscape, always on a slight incline or a steep decline. It, too, lacks substance or grip; the car seems to slip, as if on grease.

The mile signs become major landmarks. They are about six inches square.

# POSTSCRIPT

M y journal of exploration along the line ends here. It's a record of people and ghosts and stories and monuments. Stories that open like windows illuminating small differences between two cultures. Monuments recalling challenges to a thin line of distinction between two countries. Images of people whose daily lives are structured by proximity to the line but who are far removed from the game of borderline diplomacy that defines and regulates it. Images of the boundary vista, which must be tended like a garden or it will disappear.

At either end of the boundary, Machias Seal Island and the 54-40/ A-B line dangle like counterweights, the unresolved disputes. Preston Wilcox and Barna B. Norton have agreed to a schedule of alternating days during nesting season when each of them may land with a party of bird watchers on Machias Seal Island. The Canadian lightkeeper remains, and the Canadian wildlife officer returns every summer. Barna B. Norton's flag raising has become an annual event on the helicopter pad of Machias Seal Island, under the displeased gaze of Preston Wilcox.

In Dixon Entrance, the 54-40/A-B line is still the line around which flagship enforcement is maintained. Canadians take comfort from the official Canadian position that there is nothing open for negotiations. But if there were, Paddy Green insists, then the whole Panhandle issue would have to be re-examined, not just the validity of the A-B line.

Canada and the United States do not agree on how to extend the 141st meridian line out over the Beaufort Sea. The Canadians favour a straight extension; the Americans would bend the line in an obtuse angle to the east. There is also disagreement about the extent of Canada's sovereignty in the Arctic Islands, where it had not previously occurred to anyone that a border might one day be desirable. It seems there are no limits to territorial nationalism.

For two hundred years, the boundary line has been surveyed, patrolled, disputed, groomed and transgressed. What came into being as a series of arbitrary, poorly considered, unimaginative and bureaucratic solutions has acquired symbolic stature, as potent as a spell cast by a magician. It has become a permanent margin in the landscape, held open by the diligence of surveyors, held closed by a set of fragile conventions that travellers and residents heed without questioning and sometimes exploit or circumvent.

The border has become a part of travel as routine as packing a suitcase. Still, our hearts beat faster as we approach the Customs booth, fumbling in our wallets for some sure sign of identification, in our minds for some plausible excuse for crossing the line. From the corner of an eye we see guns and the border patrol cars. We tend not to see the video monitors and computer terminals, the technology that could in a trice replace the old-fashioned cut line by recording every single crossing, every licence plate and passport number.

The line that I followed is becoming increasingly irrelevant as a regulatory barrier. In a broad sense, the movement of ideas and commodities is becoming more abstract as electronic mail and bank transfers and simulcast events erase the boundaries of time and space, the conventions by which our cultures have grown. Traffic control is also more and more removed from the actual boundary, becoming instead the scrutiny and stamping of large numbers of people and their baggage at airports. There is a minor symbol of invasion in the fact that a traveller is processed through American Customs and Immigration at Canadian airports, before ever leaving Canadian soil. The subtle shift from one cultural climate to another, like moving from sunlight into shade, never happens. The childish thrill of stepping on foreign turf is withheld.

Again and again as I travelled along the border, I imagined its absence. Many Americans do not even imagine its presence. Far from bearing weight, as it does for Canadians, the boundary for most Americans is a line on the television weather maps, above which there is white space and white weather—the land of cold fronts. For Canadians it is a holding line, a sea wall, sandbags resisting America. The waters slapping against the sandbags are not threatening, but when we contemplate the potential force of the body behind them, in full flood, we take silent comfort in the sandbags.

I know Canadians who would happily fold up the boundary line and become part of the United States; I did not meet these people living close to the line.

When I asked people living along the border if they would like to see it removed—what if you woke up tomorrow, I asked, and the border had been erased, ripped out?—invariably, Canadians rejected that idea. The only people who would even spontaneously consider that possibility were Americans. We have different perceptions about what threatens our respective nations. The assumption around the border crossings is that there will be illegal passage of household goods into Canada and illegal passage of aliens and drugs into the United States. Americans, therefore, who talk about erasing the border really assume that the regulatory functions of the border will simply be removed elsewhere, that we will become one nation, a considerably larger United States of America. They do not feel threatened by Canada. Canadians, who invest relatively little in the physical defense of their border with the United States, do, however, feel threatened by the idea of losing that border. In some unarticulated and mostly polite way, Canadians feel more secure with a tidy line between them and the Americans.

We think we have claimed and tamed this continent. The border is a symbol of order and mutual regulation; we think of the strip along the border as thickly populated, organized, colonized, mechanized. But you don't have to go very far to get into the bush, descend into a swamp or end up in muskeg up to your ears. And in truth we are claiming the land not by populating it but by polluting it. Colonies of people can be erased by time and fresh growth—their bones become soil; their gravestones crumble into dust; their borders are erased. But acid rain in common airspace, clearcut logging by multinational companies, industrial waste poured directly into shared rivers—by these acts we are altering the chemical balance of the landscape. The border has failed to prevent infiltration of contraband more dangerous than handguns or aliens. Somehow this conspiracy of vandalism has to be dealt with on the border, with more tangible initiatives than peace gardens and peace parks and peace arches, and anachronistic rhetoric about being undefended and unfenced.

The border is a richly annotated margin in North American history, a fine line drawn through the collusion of surveyors with the sun and the stars, a procession of monuments springing from a single, precise point near the yellow birch tree hooped with iron.

# CHRONOLOGY

*1713: Treaty of Utrecht.* Following the War of the Spanish Succession, the Treaty of Utrecht was one of the first treaties to deal with allocation of land in North America and marked a clear shift in domination from France to Britain. The Hudson Bay drainage basin, Newfoundland and Acadia were restored to Britain from France; France retained territories around the Gulf of St. Lawrence.

*1763: Treaty of Paris, after the Seven Years' War.* By 1760, France was no longer a colonial power, losing to Britain in the series of battles culminating in the fall of Quebec in 1759 and the capitulation of Montreal in 1760. Britain acquired another large chunk of North America, including the Great Lakes drainage basin from France, and Florida from Spain.

*1775–83: War of Independence.* Between the signing of the Declaration of Independence, 4 July 1776, and the Treaty of Paris ending the American Revolution, the balance of power in North America was again radically altered. British territory became British North America; the Thirteen Colonies became the United States of America. During the war, the role of the British settlers north of the Thirteen Colonies was ambivalent; the Americans invaded Montreal and laid siege to Quebec in 1775 but eventually withdrew. Some forty thousand Americans came to British North America as Loyalist refugees.

*1783: Treaty of Paris, after the American War of Independence.* The territories of British North America and the American colonies were roughly defined between the Atlantic Ocean and Lake of the Woods and from that point "due west" to the imagined source of the Mississippi River.

*1794: Jay's Treaty.* The first international boundary commission was appointed to identify and locate the St. Croix River, named in the 1783 Treaty of Paris as the starting point for the Atlantic portion of the boundary. The British were given two years in which to evacuate frontier posts such as Detroit. The Mississippi River was declared open to both Britain and the United States.

*1812–14: War of 1812.* War was declared by the United States on Great Britain and carried out along the international border, mostly on the Great Lakes and on the Niagara Peninsula. There were also battles on the Mississippi and Columbia rivers; after the war had officially ended, the Battle of New Orleans was won by the Americans.

*1814: Treaty of Ghent.* At the end of the War of 1812, the *status quo ante bellum* was declared; all captured territory was given up. A joint commission was set up to survey those portions of the boundary defined in 1783. The survey was carried out between 1817 and 1827.

*1817: Rush-Bagot Agreement.* The treaty guaranteed the balance of naval power on the Great Lakes. However, both the United States and British North America continued to build and maintain fortifications on land.

*1818: London Convention.* After years of negotiations, it was agreed that the 49th parallel of latitude would form the international boundary from Lake of the Woods to the summit of the Stony (Rocky) Mountains, and that the land between the Rockies and the Pacific Ocean would be "free and open" to both powers for ten years.

*1825: British/Russian Alaska Treaty.* Following Czar Alexander's ukase of 1821 closing the North Pacific Ocean to all foreign ships, Britain and Russia agreed on the boundaries of Russian land in the Northwest, including the 141st meridian and summits along the Panhandle.

*1831: Boundary Arbitration.* The king of the Netherlands was asked to settle boundary disputes in Maine/New Brunswick and along the 45th parallel. Neither the United States nor Britain accepted his decision.

*1837–38: Formation of the Hunters' Lodges.* Following the Mackenzie Rebellion in Upper Canada, American sympathizers joined exiled rebels and formed the Hunters' Lodges in the border states; their intention was to liberate Canada from the tyranny of British rule. There were a number of small invasions before the American government intervened.

*1839: Aroostook War.* Ten years of hostilities between Maine and New Brunswick lumbering communities along the Saint John River culminated in preparations for a full-scale war. Sir John Harvey of New Brunswick and General Winfield Scott of the United States achieved an uneasy armistice before a shot was fired, but skirmishes continued until 1841.

*1842: Webster-Ashburton Treaty.* Daniel Webster of the United States and Lord Ashburton of Britain negotiated the Maine/New Brunswick boundary. With the help of secret agents and substantial cash settlements, they were able to placate local residents. The treaty also stipulated that all channels in the Great Lakes would be international waters and named the Pigeon River as the link between Lake Superior and Lake of the Woods.

*1846: Oregon Treaty.* In 1827, the ten-year provision of the 1818 London Convention was extended indefinitely, and serious negotiations began for possession of the Oregon Territory. Between 1818 and 1828, both Britain and the United States asserted claims through settlement and trading posts. American settlers requested annexation, and the Democratic presidential candidate, James Polk, won the 1844 campaign with the slogan "54-40 or Fight!" The treaty finally defined the 49th parallel as the boundary line, extending it to the Pacific coast from its previous terminus at the summits of the Rocky Mountains. Vancouver Island remained part of British North America. The 49th parallel was surveyed from the Rocky Mountains to the Pacific between 1856 and 1861.

*1861–65: American Civil War.* The conflict between the Confederate and Union states reverberated on the border. Fugitive black Americans fled in large numbers to Canadian border communities, where slavery had been illegal since 1790. But Britain and British North America were generally sympathetic to the Confederates; in 1864, there were raids on St. Albans, Vermont, by Confederates based in Montreal. After the war, lingering hostility along the border created a propitious climate for the Fenian raids, invasions by Irish-Americans sympathetic to Irish nationals seeking independence from English rule. The continuing threat of invasion from the United States made the idea of Confederation increasingly attractive to Canada East and West (modern Quebec and Ontario, respectively) and the Atlantic colonies.

*1867: British North America Act.* Through the confederation of Canada East, Canada West, Prince Edward Island, Nova Scotia and New Brunswick, the Dominion of Canada was created. (The BNA Act was renamed the Constitution Act in 1981.)

*1867: Alaska Purchase.* The United States of America purchased Alaska for $7 million. The boundaries were those defined in the British/Russian Alaska Treaty of 1825.

*1869: Red River Rebellion.* Under the leadership of Louis Riel, the Metis settlements rebelled against the proposed transfer of Rupert's Land (the Northwest) from the Hudson's Bay Company to Canada after two hundred years as a fur-trading empire. The Metis enlisted the sympathy of American proponents of Manifest Destiny. The Canadian government was forced to negotiate self-government, and the province of Manitoba was created.

*1871: Treaty of Washington.* American, British and Canadian negotiators dealt with a ragbag of issues—the Fenian raids, disputes from the American Civil War and the obscure definition of the boundary through the Gulf Islands between Vancouver Island and the mainland. There was some suggestion that Britain might give up all of Canada to the United States. Instead, there was a series of arbitrations and cash settlements, and in 1872, the San Juan Islands were awarded to the United States.

*1872–76: Boundary Survey of the 49th Parallel.* Britain and the United States conducted the boundary survey of the 49th parallel from Lake of the Woods to the Rocky Mountains.

*1903: Alaska Boundary Tribunal.* Establishment of the international boundary in Yukon/Alaska became important after the Klondike gold rush of 1896–98. An international tribunal of six jurists—three American, two Canadian and one British—interpreted the obscure terms of the 1825 Anglo/Russian treaty, also the terms of the Alaska Purchase. The tribunal's decision concerning the Panhandle and islands in Dixon Entrance was never accepted by the Canadians.

*1908: International Boundary Treaty.* The first bilateral boundary commission was appointed, and regular mapping and surveying of the boundary was instituted.

*1909: Boundary Waters Treaty.* To deal with disputes about international boundary waters, the International Joint Commission, a permanent body, was established.

*1925: Boundary Demarcation Treaty.* The International Boundary Commission was established to repair monuments, clear the vista, and survey and maintain the international boundary.

# FOR FURTHER READING

Classen, H. George. *Thrust and Counterthrust: The Genesis of the Canada–United States Boundary.* Don Mills, Ont.: Longmans Canada, 1965.

Corey, Albert B. *The Crisis of 1830–1842 in Canadian–American Relations.* New York: Russell & Russell, 1970. (First published in 1941 by the Carnegie Endowment for International Peace.)

Dawson, George M. *Report on the Geology and Resources of the Region in the Vicinity of the Forty-Ninth Parallel.* Montreal: Dawson Brothers, 1875.

Featherstonhaugh, A. *Narrative of the Operations of the British North America Boundary Commission: 1872–76.* Woolwich, Eng.: 1876.

Ganong, William F. "Monograph on the Evolution of the Boundaries of the Province of New Brunswick." *Transactions of the Royal Society of Canada,* 1901, Section II, pp. 139–449.

Gibson, Dale. *Attorney for the Frontier: Enos Stutsman.* Winnipeg: University of Manitoba Press, 1983.

Gluek, Alvin C. *Minnesota and the Manifest Destiny of the Canadian Northwest.* Toronto: University of Toronto Press, 1965.

Green, Lewis. *The Boundary Hunters.* Vancouver: University of British Columbia Press, 1985.

Hutchison, Bruce. *The Struggle for the Border.* Toronto: Longmans Canada, 1955.

Merk, Frederick. *Manifest Destiny and Mission in American History.* New York: Alfred A. Knopf, 1963.

Parsons, John E. *West on the 49th Parallel: Red River to the Rockies.* New York: Morrow, 1963.

Savelle, Max. *The Diplomatic History of the Canadian Boundary: 1749–1763.* New York: Russell & Russell, 1968. (First published in 1940 by the Carnegie Endowment for International Peace.)

Thompson, Don W. *Men and Meridians: The History of Mapping and Surveying in Canada.* 3 vols. Ottawa: Ministry of Supply and Services, 1969.

U.S., Department of State. *Reports upon the Survey of the Boundary between the Territory of the United States and the Possessions of Great Britain from the Lake of the Woods to the Summit of the Rocky Mountains.* Washington, D.C.: 1878.

# INDEX